'Of Good and Ill Repute'

'Of Good and Ill Repute'
Gender and Social Control in Medieval England

Barbara A. Hanawalt

New York   Oxford
OXFORD UNIVERSITY PRESS
1998

Oxford University Press

Oxford   New York
Athens   Auckland   Bangkok   Bogota   Bombay
Buenos Aires   Calcutta   Cape Town   Dar es Salaam
Delhi   Florence   Hong Kong   Istanbul   Karachi
Kuala Lumpur   Madras   Madrid   Melbourne
Mexico City   Nairobi   Paris   Singapore
Taipei   Tokyo   Toronto   Warsaw

and associated companies in
Berlin   Ibadan

Copyright © 1998 by Oxford University Press, Inc.

Published by Oxford University Press, Inc.
198 Madison Avenue, New York, New York 10016

Oxford is a registered trademark of Oxford University Press

Six of these chapters have been previously published as essays in various journals
and volumes and are reprinted here by permission: "Fur-Collar Crime: Criminal Activity among the Nobility of Fourteenth-Century England," *Journal of Social History*, 8
(1975): 1–17; "Men's Games, King's Deer: Poaching in Medieval England," *Journal of
Medieval and Renaissance Studies*, 15 (1988): 137–48; "At the Margin of Women's Space
in Medieval Europe," pp. 1–17, in *Matrons and Marginal Women in Medieval Europe*,
ed. Robert R. Edwards and Vickie Ziegler (Woodbridge: The Boydel Press, 1995);
"Narratives of a Nurturing Culture: Parents and Neighbors in Medieval England,"
Essays in Medieval Studies: Proceedings of the Illinois Medieval Association, 12 (1996): 1–21;
" 'The Childe of Bristowe' and the Making of Middle-Class Adolescence," in *Bodies and
Disciplines: Intersections of Literature and History in Fifteenth-Century England*, ed. Bar-
bara A. Hanawalt and David Wallace (Minneapolis: University of Minnesota Press,
1996, pp. 155–69; and "Separation Anxieties in Late Medieval London: Gender in 'The
Wright's Chaste Wife,'" *Medieval Perspectives*, 11 (1997): 23–41.

Library of Congress Cataloging-in-Publication Data
Hanawalt, Barbara
'Of good and ill repute': gender and social control in medieval
England / Barbara A. Hanawalt.
p.   cm.
Includes bibliographical references and index.
ISBN 0-19-510948-1 (alk. paper). — ISBN 0-19-510949-X (pbk. :
alk. paper)
1. Social status—England—History.   2. Reputation (law)—England—
History.   3. Social control—England—History.   4. Sex role—
England—History.   5. Social history—Medieval, 500–1500.
6. England—Social conditions—1066–1485.   I. Title.
HN398.E5H35   1998
305.5'12'0942—dc21   97-27325

1 3 5 7 9 8 6 4 2

Printed in the United States of America
on acid-free paper

Contents

Acknowledgments

This collection of essays clusters around a unified theme: the importance of reputation in establishing social order in the Middle Ages. The essays are based on extensive archival work that I have undertaken with a number of grants, including a Guggenheim fellowship, an NEH Senior Fellowship through the Newberry Library, and research grants through the University of Minnesota, including Graduate School grants-in-aid of research, the McKnight Summer Professorship, and Scholar of the College. I am very appreciative of the help of Anna Dronzek, Amy Brown, and Jeffrey Brunner in preparing the manuscript for publication.

My largest debt, however, is to my colleagues in medieval literature who have taught me, as a historian, to read medieval texts—be they literary or historical—with a more critical eye. It is with profound gratitude for this great lesson in reading that I dedicate this collection of essays to my colleagues in medieval studies at Indiana University and the University of Minnesota. It is because of such people as Lawrence Clopper, Paul Strohm, Susan Noakes, David Wallace, Rita Copeland, and many others who have lectured at the Center for Medieval Studies at the University of Minnesota that I received a real education in reading texts. I suppose that many of my instructors will never know that I listened eagerly to the talks and gleaned insights into my own textual interpretations from their stimulating revelations. The step from the text to interpretation was easier because of their guidance.

Introduction

The essays in this volume investigate the ways in which late medieval English society drew boundaries that separated those of good repute from those of ill repute. The stakes were high for medieval citizens in drawing those distinctions, because members of society who were well regarded could maneuver through life using their social networks for advancement or for clearing their names if they were charged with crimes, trespasses, or debts. The emphasis on "repute" came about because late medieval society was still largely an oral culture,[1] and the general "rumor" about a person's reputation could make or break his or her chances in society. While, increasingly, written records from medieval times documented those whose behavior deviated from the prescribed laws and social norms, the general reputation of a person in his or her community could still be the dividing line between hanging and going *sine die* ("without day," or being acquitted), between being released on bail or put into prison, or between getting a loan or becoming impoverished for the lack of one. Persons of "good repute" could rely on members of their community and even their superiors to support their good name in a variety of cases, whether they needed oath-helpers to swear that they were telling the truth and had always done so, to stand surety for them that they would appear in court to answer charges, to guarantee their reputation for an apprenticeship contract, or to assure the parties to a contract or loan that their word was their bond and that they firmly believed that this was true. The community members who swore that they would back their word had to be sure that they were reliable, because they agreed to pay a fine if they did not appear, to guarantee their loans and contracts should they default, and to watch out for their good behavior in the future if others suspected that they might cause further damage. The use of mainpernors, or those who stood surety, was crucial for all aspects of life.

But what of those who were of ill repute, and how did society define and separate out the marginals from the included? Rather than emphasizing formal legal codes, common law, guild ordinances, village by-laws, and court verdicts that distinguished the law-abiding from the law breakers, the essays in this volume explore the more subtle ways in which the society made and enforced its distinctions. A complex system of responses and initiatives characterize the rich culture of social difference in the Middle Ages. In analyzing the various examples in these essays, I have drawn upon an-

thropology, sociology, and literary criticisms. The first essay, " 'Of Good and
Ill Repute:' The Limits of Community Tolerance" serves as an introduction
to the volume for both the methodological and interpretative tools that I
have used, the legal contexts in which communities functioned, and the types
of distinctions that communities used in defining behavior and establishing
the subtle distinctions between the good and the bad, the included and the
excluded.

The first group of essays investigates the informal mechanisms that mayors, guilds, and kings used to establish distinctions in society and to arrive
at compromises on punishment that would bring about compliance with the
law without necessarily administering the letter of the law. In "Rituals of
Inclusion and Exclusion: Hierarchy and Marginalization in Medieval London," I have looked at the processes of law that include both social interaction and social signification. London mayors had to establish their own authority at the same time that they had to impress on others that their position
was greatly superior to even that of an earl within the confines of the city.
Rituals of behavior helped to define the boundaries of those in power from
those who were excluded from it. "The Power of Word and Symbol: Conflict Resolution in Late Medieval London" discusses how a culture of shared
values in both guilds and the city fostered the use of arbitration and mediation in settling disputes. The fear that the king would intervene and revoke
the city's charter provided further impetus to informal dispute settlement.
To make the settlements public and binding, shared drinks, religious sym-
bolism, or ceremonies of reincorporation into the community were common.
"Fur-Collar Crime: The Pattern of Crime among the Fourteenth-Century
English Nobility" points to parallels between the pattern of crime of those
of hierarchical privilege in the Middle Ages and that of corporation executives that Edwin Sutherland described in his famous study, *White Collar
Crime.*[2] The nobility, those who could wear fur on their cloaks as opposed
to shearling, committed a different sort of crime than that of ordinary criminals, because their crimes were extensions of their privileges and powers
associated with their status. The crown, confronted with the misdeeds of
those mighty subjects, likewise devised different ways of punishing them
so that they would not suffer hanging as a common criminal or even beheading as would have been more common for offenders of their class. They
suffered, instead, honorable exile that got them out of the kingdom on official duty or stationed in remote castles.

One way of separating the included from the excluded is to designate
the space that each could occupy. "Rituals of Inclusion and Exclusion" looks
at spatial divisions in the elevation of the mayor, the divisions of authority
within London and outside of it, and the ultimate punishment of exclusion
or exile from London. The boundaries of space were perhaps more subtle,
but more binding for women in the Middle Ages. They occupied the space
of the home and village if they were peasants, the castle if they were nobles,
the cloisters if they were nuns, and the home and the town quarter if they

were of the bourgeoisie. To move beyond this routine space designated for women of good repute meant traveling with appropriate dress (including veils and other headdresses that restricted viewing) and with appropriate escort. Women who moved out of appropriate space were suspect. Thus the Beguines, who refused to be cloistered and practiced their religious vocations in their communities, aroused the suspicion of church officials. Women outside of their socially allotted space were threatened with rape or were mistreated.

Several of the essays investigate the importance of gendered spatial designations. The most general exploration is "At the Margins of Women's Space in Medieval Europe." Pierre Bourdieu has pointed out that space is divided not only by gender, but also by value judgments that are put on the spaces that men and women occupied. But spatial segregation does not necessarily obviate the exercise of power. In "Separation Anxieties in Late Medieval London: Gender in 'The Wright's Chaste Wife'" I have looked at the problems women faced when left alone to cope in the wider world and at the ways that they might exploit their situation to their advantage. In "The Wright's Chaste Wife" the female voice is clear in a story of a woman who used her control of the house and the keys to punish her suitors, enrich herself, and preserve her chastity while her husband was away. Although books of advice suggested that women remain silent and in their place or they would be punished, the poem offers an alternative story of power and articulation of the female role. "The Host, the Law, and the Ambiguous Space of Medieval London Taverns" also plays with the gendered division of space. Brewing was closely associated with women in the Middle Ages, and taverns were extensions of domestic space in which beer and food were served, often by women. The clientele were predominantly male, and the women serving them often acquired a bad reputation. The space of the tavern was, therefore, ambiguous, since it was an extension of domestic, female space but had strong male connotations. The law gave taverners considerable control over and responsibility for their clientele, but Chaucer's Host finally admits that within the space of his own tavern his wife rules and he is powerless.

The tensions between men and women were played out not only in space, but also in the voice that tells the tale. "The Wright's Chaste Wife" comes from a tradition of women's stories that can be found as far back as ancient India. But the voice of the rape victim in late medieval England is more difficult to detect even though, in law, the rape victim had the right to appeal her rapist in her own voice. "Whose Story Was This? Rape Narratives in Medieval English Courts" investigates the rape of an eleven-year-old London girl in the context of a folkloric analysis of New York crime-victim stories in which the telling may be more important than the ultimate arrest of the culprit. The rape victim tells her side, but her rapist tells an exculpating story of his own, and, finally, a court official tells a titillating story of the same rape. The struggle over controlling the narrative of this violent event disintegrates into a fight over legal points that obviate the crime and the victim. In all these tales, what has happened to the victim's voice, and what purpose do the other narratives play?

Much recent exploration of gender has focused on the female voice and women's experience of being female in a male environment. Only recently has the exploration of gender extended to an analysis of maleness. "Men's Games, King's Deer: Poaching in Medieval England" explores aspects of men's relations with each other and societal perceptions of male roles. The Robin Hood poems, first written down in the fifteenth century, extol the sense of freedom ideally represented by the forests in male myths, but they gained part of their popularity from fights with a law that infringed on the presumed, primitive rights of all males to hunt. The forest laws represented the first encounter of Englishmen with a regular, patrolling force of law-keepers. The hostility of Englishmen to forest law was apparent, but, as in most poaching situations, a state of play also entered into the relationship, so that outwitting the foresters was as much a sport as hunting the king's deer. The more masculine won the triumph of the hunt. The sexual sym-bolism of breaking or stealing the forester's hunting horn or putting a fe-male symbol, the spindle, in the mouth of a stag's head were part of the game for establishing superiority over the forest law and over the contested space of the forest.

The volume concludes with a return to the definition of "good repute" and an analysis of how, in the instances of childrearing and integrating the new category of adolescence into adult society, the intermingling of story-telling and law helped to provide a didactic message to society for estab-lishing the parameters of behavior that constituted good repute. "Narratives of a Nurturing Culture: Parents and Neighbors in Medieval England" ex-plores how coroners' inquests, laws to protect orphans, directives in wills, and even miracle stories collected for the sanctification of Henry VI rein-forced protective behavior toward children. Not only parents, but neighbors were enjoined through these varied narratives to take responsibility for the children of the community and to recognize the risks that might befall the innocents among them. Those of good repute imbibed implicit or ex-plicit instructions inherent in the many positive and negative examples. The rewards for adopting these norms of good behavior were taught through these stories and through the benefits society offered to those of good re-pute.

As society changed drastically in the period following the revisitations of the plague from 1349 onwards, concern about acculturation of the small pool of youth during the late fourteenth and fifteenth centuries began to play a role in society's thinking. " 'The Childe of Bristowe' and the Making of Middle Class Adolescence" investigates a poem that posed a paragon of middle-class virtue and its close relationship to the proliferation of books of advice that was common to the fifteenth century. The desired model for middle-class youth was conventional religious virtues, devotion to master and father, courteous behavior, superior education, and a "sad and wise" demeanor. Youth who imbibed these middle-class virtues were rewarded with plum apprenticeships, close relationships with masters, financial reward, and good marriages. The transition from chivalric values to those of the middle class is already amply apparent in the behavior advocated in poems, advice literature, and guild regulations.

While law, legal history, and administrative processes are adequate to analyze formal procedures and precedents in crimes and punishments, informal justice and the establishment of customary interactions and subtle distinguishers of the included and excluded, the marginal and the mainstream, require different methodologies to tease out the parameters of practices and the desired consequences in the interrelationship among the parties to a dispute or a settlement. I view the whole process of establishing boundaries and barriers, of making such walls permeable or penetrable, as a matter of great complexity. In ongoing, social processes a whole range of factors play roles: Social class, gender, and access to power are only the most obvious of these elements in regulating social intercourse. Beyond these are the subtle literary/folkloric stereotypes of a chaste wife as opposed to the promiscuous wife in a *fabliaux*, a poacher in a dream sequence compared to the male myths of real poachers, and an idealized youth in advice literature as opposed literary models of "wanton and wild" adolescents. In the creation of social boundaries, humans are ingenious. In establishing ways for offenders to recross these boundaries, human societies seek to reestablish an equilibrium that they perceive was breached. Ceremonies of forgiveness and reintegration provide for symbols of contrition or resumption of former social roles.

The players in the subtle games of establishing good and ill repute employed many devices. These could be violent ones, but on the whole, medieval society looked for ways of expressing its desired outcomes in a range of activities. Control over narratives was obviously very important. A raped woman could tell her tale, but the constraints that male society put on how she told it could spell her defeat in court. On the other hand, she might succeed in rendering her assailant a man of "ill repute." A clever woman could act within a limited space and discourse, but could still tell her tale with eloquence if she knew the game and played it well, as can be seen in "The Wright's Chaste Wife." Symbols spoke volumes. The shared meal and drink signaled a reconciliation; the shaving of a head was a sign of humiliation; the exile of a noble to Ireland meant the end of his ability to tamper in local crime; the inversion of sexual symbols such as sticking a spindle down the throat of a poached deer or forcing a man to work with women's tools indicated profound insult in a society that recognized a strict gender hierarchy; the very dress and distance of the mayor separated him from the populace; the humiliation of holding a stirrup for a superior to mount indicated the delicate and subtle equations of words, actions, and symbols that established the good, bad, and indifferent in medieval society.

NOTES

1. Michael Clanchy, *From Memory to Written Record* (Cambridge, Mass.: Harvard University Press, 1979).
2. Edwin H. Sutherland, *White Collar Crime* (New York: Dryden Press, 1949).

'Of Good and Ill Repute'

1

'Of Good and Ill Repute': The Limits of Community Tolerance

Not all crimes, trespasses, slanders, and irritations are prosecuted or end in some sort of settlement; this is a given in studying the latitude of social behavior in enforcing laws, getting satisfaction, or even registering disapproval. To be labeled "of ill repute" or "of no account" in medieval society or in any society implies that the person has committed a violation of accepted standards of social interaction and has stepped beyond the bounds of permissible behavior. Labeling is complex, because members of the medieval nobility committing "fur-collar crime" might have had considerable leeway to oppress their neighbors and countryside with violence and legal violations before they offended so flagrantly that the king had to reprimand and control them. On the other hand, a woman who was caught without appropriate attire and without the proper escort outside the milieu of her daily life hazarded the label "a woman of ill repute." To have the reputation of being of "good repute," on the other hand, was a sufficient reason for jurors to acquit suspects. Gender, class, social status, wealth, connections, bribes, friends, and community all played a role in how quickly or how permanently a person's reputation could be damaged, but so too did unwritten and sometimes written codes of behavior that determined who was of good repute and who was not. Medieval sermons, advice books, manuals of penance, ballads, laws, legal treatises, court records, and city and guild ordinances drew lines between good and bad behavior, but in practice dichotomies of behavior were less common than a range of actions that damaged a person's good name. Social regulation and stigmatization were so complex that no simple measure explains how people arrived at their decisions about condemnation and exoneration or what behavior moved a person beyond community tolerance. This chapter looks at a variety of measurements expressing the limits of medieval community tolerance.

In looking back 600 to 700 hundred years the written evidence is obvi-

1

ously limited in nature and contains fictions of its own that were added by
dominant contemporaries such as judges, village jurors, and guild masters.
Can historians separate the elite, literate voice of court records, laws, and
ordinances from that of the less-lettered community? To what extent can one
discover the cultural constructs surrounding social control and reputation
at the community level? Michel de Certeau has suggested that the historian
try to recapture or reconstruct a contemporary viewer's eye and voice as he
or she contemplated events and behavior. Such a perspective involves, in-
evitably, some reconstruction of impressions that are imaginative.[1] In reconstructing the cultural values that placed some people beyond the pale,
Certeau's concept of imaginative reconstruction can become an important
interpretative tool. In looking at cultural history, Certeau observes, contemporary fictions at those periods may be as instructive as reality.[2] The wide
range of court materials and contemporary commentary on criminal or un-
acceptable behavior provides both facts and fictions with which to assess
societal attitudes and tolerances. I have drawn on both literary works and
legal records in these essays to begin to elucidate the subtle ways in which
reputations were made and destroyed.

This essay explores some of the more direct statements made by medieval society about those who moved outside the limits of community tolerance and consequently were punished. It is designed to provide an
overview of crime and social control in order to give a context to the other
essays. The records of criminal courts are repetitive and usually have little
detail, and therefore a quantitative approach is the only way of providing a
manageable perspective on the vast quantity of data. In turning to the court
records here, my object is not to determine if the crimes actually occurred,
but rather to look at the acquittals and convictions as a way of assessing
community attitudes: which types of crime ended in conviction, and who
was more likely to be convicted?

The medieval criminal justice system placed heavy responsibility on village members and local communities for policing their own people and
space. Villagers and townspeople had the primary responsibility for insuring the good behavior of their neighbors and for identifying, pursuing, catch-
ing, imprisoning, and trying felons. Although guided by common-law traditions and the Statute of Westminster (1285) that larceny, burglary, robbery,
receiving, homicide, rape, and arson were matters to be referred to the king's
courts as felonies punishable by life or limb, the jurors had considerable latitude in interpreting categories. All males twelve years of age and older (ex-
cepting clergy, nobility, and their household servants) were bound into
tithing groups or frankpledge. Members of the group were responsible for
reporting one another's misdeeds and any crimes that occurred in their
neighborhoods. The most ancient method of detecting crime was to raise the
hue and cry (*hutesium et clamor*): anyone coming upon evidence of a felony
such as a body, a house broken open, or a person carrying stolen goods had
to rouse the neighbors in pursuit of the suspect. Most of the suspects, however, were caught through the process of indictment and arrest. Twice yearly

the county sheriff or one of his bailiffs came to "the hundred" (a division of the county) and gathered together the tithing groups or their representatives (capital pledges). At the sheriff's "tourn" the local men reported crimes and determined if there was sufficient evidence to make an indictment for felony. A select group, a grand jury, had to question the villagers and assess the presentments (cases). If they brought an indictment, the sheriff ordered the arrest and imprisonment of the suspect. The villagers and the jurors had considerable control over who was indicted, and the community could manipulate the legal system for their own ends.[3]

Local control did not end with the arrest of the suspect. Suspects were put in jail or released to sureties on bail to await trial. Two to three times a year, the justices of jail (*gaol* in the English spelling) delivery came to the county town and tried those indicted. Juries from the neighborhood in which the crime was committed determined the guilt or innocence of the accused. They were to collect evidence before they came to court and render a verdict on their prior knowledge of the case. Witnesses might be called upon to testify or the accused might offer an alibi, but the jurors had probably already made up their minds before the prisoner stood before the bar at court. Because of this dual role of juror and witness, it was possible for the indictment jury and the petty or trial jury to have the same personnel or for the victim to be on the jury. In addition to deciding guilt or innocence, the jurors might suggest extenuating circumstances that would permit the person to be pardoned or excused. On the basis of the jury's evidence, the justices of jail delivery consulted and passed sentence, designated punishment if the person was convicted, or returned the suspect to jail for further information.[4]

The justices of jail delivery spent a relatively brief time in each county, and so justice was swift and the word of the jurors was taken without much inquiry. In a sample of six deliveries of Norwich Castle jail, an average of forty-six persons were tried per day. Assuming that the justices worked at most ten to twelve hours a day (and they could have worked less), a normal day's load would allow about five to seven cases per hour or about fifteen minutes per case. The highest number of people tried per day was seventy-one in the famine year of 1316, when on March 15th through 16th 142 persons were tried.[5]

The usual punishment was hanging, although there were a few exceptions. If the accused had stolen under 12d. worth of goods, then the case was not a felony and the convicted person was released, perhaps after spending some time in the pillory. Those who were under twelve years of age were considered incapable of understanding the illegality of their actions because they had not reached the age of reason. Likewise, those whom the community judged insane could receive the king's pardon because they too did not understand the reprehensible nature of their actions. Persons killing in self defense were eligible for the king's pardon.[6] By far the largest and most slippery category of those who were convicted and escaped hanging were those who successfully plead benefit of clergy. The accused had first to prove that he was clerk, either by a literacy test, by appearing in proper tonsure and habit, or by having an ecclesiastical representative—an ordinary—come to court with notice from the bishop that he was a member of the clergy in his diocese. Clerical privilege extended to all persons who received orders and covered all cases except high treason. Clergy who were tried and convicted in the king's court were then released to their bishop, who might try them again in his court and prescribe appropriate penances if convicted.[7]

The jurors making indictments to the sheriff and rendering verdicts before the justices of jail delivery, therefore, represented not only community attitudes about the ill repute and guilt of the accused, but also about community tolerance for capital punishment. The verdicts did not necessarily represent guilt or innocence of the accused, but rather the degree to which the community felt threatened by the accused or repulsed by his or her criminal offense. Conviction/acquittal would seem to be a simple binary, but within this stark choice of life or death, the jurors made a series of distinctions that the law did not recognize as valid categories.

In the period between 1300 and 1348, in a five-county survey including 16,365 criminal indictments, the mean number of convictions was 25 percent. Those indicted for simple larceny—that is, picking up and absconding with goods not their own—were convicted in only 22 percent of the cases. Larceny is a loose category in medieval law, because it was so easy to call it "self-help" when a perpetrator would get back goods perceived as belonging to him. If the value was low, then the jurors were unlikely to call it a felony or to convict the indicted person. We might expect, therefore, that the charge of larceny would end in a low conviction rate. Burglary, with a 38-percent conviction rate, and robbery, with a 31-percent rate, seemed to have been more offensive to jurors. With both of these types of felonies, the secrecy and violence of the offense lent a sinister quality. People who should have been secure in their homes, or travelers going about legitimate business, suffered sudden and unexpected violence in burglary and robbery. Jurors added to the official records such statements as "broke a wall [or window] and entered," or "broke into the house at night," or "under the cover of darkness," "lay await in ambush," indicating a sense of helplessness and defenselessness on the part of the victim and cowardice on the part of the accused. Even though no additional punishment to hanging could be extracted from the perpetrator, the jurors and clerks recording their testimony expressed heightened disapprobation. Thus, the property crimes that were committed in stealth, under the cover of darkness, and with violence or the threat thereof were more likely to end in a conviction than were those involving simple theft. Arson, willful destruction of property by fire, was not a common crime and resulted in conviction in 23 percent of the cases.

The types of goods stolen and their value influenced the jurors' convictions as well. Thefts of household goods and clothing, typical items stolen in burglary, ended in convictions in 35 percent and 38 percent of the cases, respectively. Thefts of cloth, usually taken in burglary and robbery, also resulted in high convictions. But stealing foodstuffs including grain, bread, and meat led to convictions in only a quarter of the cases. By far the largest category of theft in larceny, burglary, and robbery was livestock. Those stealing horses were found guilty in 29 percent of the indictments, whereas those stealing sheep, cattle, and pigs were convicted in only about 20 percent of the indictments. Jurors tended to overlook thefts of poultry (15 percent convictions).

The value of the stolen goods was also a consideration for jurors in reaching their verdicts. Only 18 percent of goods worth 12d. ended in convictions compared to 26 percent of those worth 1–10s. and 22 percent of those worth 11–19s. Thefts of goods valued over one pound sterling ended in convictions in 24 percent of the cases.[8]

Accessories to property crimes, receivers of stolen goods, or even receivers of known felons were treated with the most leniency. Only 5 percent were convicted. While the receivers were certainly a threat to order in the countryside because they provided a ready market for stolen goods and a haven for notorious as well as petty outlaws, the jurors and the community could well understand their position. Fear and direct threat of violence from outlaw bands certainly led some people to give shelter to those on the run, but simple greed or even exchange of goods were also factors. The luxury items that the bandits provided might be beyond the budget of the people who received them, but the bandits needed to barter them for the ordinary items of daily livelihood such as bread, blankets, cooking pots, and so on.[9] Furthermore, most of the receivers were appealed rather than indicted. That means that the persons who appealed them had already confessed their crime and turned "king's approver," admitting their guilt and naming their associates in crime to the coroner.[10] Many of the people approvers appealed were receivers of their stolen goods. These people were among the ordinary villagers and would not otherwise have been suspect. The jurors were suspicious of the word of a person who confessed to being "of ill repute" and who would be hanged as a felon in any case. Probably jurors knew the extenuating circumstances of receivers sufficiently well, and many had even benefited themselves by obtaining cheap luxury goods at the hands of outlaws.

Crimes involving the direct interest of the king, counterfeiting and treason, frequently ended in conviction either because jurors found them reprehensible or justices clearly expected convictions. Counterfeiters were convicted in 47 percent of the cases, and those charged with treason and spying in 87 percent. Since England was engaged in warfare with the Scots throughout that period, jurors might have felt as strongly as the king about spies, and no one wanted to receive false and clipped coins. Even the fact that both these felonies resulted in a more horrible form of death—burning for women and being drawn and quartered for men—the jurors were willing to convict the accused. One factor, as we shall see, may be that most of the perpetrators were strangers to the community.

Crimes against the person, homicide and rape, did not result in widespread convictions—12 percent and 10 percent respectively. The reasons for the low convictions in rape are discussed in chapter 8, "Whose Story Was This? Rape Narratives in Medieval English Courts." Homicide has its own complex story.

Looking at the percentages of convictions, it would appear that the jurors had more of an abhorrence for those committing property crimes than for those committing personal ones. The figures point to a higher value on material possessions than on life. But a closer analysis of the pattern of homicide points to the interpretation that murder was comprehensible at the community level and not a general threat to community well-being. Random violence—the ride-by bow-and-arrow attack—and even psychopathic violence were unusual in medieval communities. Homicide was more typically a crime of passion, and tempers are more likely to rise between people who know each other than between strangers. The close ties between victim and accused are apparent from a number of indices. The majority of actors in the homicidal drama were neighbors and acquaintances: Forty-six percent came from the same village, 18 percent from a radius of five miles from each other, and another 18 percent from a distance of six to ten miles apart. About a fifth of the suspects came from other counties and from distances farther than ten miles from the victim's home. Some of these people met their victims on the road or in market towns, so each of them had traveled. Although victims and suspects usually knew each other, they were not as a rule members of the same family. Only 2 percent of the homicides tried in jail delivery, and 8 percent in the coroners' rolls, involved family members.[11] The most common pattern of intrafamilial homicide was the husband killing the wife, fights between brothers, and the wife killing the husband.

The place of homicides, the weapons used, and the motives ascribed to the perpetrator indicate the spontaneous nature of the act. About a third of all homicides in rural society and about a quarter in urban ones occurred in the victim's home, usually in connection with a burglary. Robbery accounted for practically all slayings in woods and some of those on the king's highway. But for the most part, medieval society was accustomed to make social contacts on the streets and in the fields. In London 61 percent of the homicides occurred in streets, and in rural society streets and fields were the place of over 50 percent of homicides. Although the motive for a homicide was not a necessary part of the record, about 84 percent of urban murders and 60 percent of rural ones mention a quarrel. The tensions over land boundaries, harvests, grazing of animals, and use of streets and highways gave rise to many of these violent arguments. Men struck out with the weapons that they had to hand—knives and daggers were the murder weapons in 73 percent of the cases and staffs in 27 percent. Tools were used in only 18 percent of the deaths, and weapons of war (bows and arrows, lances, swords) were used in 12 percent.[12]

To the jurors, who knew the victim and the accused in most cases, the tensions leading up to the homicides and the personalities involved would have been well known. The community had little to fear of a repeat homicide from such specific quarrels. In the case of homicides connected with burglary and robbery the local people would convict the perpetrators if they could be caught. Most of these people were strangers, and as we shall see, strangers got scant mercy from local jurors.

Women, on the other hand, were infrequently indicted (only 10 percent of all indictments involved women), and only 12 percent of those indicted were convicted. A number of factors could help to explain the low participation of women in crime. They certainly had fewer opportunities to move about society and, therefore, fewer opportunities to commit crimes, as the essay, "Women's Space," in this volume, suggests. On the whole, they stole items of less value than those stolen by men and tended to steal such objects as food, poultry, clothing, and other goods that might contribute to provisioning their families. The only period in which female crime rose beyond 10 percent was during the great famine of 1315 to 1317. Jurors did not fear women's crimes as much as those committed by men. A woman "of good repute" was under the domination of her husband or other male relative, and for this reason there was no need to have women in tithing groups. Keeping women in their place could be accomplished through a cultural dominance that did not rely on the judicial system.[13]

Clergy formed an odd category in the criminal courts. While they were charged with 4 percent of all felonies, they were convicted in 64 percent of the cases. Clergy were suspected of robbery and burglary far more than laymen, and their thefts were high-profit goods. Larceny was less to their taste, and their pattern of crime in homicide and rape was similar to that of laymen. The high conviction rate does not necessarily indicate anticlericalism. When the jurors convicted a layman, hanging would be the most common punishment, but when they convicted a clergyman he would be turned over to his ordinary. The 64-percent conviction rate could, therefore, be closer to a truer assessment of the jurors' knowledge about guilt. Alternatively, if many of the hard-core robbers and burglars took the precaution of entering lower orders of clergy or learned to read in order to plead benefit of clergy, then the figure may represent the jurors' treatment of the dangerous criminal element. Clergy formed a large element in bandit gangs.[14]

Moving the inquiry to the village level gives another perspective on the limits of community tolerance. The study of village dynamics in the commission and punishment of crime comes from a comparison of the Huntingdonshire jail delivery rolls with the village reconstitution studies undertaken by J. Ambrose Raftis and his students at the University of Toronto.[15] In all, eighty-nine of those indicted for felonies and forty-three victims of felony were positively identified in the manorial or village court rolls either as individuals or as members of village families. Identifying those people with their record of participation in community governance, their economic transactions, and their misdemeanors provides a rare glimpse into the background of those indicted for crime or of victims of crime.

Raftis and his students have reconstituted families in a number of Ramsey Abbey villages. Their studies show that village families fell into three main classifications: primary, secondary, and intermediate villagers.[16] The primary village families lived in the villages for generations, held from fifteen to thirty acres or more of land, dominated the juries and village offices such as reeve and capital pledges, and used the manorial court aggressively in pursuing debts and trespasses against them. They were frequently cited in the court for flaunting rules such as work owed to the lord and for infractions against fellow villagers including assaults, trespasses, and petty thefts.[17] Primary villagers contributed 38 percent to the pool of those indicted for felonies. Secondary villagers resembled the primary ones in the longevity of their residence in the village, but they had less land and moveable wealth and only occasionally served on village juries and in other official capacities. They too were aggressive toward their neighbors at the village level, constituting 42 percent of the indicted. Both these groups were well enough established economically and socially to have a number of interactions and to pursue their disputes aggressively in court or in crime. They probably also made up a percentage of the village population similar to their indictments. A dramatic drop in indictments comes with the cottagers or intermediate villagers: only 20 percent of this group could be identified in both jail delivery and manorial courts. This group did not have long residence in the village, and they either held little land or worked as laborers and craftsmen. They never held village office. A typical example was Richard Tynkere of Hemmingford Grey, who was tried in 1329 for stealing from a barn. His name probably indicates his occupation.[18]

The crimes that led to indictments indicate a village culture of self-help in which arguments could end in assaults. Homicide was the most common crime (40 percent of the total) for villagers of all status groups, but the majority of them were committed by the primary and secondary villagers (29 out of 37 homicides), who also predominated in charges for assaults in the manorial courts. Those well-fed, prosperous, aggressive villagers had potentially volatile interactions with fellow villagers, and their solution to anger was often physical assault. In property crimes, as well, the primary and secondary villagers committed burglary rather than larceny. While 39 percent of the indictments of the cottagers was for larceny, only 23 percent of the primary and secondary villagers were charged with this felony. But in burglary only 6 percent of the cottagers were indicted compared to 16 percent of the primary villagers and 19 percent of the secondary villagers. The primary and secondary villagers were also more likely to be the receivers of stolen goods and known felons. Arson, robbery, and rape did not appear among villagers' felonious actions.[19] The property crimes, therefore, represented the economic needs and perceptions of villagers. The poor picked up items of little value and usually those things that could supplement their diets while the wealthier villagers committed burglary and took items of greater value. Some of these burglaries were, no doubt, perceived as taking what was owed to them. In other words, their violent relationship to property was an extension of notions of self-help also leading to assaults and homicide.

An analysis of the victims of village crime helps to elucidate the violence. As in the general overview of homicide, crimes among villagers were neighborhood affairs, with 45 percent coming from the same village, 18 percent from a village a mile or less away, 14 percent from two to five miles, 8 percent from six to ten miles, and the rest from more than eleven miles away. If the accused had accomplices, they tended to be neighbors from their own status groups in the village or in a neighboring village.

When the victims are matched with the accused, a definite village pecking order appears. The prominent villagers overwhelmingly chose their victims from the clergy (very frequently their overlord, the abbot of Ramsey, or a local parson). After the clergy, they attacked each other and the secondary villagers equally. Since the Ramsey villages were ecclesiastical estates, it is obvious that the abbot's property would be attacked—it was both an object of resentment and the richest in the neighborhood. The attacks were not only for personal enrichment, but also indicated resentment against the abbot.[20] Secondary villagers could also find themselves at odds with the clergy, but their chief object of attack was their immediate social superiors, primary villagers, and each other. In both the manorial courts and in jail delivery indictments, the tensions between these two groups emerged repeatedly. The secondary villagers struggled harder for a living and resented the dominance that primary village families had over village offices and juries that extracted fines and labor from them. The cottagers confined their hostile attacks and criminal actions to the primary and secondary villagers. Wealthy villagers were more likely targets for theft, but even in homicide, the cottagers victimized primary and secondary villagers rather than each other.

Intergroup rivalry, of course, did not account for all the hostilities and criminal actions. Individual antisocial tendencies also motivated crime and aggression. A man who was killed in a tavern fight had a record of assaults and had the hue and cry raised against him twice. When he lost his life in a tavern fight in 1333, the jurors recommended that the murderer be pardoned in a plea of self-defense. Two brothers, John Porthors major and John Porthors minor came from a prominent family and also had a record of aggressive behavior. Their assaults, defamations, and disputes were unusual in that they were directed at family as well as other villagers. Sibling rivalry had been building up between the two brothers, and finally one brother murdered the other. In the case of one of the cottager families, a whole string of petty thefts and trespasses committed by a mother and daughter led to the expulsion of the mother from the village and, finally, the indictment and trial of the daughter in jail delivery.[21]

Status played a role once again at the suspects' trials. The primary villagers served on the juries and would be the ones determining the fate of their neighbors. Although they were willing to indict people in roughly the same proportion as their numbers in the village, when it came to actually convicting people, their prejudices again emerged. Only two of the thirty-four prominent villagers and six of the thirty-seven secondary villagers were

convicted, while eight of the eighteen intermediate villagers were convicted.
Status also determined punishment. Only one prominent villager was
hanged—John Gere who confessed his crime and became an approver. The
other one, a Porthors brother, was a member of the clergy and released to
the bishop. Of the secondary family members convicted, three were hanged,
two pardoned, and one sent to the pillory for a theft under 12d. Members
of the intermediate group were treated more harshly—five were hanged,
two released because of the low value of goods stolen, and one was pardoned. Strangers to the community were convicted in 38 percent of the cases.

The pattern of convictions and punishments tells us much about community tolerances, intolerances, and tensions. People with a record of community irritation were more likely to be convicted than those who had been
good neighbors all along. The former had already earned the label of "being of ill repute." Strangers to the community who committed crimes could
not be trusted. They could not find sureties in the community who would
guarantee their good behavior and they did not have a network of mutual
obligations to give them protectors. Furthermore, they were more likely to
be the ones who committed robbery, burglary, and larceny of expensive
goods. The deficiency of strangers in the eyes of jurors was that they could
not prove that they were "of good repute."

The use of indictments, courts, and convictions, however, points to a sophisticated manipulation of the judicial system. Why did the jurors indict
so many of the primary and secondary villagers when they would only acquit them in the end? The villagers were jointly responsible, under pain of
fine, for reporting to the sheriff's tourn all felonies committed in their village and suspects in the cases. All homicides had to be reported directly to
the coroners. The fines for not reporting were not large, but it would have
taken joint agreement of at least the prominent families to risk suppressing
a case. But there were other reasons for indicting the main village families.
Unlike the intermediate villagers, they could not be expelled from the village because they held land there. They could be fined in manorial court or
they could be put through the expense and trouble of jail delivery. The whole
process of indictment and trial was expensive and bothersome: A person indicted for violent crimes would be held in the dungeon of the local county
castle until the justices arrived and, depending on the time of arrest and the
frequency of judicial circuits, this could be as long as six months. Prisoners
had to pay for their food, bed, and the right not to be fettered in prison. Altogether the dungeons were a bad experience in which men and women
were mixed together in rooms with no windows.[22] If the offense was not so
serious or the person was of good repute, then he or she had to find sureties
for appearance at trial. During the period prior to the trial, the indicted person had to be on best behavior because he or she was at the mercy of the
jurors.

Since conviction implied hanging, no doubt family and friends did fa-
vors for the jurors and perhaps even bribed them. But the jurors had other
considerations as well. If they convicted and condemned to death one of

their fellow villagers, then they risked starting a vendetta. The case of John Gere, who turned approver, is instructive. He was accused in 1336 of stealing five horses worth £1 6s. 8d. He was either guilty or sure of a hostile jury, because he agreed to name his accomplices. His family were primary villagers, and his record of trespasses was no worse than others in the village. In his appeals he named a number of people, among whom was the secondary villager, Nicholas atte Crouch. He turned approver himself and got his revenge by naming a number of primary villagers, including two members of the Gere family and two members of other prominent families. For the jurors the most cautious procedure was to indict their neighbors, but to see that they were acquitted or recommend for pardon so that families and individuals would not seek revenge. Even if they were releasing felons back into their community, they had made the point that future bad behavior might result in hanging and everyone would be watching. Cottagers (intermediate villagers), on the other hand, posed no problems for punishment, since they would never serve on juries and never be in a position to indict their social superiors.[23]

If jurors from the village communities and towns worked out their own hierarchy of the crimes that they thought were most serious and individuals who had to die, the general discourse of the realm spoke to a more generalized fear of crime. The establishment of commissions of peace and justices of peace, statutes, parliamentary petitions, and directives from the king to justices and local officials all emphasized a fear of crime and disorder. Civil wars during the reign of Edward II, invasions of the Scots, and Edward III's long absences abroad for campaigns in the Hundred Years' War all brought comments from parliament and chroniclers.[24] Evidence from trends in indictments shows a steep rise during the famine of 1315–17 and again in the famine of the early 1320s, but the correlation of a rise in crime with civil war or foreign wars is less clear. Criminal indictments did increase in general in the 1340s and may have been related to war. In those counties most directly affected by war, particularly Yorkshire, crime did appear to rise.[25] The king complained to the mayor of York in 1334 "that several malefactors and disturbers of the peace . . . making assemblies and illicit gatherings both by day and by night in York, its suburbs and neighborhood, go armed and lie in wait for those coming and going to and from the city, and staying there, both the king's ministers and other lieges, and beat, wound and rob them."[26]

Contemporaries were particularly concerned about the lawlessness of the troops returning from the French campaigns. Indicted felons and outlaws could obtain a pardon by serving in the king's army for a year and a day, and even those who were not already used to the criminal life learned it in the king's campaigns in France, where plunder was an ordinary means of provisioning.[27] A statute directed the justices of the peace to "inform themselves . . . touching all those who had been plunderers or robbers beyond the seas and are now returned and go wandering and will not work as they were used to." Special measures were apparently needed, for the counties

of Wiltshire, Berkshire, and Hampshire informed the king that a body of returned soldiers had formed an armed band with other criminals and rode
in warlike array robbing, ransoming, and maiming inhabitants.[28] In a peti-
tion to the king and council in 1347 the Commons complained that "many
murders, woundings, robberies, homicides, rapes, and other felonies and
misdeeds without number are done and maintained in the kingdom because
the evil doers are granted charters of pardon . . . to the great destruction of
the people. May it please the king to provide a remedy through a statute . . .
and order that charters of pardon not be granted without the assent of Parliament.[29]" This protest was made after three previous statutes had failed to
remedy the problem. The language of the statutes also reflects the general
view that "Murderers, Robbers, and other Felons, be greatly encouraged to
offend, by reason that Charters of Pardon . . . have been granted so lightly."[30]

As the fourteenth century wore on, other fears, associated with the fear
of crime, began to influence people's language and actions.[31] The plague of
1349 and repeated outbreaks obviously brought fears of mortality and God's
punishment, but the disruptions of the depopulation also began to influence
the very hierarchical nature of society. Peasants and wage laborers were
quick to realize that they could charge more for their labor now that there
were fewer of them. The landlords were equally swift in passing the Ordinance of Laborers and the Statute of Laborers to preserve manorialism,
prices, and wages just as they had been in 1347. The meaning of "ill repute"
began to broaden beyond application to individuals to groups and classes.
"Good repute" also began to apply to groups such as members of guilds or
of social classes or status groups.

Norbert Elias observes at the end of his book, *The History of Manners*,
that in art works commissioned by elites and foregrounding aspects of their
lives, peasants are represented as part of a backdrop landscape, be their role
that of laborers in rags, participants in rustic merriment, beggars, victims of
pillage and rape, or as felons hanging and rotting on wheels and gallows.
The landscape with peasants, as in the Duke de Berry's book of hours, treats
them as an ordinary, nonthreatening part of the background that served to
set off the elegance of the elite.[32] The elite of England and London shared
this view of peasants as in-their-place or suffering due punishment should
they deviate from the controlled environment. The urban centers of Europe,
including London, customarily assimilated large numbers of peasants into
their ranks, but they did so through apprenticeship contracts, service contracts, marketing arrangements, and other such means that kept the newcomers and country bumpkins within control.

Late medieval revolts of the lower orders changed the managed landscape and brought images to the minds of the elite that evoked animal images. The metaphor, which had been used earlier, reappeared in the Revolt
of 1381. Already in the thirteenth century, when the London craftsmen and
laborers physically attacked the queen, mayor, and aldermen, the chroniclers described those people as "roaring abuse" and using "all sorts of dis-
gusting projectiles" against "the senior and wisest men of the city." The

chronicles used barnyard imagery with ease, calling the commons "fools of the vulgar herd." The rebels were not articulate in language as were their betters, but were capable only of confused, loud sounds.[33] One disgruntled rebel was described as standing at the roadside and neighing like a horse every time an alderman road by.[34] The chroniclers and the oligarchy of London saw a savage threat emanating from the unleashing of peasants and the breakdown of boundaries imposed by social hierarchy and law.

Existing accounts of the peasant revolt of 1381 indicate that the designation of primitivism had become a major theme among chroniclers. Added to the image of the peasantry and urban commons as negative and inarticulate was the great divide of literacy. Commons "roar" rather than talk; they attack literacy by destroying court records that are their written oppressors; they assault anyone who appears with an ink pot at his arm. These are the barnyard animals let loose to destroy the culture of the literate. When one of the chroniclers described the scene in which Richard II repudiates the charters he has given to the peasants to disperse them at Mile End he gave Richard the speech:

> Rustics you were and rustics you remain. . . . For as long as we live . . . we will strive to trample on you so that your slavery may be an example to posterity, and so that those like you may now and in future have always before their eyes as if in a book your misery and reasons for cursing you.[35]

Literacy, however, was increasing in the late fourteenth and fifteenth centuries and provided yet another way of being identified as "of ill repute." By the fifteenth century a relatively large public could read, and poets were hung, drawn, and quartered for their gift of writing doggerel against the king. William Collyngbourne, for instance, was "put to the most horrible death at the Tower Hill. . . . After being hanged a short season he was cut down, being alive, and his bowels were ripped out of his belly and cast into the fire before him." While still alive, the executioner thrust his hand into his body cavity again and Collyngbourne exclaimed that he had had enough and died. The remarkable cruelty of the punishments for this step from illiterate to literate protester indicates how significant and terrifying such a step was for the elite.[36]

If illiterate peasants and increasing literary political critics disturbed the perceived order of society, so too did heresy. Lollardy and the Revolt of 1381 became inextricably entwined because of John Ball's Lollard preaching. In the fifteenth century the Commons complained about disturbances to the peace caused by violent breaking of forests, chases, and parks. They suggested that the offenders were "probably of the opinion of Lollards, traitors and rebels." By 1423 Lollardy was mentioned with treason and felony. Fear of heresy became entangled with the fear of revolt, crime, and attacks on the hierarchical nature of medieval society. Lollardy was threatening. Wycliffe had urged the disendowment of ecclesiastical establishments, and his suggestion for land redistribution began to be applied more broadly to the possessions of kings, dukes, and other laymen. His theology was also radical, suggesting the elevation of scripture and preaching over the sacraments and the church hierarchy. As one of their detractors wrote of Lollards: "They were always spreading dissension and inciting the people to insurrection, so that it was hardly possible for anyone of them to preach without their hearers being provoked to blows, and discord would arise in towns."[37]

Disorder and violence, particularly when exercised by those who fell outside the knighthood or nobility (i.e., those who had long been classified as legitimate fighters), raised alarm. While the society tolerated homicide when it was understandable within the context of the community as they knew it, outsiders who incited violence had to be punished. Jack Cade's entry into London, for instance, showed a man acting outside his rank. As one chronicler observed, he "rood aboute the cite berying a nakid swerd in his hand, armed in a peire of brigaundynez, werying a peire of gilt sporis, and a gilt salat, and a gowne of blew veluet, as he hadde be a lord or a knyght— and yit was he bit a knaue,—and hadde his swerde born befor him."[38] Anyone who imitated the mayor in his own town was sure to be "of ill repute."

Medieval people's attitudes toward the unlawful and rebellious were far from entirely negative, however. Medieval popular culture had a long tradition of outlaw poems that glorified the feats of lawlessness, guile, violence, disguises, adventure, and bravery.[39] The Robin Hood poems and ballads represented a male culture (Maid Marion was a sixteenth-century addition) that celebrated freedom from the constraints of law. Rather than being hunted down by the law enforcement officials, outlaws turned the tables on them. The outlaws' life is one of freedom. Not only do they have no overlords, but they have no other responsibilities: it is always May, there are no women demanding domesticity, no children, no house to repair, no fields to plow, no animals to milk. "Men's Games, King's Deer" likewise plays with the theme of male freedom from the constraints of law. Literature accorded a rebellious role to women as well. Even within the spatial and customary restraints on women, the manipulation of the home environment that appears in the fifteenth-century poem, "The Wright's Chaste Wife," shows that women had their own versions of resistance stories. While the *fabliaux* dwell on the resourcefulness of wives in finding satisfaction in illicit sex, the poetic tradition from which the "Chaste Wife" comes depicts clever women preserving their chastity by duping their suitors. Both the outlaw poems and those dealing with clever women show an enjoyment in hierarchical inversions.

Although expressing anxieties over crime, rebellion, and heresy, medieval English communities actually accepted a considerable latitude of behavior between the categories of good and ill repute. Popular poetry showed a relish for those who bent the rules. Jurors were lenient in using capital punishment for felons, officials did not use torture to extract confessions, the king hanged remarkably few peasant rebels, and bishops burned relatively few heretics. But the society also placed a very high value on a person's reputation. To be "of good repute" meant living by the community norms and to be "of ill repute" removed societal protections from the miscreant.

NOTES

1. Michel de Certeau, *The Writing of History*, trans. Tom Conley (New York: Columbia University Press, 1988), pp. 19–55.
2. Michel de Certeau, *The Practice of Everyday Life*, trans. Steven R. Rendall (Berkeley: University of California Press, 1984), pp. xii–xv. He has criticized Michel Foucault's position as too static to describe the varieties of power relationships.
3. Barbara A. Hanawalt, *Crime and Conflict in English Communities, 1300–1348* (Cambridge, Mass.: Harvard University Press, 1979). See pp. 32–39 for a more detailed description of the community-based policing system.
4. Ibid., p. 41.
5. Ibid., p. 13. The sample of six deliveries was carefully selected: They all were followed immediately by a delivery of Norwich City jail so that the beginning and end of the delivery could be determined exactly.
6. Naomi D. Hurnard, *The King's Pardon for Homicide before A.D. 1307* (Oxford: Oxford University Press, 1969), pp. 68–108, 152–170. For a discussion of the pardon for self-defense see Thomas A. Green, "Societal Concepts of Criminal Liability for Homicide in Medieval England," *Speculum*, 47 (1972): 669–94.
7. Leona C. Gabel, *Benefit of Clergy in England in the Later Middle Ages* (Smith College Studies in History, 14, nos. 1–4, Northampton, Mass., 1928–29), pp. 31, 61–91.
8. See Hanawalt, *Crime and Conflict*, pp. 59–62 for discussion of convictions for types of crimes and goods stolen.
9. Barbara A. Hanawalt, "Ballads and Bandits: Fourteenth-Century Outlaws and the Robin Hood Poems," in *Chaucer's England: Literature in Historical Context*, ed. Barbara A. Hanawalt (Minneapolis: University of Minnesota Press, 1992), pp. 154–57.
10. F. C. Hamil, "The King's Approvers," *Speculum*, 11 (1936): 238–58.
11. For a more complete discussion of family involvement in crime between family members see Barbara A. Hanawalt, "The Peasant Family and Crime in Fourteenth-Century England," *Journal of British Studies*, 13 (1974): 1–18.
12. For a more detailed discussion of homicide see Barbara A. Hanawalt, "Violent Death in Fourteenth- and Fifteenth-Century England," *Comparative Studies in Society and History*, 18 (1976): 297–320.
13. Hanawalt, *Crime and Conflict*, pp. 115–25. Barbara A. Hanawalt, "The Female Felon in Fourteenth-Century England, 1300–1348," *Viator*, 5 (1974): 253–368.
14. Hanawalt, *Crime and Conflict*, pp. 54–55, 136–38.
15. This study was made possible through the generosity of J. Ambrose Raftis. I contributed the Huntingdonshire jail delivery materials to the Regional Data Bank at Toronto in exchange for use of the data on village reconstitution. The Huntingdonshire jail delivery rolls for the study are sporadically preserved for 1290–1300, but there are good runs for 1309–13, 1228–33, and 1335–53. The Ramsey Abbey manorial court rolls included in the Regional Data Bank at Toronto cover the Huntingdonshire towns and villages of Broughton, Godmanchester, Holywell-cum-Needingworth, Hemingford, Houghton, Wyton, Ramsey, Ripton (Abbots and Kings), Little Stukeley, St. Ives, Upwood, Warboys, and Wistow. The results of this comparison were first published in Barbara A. Hanawalt, "Community Conflict and Social Control: Crime and Justice in the Ramsey Abbey Villages," *Mediaeval Studies*, 39 (1977): 402–23.
16. J. Ambrose Raftis, "The Concentration of Responsibility in Five Villages," *Mediaeval Studies*, 28 (1966): 93–118.

17. Edwin B. DeWindt, *Land and People in Holywell-cum-Needingworth* (Toronto: Pontifical Institute of Mediaeval Studies, 1972) and Edward Britton, *The Community of the Vill: A Study in the History of the Family and Village Life in Fourteenth-Century England* (Toronto: Macmillan, 1977) have both studied the infractions of manorial rules, misdemeanors, and trespasses of the peasants of those villages.

18. Public Record Office Just. 3/24/4 m. 3d.

19. Hanawalt, "Crime and Justice in Ramsey Villages," p. 412. The indicted consisted of 12 primary villagers, 17 secondary villagers, and 8 cottager villagers for homicide; 6 primary, 15 secondary, and 1 cottager for burglary; 8 primary, 9 secondary, and 7 cottagers for larceny; and 7 primary, 7 secondary, and 2 cottagers for receiving.

20. Ibid., pp. 414–15, forty-three victims were identified in the data bank.

21. Ibid., pp. 417–18.

22. For a study of prison conditions, see R. B. Pugh, *Imprisonment in Medieval England* (Cambridge: Cambridge University Press, 1968).

23. Hanawalt, "Crime and Justice in Ramsey Villages," pp. 419–23.

24. See, for instance, Bertha Haven Putnam, "Transformation of the Keepers of the Peace into Justices of the Peace, 1327–1380," *Transactions of the Royal Historical Society*, 4th ser., 5 (1920), pp. 23, 41–48; Dorothy Hughes, *A Study of the Social and Constitutional Tendencies in the Early Years of Edward III* (London: University of London, 1915), p. 227; May McKisack, *The Fourteenth Century, 1307–1399* (Oxford: Oxford University Press, 1959), pp. 50–51, 158; and *Rotuli Parliamentorum et Petitiones et Placita in Parliamento*, 2 (London, 1832), 140.

25. Hanawalt, *Crime and Conflict*, pp. 222–32.

26. *Calendar of Patent Rolls, 1334–1338*, 3 (London: Public Record Office,), pp. 294–95.

27. Herbert J. Hewitt, *The Organization of War under Edward III* (Manchester: Manchester University Press, 1966), 173–75.

28. Charles G. Crump and C. Johnson, "The Powers of the Justices of the Peace," *English Historical Review*, 27 (1912): 227, 236.

29. *Rotuli Parliamentorum*, 2, p. 172.

30. *Statutes of the Realm 1238–1713*, I (London: 1810), Statute of Northampton 2 Ed. III, c. 2; 10 Ed. III, st. I, c. 2–3; 14 Ed. III, st. I, c. 15.

31. For an excellent discussion of the French experience of fear of crime and hierarchies of crimes see Claude Gauvard, *"De Grace Especial:" Crime, état et société en France à la fin du moyen âge*, 2 vols. (Paris: Publications de la Sorbonne, 1991).

32. Norbert Elias, *The Civilizing Process: The History of Manners*, trans. Edmund Jephcott (Oxford: Basil Blackwell, 1978), pp. 206–17.

33. Antonia Gransden, *Historical Writing in England*, 1 (Ithaca, N.Y.: Cornell University Press, 1974), pp. 466, 515.

34. Gwyn Williams, *Medieval London: From Commune to Capital* (London: Athlone Press, 1963), p. 201.

35. Susan Crane, in "The Writing Lesson of 1381," in *Chaucer's England: Literature in Historical Context*, ed. Barbara A. Hanawalt (Minneapolis: University of Minnesota Press, 1992), pp. 201–21, has explicated the play between writing and the rebellion. See also Steven Justice, *Writing and Rebellion: England in 1381* (Berkeley: University of California Press, 1994).

36. V. John Scattergood, *Politics and Poetry in the Fifteenth Century* (London: Blandford Press, 1971), pp. 20–22.

37. Margaret Aston, "Lollardy and Sedition, 1381–1431." in *Lollards and Reformers: Images and Literacy in Late Medieval Religion* (London: Hambledon Press, 1984), pp. 1–18.

38. Philippa C. Maddern, *Violence and Social Order: East Anglia 1422–1442* (Oxford: Clarendon Press, 1992), pp. 93–94.

39. Maurice Keen, *The Outlaws of Medieval Legend* (Toronto: University of Toronto Press, 1961).

2

Rituals of Inclusion and Exclusion: Hierarchy and Marginalization in Medieval London

Most approaches to studying marginalization in medieval society have been too rigid and have failed to fully appreciate the nuances, the rituals, and the processes that were involved in creating marginals. The dominant approach has been a legalistic one that foregrounds hierarchy as the power that excluded the undesirables and made law its tool in enforcing the exclusion. Marginals have been seen as poor, of low status, and as lawbreakers. Bronislaw Geremek added a social dimension to this argument in his study of the low life of late medieval Paris by looking at marginals as a class.[1] They were not only people and groups who fell outside the social and economic or the legal and political mainstream, but also formed an underclass with rendezvous in taverns and other gathering places. Contemporaries described them as "of no account" or "not of good fame."[2] Such a definition contains a structural limitation, for it presumes that only the social outcasts will be marginalized. In this essay "marginalization" moves beyond a "lower class" and suggests, instead, processes that elevate people in rank and also temporarily or permanently exclude them from their social rank.

The hierarchical/social class view of marginalization simplifies the social process to the point of undervaluing its complexities. As we move away from the traditional Marxist and structuralist models of class formation and social class identity that have so long dominated historical analysis, scholars are demonstrating the permeability of class and the ebbs and flows of identity and membership. Analysis of words, gestures, tensions over space, and status add new dimensions to the older views of stable hierarchies. Ronald Weissman, for instance, has argued for a new sociology of the Renaissance that would "focus on the twin processes of social interaction and social signification."[3] Medieval society formed many social groupings and was adept at creating boundaries around them; those thrust outside the group's borders were on the margins whether they were elites or vagrants.

We are used to thinking of medieval society in vertical terms in which exclusion from one social class means the excluded drop to a lower one. While not arguing against the essentially hierarchical nature of medieval society, I am suggesting that medieval social and political arbiters drew horizontal boundaries within their social class and status groups. The patterns of inclusion and exclusion look more like a crosshatch than a single, vertical line. While to Geremek only those on the bottom could be marginals, a liveried guildsman in medieval London regarded his apprentices as marginals who might some day cross the social boundaries into his status, but considered his scullery maids as permanent marginals. If the visual image of a social landscape done in crosshatching (involving both vertical and horizontal lines) seems complex, it is probably closer to reality than that of simple social hierarchies. As Weissman suggests, process should be part of our model for people in groups, and adding that component makes the picture more blurred because it is more dynamic.

In exploring the boundaries that medieval London society created and the rituals that it used to police the borders, a primate anthropologist, Frans B.M. De Waal, provides valuable insights. He observed that "status rituals are the backbone of every established hierarchy." When a subordinate stops performing these rituals, the action results in punishment that will return the offender to submissive status once again.[4] The rituals are those of both inclusion and exclusion; that is, they are indicators of the privileged and dominate as well as of the subordinate and excluded. Social rituals among humans are similar to those of primates in that rituals are two-sided—a ritual of submission also reinforces the position of the dominate and a ceremony reinforcing dominance underscores the exclusion of those of lesser social status.

The range of ritual at medieval social boundaries is vast, and some of the more obvious ones such as excommunication with bell, book, and candle or entry ceremonies that welcome monarchs and include them in the city cannot be treated here.[5] Instead, I will look at the public humiliations such as pillories and parades with rough music, private actions that marginalized a rival or enemy, reconciliation ceremonies that reintegrated someone who had been marginalized, and initiation ceremonies that separated the urban elite from the common people. Those social rituals are interesting in themselves, but they reveal a deeper meaning when one looks at the ways in which they inscribed their message on the marginal and attempted to create public acceptance of social boundaries. The shaving of a bawd's or prostitute's head inscribes the message of marginality directly on the offender's body; reconciliation ceremonies involving gifts of wine or shared banquets use food and drink as time-honored symbols of a coming together; clothing in the form of livery or robes of state plays a significant role in defining membership in the elite. The ceremonies, therefore, reveal attitudes toward people's bodies as well as their honor and their place in society.

Finally, boundaries also imply an idea of space. People group themselves or are grouped in the boxes of the social crosshatching. Examination of these spaces helps us to understand not only what is public and private or what is more powerful or less powerful, but also what people's attitudes were toward their social space as opposed to that of others.[6] Since bodies and dress also partake of spatial relations to the inward self and the outward perception of the individual, these too are related to social conceptions of central versus marginal space. The physical gestures that people used to insult, to debase, to make sacred, to reverence, to bestow friendship and status are a use of body and space to include and exclude. This wealth of analytical approaches helps us to see that there is more to marginality than taverns and low public esteem.

ESTABLISHING AND MAINTAINING OFFICIAL SPACE

Official space, including the problems of defending it against marginals and marginalization, is a convenient place to begin the investigation because it provides a background for the social process among London's highest status groups, thereby extracting the concept of marginals as dealing only with "those of no account" or those of "ill repute." City ceremonials for the elevation of sheriffs, aldermen, and liveried guildsmen would all demonstrate the elite's prickly concepts of social and physical space, but the election of the mayor provides a concise example, since he was the highest ranking official in the city. In London, only the king had a higher rank than the mayor. As the *Liber Albus* of 1419 put it: "the sword is born before him [the mayor], as before an Earl, and not behind him."[7]

The selection of the mayor demonstrates the delineation of space both in terms of power and territory. When the *Liber Albus* was compiled, London was still recovering from the struggle between mayors Brember and Northampton, which revolved around the inclusion of a larger portion of the city population in governance at the expense of the elite. The argument ran parallel to and was exacerbated by the struggle between Richard II and the Lords Appellant.[8] To establish an electoral system that would both reach a compromise but at the same time make the boundaries between the elite and the commons clear, the ceremony of selection divided the physical space and power spheres of the Guildhall, or in modern terms, the city hall.

First, not all of the commons could appear as a large crowd at the elections (for fear of riot) and, second, the space in which the commons and the elite were to stand and the types of interactions that were to occur there were carefully delineated. The representatives of the commons were to meet on the eastern side of the Guildhall where the sheriffs were reputed to have held their courts. In other words, they met on the less prestigious end of the hall. They were to select the names of two aldermen as candidates and instruct the Common Pleader to traverse the space between them and the current mayor and aldermen, who stood at the opposite end of the hall (west end) where the mayor was accustomed to hold the Husting Court. The Common Pleader's office permitted him to move between the lower status space to the higher status space to make nominations. The elite received the nominations and ascended into an even more restrictive and exalted space, the chamber above, where they held the actual election. Descending back into the main hall, they reported the outcome to the Recorder, who conveyed the name of the mayor elect to the commons at the other end of the hall. The old mayor then took the newly elected one by the hand and led him down to the hall to announce his election and instruct the commons to hold themselves in readiness for his installation on the Feast of Apostles Simon and Jude.[9] This hand clasp, the first public, physical contact in the ceremonial process, indicated a passing on of power through the elite. A detailed description of an early sixteenth-century mayoral election demonstrates that the election process actually occurred.[10]

The rituals accompanying the mayor's installation reinforced the office's high status. Appropriate gestures joined the apportionment of physical space in the ceremonies establishing the mayor's elevated status. A larger public was included and had to be informed about the elevation of a well-known figure to official rank. Jean-Claude Schmidt has analyzed three notions of gestures in the Middle Ages: expressivity or showing of emotions and inner feelings and values of individuals; nonverbal communication including such gestures as crossing one's self; and efficacy, which has a double meaning—practical gestures such as sawing or writing and symbolic gestures that are essential for making political or sacramental rituals efficacious. We will have occasion to come back to the first two types of gesture as we look at other rituals of marginalization, but those employed in the mayor's installation pertain to the efficacy of establishing his office. Such gestures had to be executed accurately in the minute, scripted details established by both law and custom; their strict performance contained a sacral element.[11]

At the Guildhall installation of the mayor, the aldermen, the mayoral candidate, city officials, and the commons met for the ceremony. The Common Crier called for silence. The Recorder, seated to the right of the mayor, announced that, in conformity with the ancient usage of the city, a new mayor was to be installed. He spoke of the accomplishments of the outgoing mayor, to which the mayor could respond if he wished. Then the mayor vacated his seat to make way for the new mayor and sat on his left. The traditional words and gestures of efficacy followed. The Common Sergeant-at-arms held the gospels ("the book with the Kalendar, with the effigy of Him Crucified on the outside thereof"), and the new mayor placed his hand on the book. The Common Sergeant read the oath that the mayor would take the next day at the king's Exchequer. Promising to uphold the oath, he kissed the book. The new mayor addressed the people and city officials about the needs of the city. The sword of the city was borne at the head of a procession in which the old mayor again took the new mayor by the hand and led him to his home followed by the aldermen, city officials, and the commons. The sword then preceded the old mayor to his home, since he would carry out the duties of office until the next day.[12]

Since the mayor held office at the sufferance of the crown, the oath was repeated the next day before the king's Exchequer. The royal ceremony established the dependency of the mayor and the city's freedoms on the king's pleasure, thereby confirming the position of the mayor in the broader hierarchy. On the procession to Westminister and back to the city, the space around the mayor was ritually established in order to reinforce the status boundaries that separated the mayor from all others in the city. On the way down the Chepe the sword was borne before the mayor elect with the past mayor, the aldermen, sheriffs, and those wearing the personal livery of the mayor coming next. All of the aldermen were dressed in the same robes. (On the day of the oath at Guildhall, they were to wear violet robes.)[13] Then came the livery companies dressed in their company's robes and then the commons. The procession was reversed on the return.

The space maintained around the mayor as he returned to the city set him and his special dignity of office apart. Since he had no equal in the city, his space was protected: "No person . . . moved so close to the Mayor but that there was a marked space between." To insure and preserve the special space, the sergeants-at-arms, the mace-bearers, and the mayor's sword-bearer went before him. The two sheriffs were on either side bearing white wands. The Recorder and aldermen brought up the rear.[14] More festivities, of course, followed but for our purposes, we may leave them to their feasts and religious services, because we have amply demonstrated the use of space, clothing, and gesture in assuring the efficacy of the election and oath taking.

Public recognition of the oath was but one aspect of maintaining the mayor's exalted dignity. He also had to work at preserving that position against all challengers, be they from above his social rank or below. We immediately assume dramatic events such as rebellions, coups, or assassinations when thinking of the marginalization of an elected official, but in a society in which the symbols of rank are integral to the concept of power, an attack on the dignity of office was a major threat. In a society in which orality and gesture remained strong weapons of insult, people were quick to see nuances of vulnerability or signs of strength.

Of major symbolic importance in rank and dignity was seating at the table. Not only did one want to be seated above the salt, but the highest social status determined the position at the head table. In the city of London the mayor's rank was "next unto the king in all manner of thing" and so he had precedence over an earl.[15] But at a banquet given by the Sergeants-at-arms at the Bishop of Ely's hall in 1464, the Earl of Worcester came from the washing of hands before the banquet first and took the seat of state in the hall. When the mayor "seynge that hys place was occupyd hylde him contente, and went home a gagne with owt mete or drynke or any thonke, but rewarded hym he dyd as hys dygnyte requyryd of the citte." He took with him the aldermen and all the other city officials that he could find and served them a banquet as magnificent as the one they had just left. The menu included swan and other delicacies and the table appointments of gold and silver plate were equally grand. When the hosts discovered the mistake, they tried to make amends by sending meat, wine, bread, and "many dyvers sotelteys." But when their spokesman came to present their gifts, "he was fulle sore a schamyd that shulde doo ye massage, for the present was not better thenn the servyse of metys was by fore the mayre, and thoroughe owte the hyghe tabylle." The mayor magnanimously thanked the messenger for his concern, but clearly indicated that a mere earl was not going to ruin his dignity by invading his official, social space. As the record notes, the offense against the mayor was not simply against his personal dignity, but against that of the city. His office required this show of "living well is the best revenge." The chronicler noted with approval: "and thys the worshippe of the citte was kepte, and not loste for hym."[16]

What happened to an ordinary citizen of London if he attacked the dignity of the mayoralty? Insults to the dignity of any official were taken extremely seriously, and the miscreant was subjected to crippling punishment, unless the offender made elaborate apology. The records are replete with cases of people who objected to the mayor's handling of individual cases or who were general critics of his policies. The problem is to choose, among the many, a case that exemplifies the treatment of a lower-status citizen who insulted the mayor.[17]

One of the most interesting is that of John Walpole, a tailor, who on January 29, 1395 had a prolonged confrontation with Mayor John Fressh. The words of his insult are repeated in what was intended to pass for a verbatim account. The political situation was the highly charged one that surrounded the last years of the reign of Richard II.[18] According to the jurors' account, the miscreant made a number of assaults on the mayor's dignity. First, he invaded the mayor's space as he left St. Paul's Church by approaching him and actually taking hold of his sleeve (the sleeves were of exaggerated length in this period so that the intimacy may not have been as great as pulling a shirt sleeve today). Not only the gesture but the accompanying words were offensive and described by the jurors as "derisive": "Oh mayor, do justice to me." The mayor told him to put his problem in a bill and justice would be done. Walpole was not content, but began to attract the attention of passers by with noisy insults. This partisan shouted: "What use is it to make you a bill when all the magnates of England have made my plea and acknowledge my action?" He is probably referring to the magnates who rose against Richard, since Mayor Fressh was on his way to meet Sir John Bushbeye and Sir William Bagot, intimates of Richard II. The shrill-voiced critic continued to badger, calling a sergeant "a false ribald and harlot" and saying that if he were not one he would make him one. He then attacked the mayor again saying that he played at tables with his sergeant "harlot as he is." He continued harassing the mayor, taking him by the sleeve and shouting at him and threatening mob justice against him. At these words of insurrection, the mayor had him arrested and taken to Newgate. But he protested the whole way, indicting six mayors as he raised the hue and cry. The jurors said that "a great part of the uproar and rancour in the city . . . was spread by the ill-will of John Walpole." He was fined the large sum of £100.[19]

The case underscores a number of points we have observed about the boundaries surrounding the mayor's particular box in the social crosshatch. Both gesture and space are significant. Walpole moved into the mayor's space and presumed the intimacy to pluck his sleeve as well as to shout at him. Both the robes and the space surrounding the mayor should have been off limits to Walpole. But, as in the case of the banquet snub by an earl, the mayor is made out to have maintained his dignity by magisterial forbearance and an appeal to the usual procedures. Only when confronted with a threat of an insurrection did he have the offender thrown into prison. The prison selected was an important symbol as well. Newgate was the prison where felons and traitors were held awaiting trial. Other prisons referred to in this chapter existed for lesser offenders and debtors. An approach to the mayor's body, official dress, and space meant that the offender might end up with his own spatial movement confined in a holding cell with other, violent prisoners.

MARGINALIZATION OF PUBLIC OFFENDERS

The rituals of exclusion from community or status group were as important in establishing boundaries as were those that elevated and enclosed the space around the elite. Rituals of exclusion can, of course, take many forms, and, again, a few must serve as an indication of the symbols and acts that marked the offender as undesirable. London law and custom ranged from the subtle to the obvious in punishing offenders, depending upon the types of offenses and the social status of the offender.

Moving down into the social ranks with which Geremek has dealt—pimps, prostitutes, and bawds—the rituals of exclusion were maximally public and personally humiliating. Beginning with these rituals and some examples of those who suffered them, we can then proceed to the meaning they held for the community in its attempt to define marginals and educate a public made up of foreigners and young country bumpkins. The punishment of bawds and whores permits us to look at gender differences in punishments as well as the spatial, gesticular markers of boundaries.

The *Liber Albus* dealt first with bawds (procurers of prostitutes). In the gender hierarchy male offenders had pride of place to be dealt with first in the law. A bawd convicted on the first offense was to have "his head and beard . . . shaved, except a fringe on the head, two inches in breadth." He was to be taken to the pillory accompanied by minstrels and set thereon for a period determined by the mayor and aldermen. For a second offense he was to undergo the same public rituals of humiliation but also have ten days of imprisonment. A third conviction brought the same punishment, after which he was taken to a city gate and "there let him forswear the city for ever."[20]

These rituals of humiliation were not simply the stuff of legal texts and customary civic recitations of laws. One particularly vivid example from 1517 jolts us into an understanding of how bodies and their articulation became part of the language of medieval rituals of marginalization. Joan Rawlins wanted to go to London to earn the higher wages as a servant that the city afforded. Her patroness, the Lady of Willesdon, had connections with a tailor, John Barton, and asked him to conduct Joan to London and find her "good and honest service." He took her to the city but left her at a waterman's house while he went to a bawdy house "where he proposed to put her." Realizing his designs, she "begged the waterman's wife on her knees" to have her taken to the authorities, which the older woman did. John Barton was convicted and, since he had a previous record of "dishonorable transactions with women," he was imprisoned at Newgate. His punishment was to be paraded about town with a paper on his head explaining his crime as he held on to a horse's tail. At various public places the proclamation of his villainy was read so that the illiterate, most probably the young serving women who were possible victims, would be warned. He was then pilloried for a time and conveyed out of the city.[21]

The case not only confirms the nature of the legal sanctions, but also indicates the importance of various verbal and nonverbal symbols of marginalization. Joan Rawlins used the time-honored gesture of a supplicant by kneeling in humiliation at the knee of a possible benefactor in an expression of her moral values and goals for personal liberty. The waterman's wife availed herself of an access even women had to aldermanic authority to request magisterial justice. Barton, being a repeat offender, had to undergo the rituals of both verbal and nonverbal marginalization. His humiliation was inscribed on his body by way of shaving and publicized by stumbling after a horse's ass and public shaming (probably accompanied by rough music, cries of shame, and lobbed, offensively decaying material objects). Finally, he was expelled from the city. A written indictment, a more elite form of expressing insult, was pinned to his attire so that all means of communication announced his crime. Schmitt's categories, developed from devotional and iconic sources, hardly do justice to the panoply of semiotic elements in one of London's court cases.

But I have said that there was a gender differentiation in the treatment of men and women, and thus I must return to the prescriptions against bawdy house keepers and whores. The *Liber Albus* makes subtle gender-biased assumptions. While men appear in the records accused of being pimps and keepers of bawdy houses, the laws and customs state that any woman who is a "common receiver of courtesans or bawd" and who has been attainted, "let her openly be brought, with minstrels, from prison unto the thew [a special pillory for women] and set there on" for a length of time specified by the mayor and aldermen. Her hair was to be cut around her head, but the length was not specified. For women, the cutting of the hair was both a more obvious and more subtle humiliation than for men. Women normally wore hoods or wimples that surrounded their heads, including the hair and neck. Thus these keepers of bawdy houses were being exposed as no woman, honorable or not, would be and not with long hair but with cropped hair—a primitive symbol of the marginalization of morally offensive women. Consider the pictures that immediately spring to mind: Tacitus's description of the shearing of adulteresses' hair in *Germania* and the unforgettable pictures of the shaven heads of women who took Nazi lovers, including the designer Chanel, as they were paraded through the streets of Paris after World War II. Imprisonment and exile completed the punishment for repeat offenders.[22]

The public cutting of hair must have been more humiliating for women than for men. Men were accustomed to go in public with their faces exposed, and many men, particularly among the upper-class Londoners, shaved. They might even go with their heads uncovered, although most wore hats or hoods in the street. Furthermore, those men who were shaved or had their hair cut in barber shops were accustomed to public shearing, and all men would have been familiar with seeing this small, personal ritual performed in the semi-public space of a shop. The crudity of having this ritual performed in front of a jeering mob, no doubt with many female participants, would have been humiliating, but a shaved face would not have been. The cut hair with the fringe would have been a marker of humiliation, but the very uncovering of the head would not have been as embarrassing and humiliating as it was for the women who underwent the punishment of being shorn. This public undressing and shearing offended expectations for women's normal public posture. Even for men, however, these publicly born physical markers should not be underestimated. One man, who had lost his ear through a horse bite, had asked for a charter from the king explaining that he had suffered mutilation honestly.[23] Hair might grow back, but an ear would not.

Prostitutes received somewhat different treatment than did bawds. Unlike pimping, procuring, or running a bawdy house, prostitution was acceptable in both civil and canon law. Although a necessary evil, the Church found prostitutes' activities more acceptable than adultery or other forms of sexual sins in which men, including clergy, were likely to engage. City fathers in late medieval Europe generally found that prostitutes contributed to the city coffers, and so they ran brothels themselves. London did not engage in licensing or running brothels, although they did allow prostitutes to set up their profession in certain places in the city, particularly Cokkeslane, or encouraged them to ply their trade across the river in Southwark. Those practicing elsewhere were subject to arrest and punishment.[24]

The initial offense did not require the removal of clothing or cutting of hair, but rather the addition of clothing and symbols that both covered and identified the whore. The convicted offender was to be taken from prison to Aldgate "with a hood of ray [striped cloth], and a white wand in her hand." The "hood of ray" became a symbol of the blurred and mixed status of the prostitute, just as various items of clothing identified and shamed Jews in other cities at the time.[25]

The public parade, accompanied by minstrels and rough music, preceded the offender to the thew where the cause was read and then "she was led through Chepe and Newgate to Cokkeslane where she was to take up her abode." For a servant girl or young woman from the country who entered into prostitution without an idea of becoming a professional or who was, in fact, forced into prostitution, such a ceremony would have been a horrible humiliation. The city law was intent on labeling and signifying on the first offense; only on the third conviction was a prostitute to be rendered unattractive and unmarketable by being shorn, while sitting on the thew, and taken to a city gate and made to forswear the city.[26] Actual cases confirm that the public spectacle was performed.[27]

The packaging of honest women as opposed to whores, or to put it another way, the external boundaries surrounding all women's bodies received attention in other directives, thereby indicating the importance of clothing in boundary enforcement. Already in the late fourteenth century the mayor and aldermen issued a ordinance on women's hoods and their symbolic meaning. They decreed that no women of the town should go to market or into the highway wearing furred hoods of lamb or rabbit unless they were of a status appropriate to wear fur. Those of lower status—brewsters, nurses, other servants, and women of disreputable character—had been observed to "adorn themselves and wear hoods furred with *gros veer* and minever after the manner of reputable women."[28]

The city fathers expressed a number of concerns about margins and boundaries in this revealing passage. They wanted to draw status distinctions among the urban women so that wives of the powerful could display their wealth in public, but ordinary women could not go out of their homes with furs—a tacit admission that the city fathers did not control the private space of the house and what women wore therein.

The preamble to the laws concerning bawds and prostitutes emphasized that the process of punishing them was to return the city to "cleanness and honesty."[29] The expulsion of the offenders returned the body politic to a clean and healthy wholeness. But the ritual humiliations had an educational purpose as well. They indicated to the onlookers, particularly the great number of youths and foreigners who flocked to London each year, that the city would punish those who transgressed the laws. As a byproduct, of course, they also educated those who wished to procure sex for hire about where to go, who to look up, and the explicit code of women's hoods.

It was not simply sexual offenses that threatened the city's "wholeness." All business transactions required honest dealings, because the citizens perceived that it was not only the cheated party that suffered. The whole city and its business reputation could be put in jeopardy if the offender was not punished and other potential customers not warned. Public humiliations of offenders were meant as both a deterrent and as an educational tool. As in the case of the sexual offenders, the punishments incorporated the graphic symbols of the offense—for sexual offenders the body was punished, for economic offenders the bad goods were forced on them. The man who sold sev-

enteen pigeons that were unfit for human consumption, for instance, was
paraded to the pillory and had the rotting birds burnt under his nose. A
vintner found guilty of selling unwholesome wine was sentenced to drink
a draft of it and have the rest poured over his head. Nicholas Mollere, servant of John Toppesfeld, smith, was condemned to sit at the pillory with a
whetstone around his neck (the symbol of the liar) because he was a slan-
derer.[30]

The pain and anger that such public humiliation could cause is apparent in the case of Richard Davy, a baker. In 1281 the king ordered that any
baker who produced bad products should be drawn on a hurdle from Guildhall to his home through the main streets where it was most crowded. The
deficient loaf was hung around his neck.[31] Davy had been returned to his
home on the hurdle after this unwelcome exhibition. When he got off the
hurdle he entered his home and got a bone. He threw it at the tabor player,
who had accompanied him with rough music, and broke the tabor through
the middle.[32]

It is hard to remove from our minds the idea that only the sexual offenders and small-time tradesmen could suffer public humiliation. The
guilds of London, however, had ample reason to seek to discipline their
members through rituals of mortification within their guild structure, but if
such measures failed, they were perfectly willing to go public with abase-
ment of an offending member. For instance, John Tresylton, a goldsmith, reviled Robert Rede, collector of the king's money, calling him a "false knave"
and threatening that he would "give him such a blow that he would never
recover from it." The Goldsmith's Guild tried to handle the matter within
the brotherhood and, finding him guilty, fined him 20s. When he refused to
pay, the guild wardens went to his shop in the Chepe to take surety for payment. He met them with abuse and refused to give surety. The wardens
threatened to put him in the Counter, the prison for debtors. Tresylton, the
wardens wrote, insisted "in his passion on being put into the vilest part of
the prison and his wish [was] complied with." After being there a few hours,
however, he paid his fine and was released.[33]

Again, a case such as this shows the multitude of ways that marginalization occurred. Tresylton's words of insult to the tax collector and the guild
wardens is similar to Walpole's attack on the mayor and raises a whole new
area of rituals of marginalization in medieval society—verbal, public slanders. In a society in which oral culture was still very important, the insulting word would be remembered and was perceived as damaging to the person insulted. But this whole area of words that hurt and label must be left
to another occasion for analysis. The gestures and space in which they occurred brought Tresylton's public humiliation to his very doorstep in the
busiest street of London. His insulting words had many witnesses, as did
the triumph of the guild wardens in carrying him off to prison. Nor could
he have returned to his shop a few hours later without accompanying jeers,
laughter, and gossip.

RECONCILIATION AND RECROSSING THE BOUNDARY

Modern criminal justice studies warn about the power of labeling people as undesirables or convicts. The application of such negative labels makes reentry into regular social relations difficult and leaves a cloud of suspicion over the person who has been thrust out. In order to understand the complexity of marginalization in medieval London, therefore, it is useful to look at the possibilities for reconciliation and recrossing the boundaries back into acceptable social relations. In the process of looking at these ceremonies, we need to turn again to the more traditional implications of class and status in the Middle Ages, for the possibility of moving back from a marginalized state to social acceptance depended on the nature of the offense as well as the person's social status, gender, and character.

Characteristic of reconciliations were rituals that not only reintegrated the marginalized, but also reestablished the correct social distances. For instance, when Alan Everard, a mercer of London, had a falling out with his nephew and apprentice, John Everard, the first step was to settle the dispute and the second step was to bring about an acceptable emotional and social basis for renewing the relationship. The apprentice was to pay all the money that he owed to his master, including reimbursing all the moneys he spent on his personal comfort beyond those that an apprentice could normally expect from his master. After the debts were paid, "as a sign of obedience and respect towards his uncle and master," John Everard was to contribute 40s. towards a horse and hold the stirrup when his master mounted.[34] The master's superior position was reinforced, and the rebellious apprentice could be reintegrated only with continued gestures indicating his humility and lower status.

In the reconciliation of differences between those on a more equal social footing, such as guild brothers, the shared meal or drink was the common symbol of reintegration, as can be seen in the chapter "The Power of Word and Symbol."[35] But when a guild brother had so offended the guild either by making false products or by attacking the dignity of the wardens or other guild brothers, it was common to beg to be reconciled by offering casks of wine. Thus in 1359 John de Barton was removed from the Goldsmith's company and forfeited his livery for his *mals outrages*. This action meant that he was no longer a citizen of London and could no longer trade in the city. His outrage lasted only fourteen days when he went to the church of St. Peter's Chepe and prayed for the mercy of the company, offering a gift of 10 tuns of wine to be reconciled and readmitted. The Goldsmiths took him back, but he had to pay for a pipe of wine and give 12d. a week for a year to the poor men of the guild.[36]

A colorful case involving the city of London and the Earl of Derby returns us once again to the fine-tuned posturing that was characteristic of elites dealing with boundaries of behavior. At the end of the summer of 1342, in the initial phases of the Hundred Years' War, the Earl arrived in

London with troops armed for war in France. Some of the Earl's retinue got into a skirmish with some Londoners, and a goldsmith was seriously wounded. The circumstances of the fight indicate once again the prickly relationship between Londoners and members of the nobility. A subsequent inquest indicated that on the day after the Feast of the Decollation of St. John (August 29), the goldsmith was in Friday Street when he was "struck lightly" by the hoof of a horse that the Earl's groom was riding. The goldsmith reacted in anger, calling the groom a "ribald" and striking him with his fist and then his knife. One of the groom's companions struck the goldsmith with a sword.

Fearing reprisals from the Earl's army, a delegation of the mayor, aldermen, and several commoners responded immediately and waited on the Earl at his inn. He threatened not to take his troops to France unless he received satisfaction, but to "visit his enmity upon all citizens of London wherever he found them." Although such action against London was unlikely, a hothead on his way to war was capable of anything. The mayor then called the commonality to consider what to do. This body was not very sympathetic to the Earl's complaint, but saw the wisdom of getting him and his army abroad in the service of Edward III. The only solution was to offer him a gift to avoid incurring his displeasure. The next day several aldermen and commoners were chosen to placate the Earl. One would think that this would be a most difficult assignment, but the record states that they went with "cheerful demeanour" (*vultu hillari*) and begged the Earl not to blame the whole city for the actions of one person, and they offered him a gift of 1,000 casks of wine. The Earl, "highly delighted" (*letus et jocundus*) accepted the gift and "insisted on them dining with him, though they begged to be excused." This polite exchange ended with the Earl's decision, after dinner, to meet the mayor, aldermen, and commonality at Clerkenwell that evening. His honor having been assuaged, he thanked them for the gift, but released them from giving it, and he immediately left for the continent.[37]

Common to the reconciliation cases among these closer social equals was the offer of propitiation and recompense with a ceremonial and a feast item, wine. For the offended party, particularly if perceived as a social superior such as an earl, mayor, or the guild masters, the magnanimous response was to forgive or lessen the penalty. In the case of the offended Earl of Derby, the situation was delicate indeed. The mayor, as we have seen, had precedence over an earl in the city so that he could not go on bended knee to the earl in London. Instead, some of the aldermen and commons undertook the task. Because of the near equality of the mayor and earl, to accept 1,000 casks of wine would insult the mayor. The impasse was overcome with a good-humored offer, a jocular acceptance, a shared meal, and a magnificent gesture of release from both the promised gift and the threat of destruction. The Earl, in the end, had traversed the space between his lodgings and the mayor's congregation in order to show how generous and truly noble he was. The rejoicing citizens accompanied the Earl out of the city, thereby removing him from their space and preserving that of the mayor and citizens.

The wounded goldsmith bore the brunt of blame at an inquest a few days later. All faces were saved, save his.

The rituals of exclusion could create permanent marginals or they could create a temporary state in which the marginalized were to suffer enough humiliation or threat thereof so that they were willing to be reintegrated on the terms that the community, a social group, or a powerful personage wished. Some people were more likely to end up permanently on the margins because they had no ability or possibility to perform rituals of reconciliation and reintegration. Women, being in a generally weak position in the society, worried about being labeled as prostitutes or adulteresses, because they had little recourse to removing the stigma and being reintegrated.[38] Like Paris, London had a group of residents who were "of no account" or "of bad fame." They were people who had little credibility and bad reputation in the city and could not find sureties for their good behavior if they were arrested or had a bad debt. But the group was amorphous, including scoundrels and the unfortunate poor, and did not develop a class consciousness or identity. Nor were they regarded as a group or class by those who refused to do business with them.

Wealth, high social status, and a generally good reputation helped to remove the humiliations of marginalization, but they did not make a person immune from exclusion or insure reintegration. Violations of space, official dignity, publicly held moral views, and good business practices could threaten the "cleanness and honesty" of the city, its officials, and its corporate bodies. The city's laws and practices clearly expressed a need to preserve its moral cleanness and teach both offenders and observers correct behavior. Rituals of inclusion and exclusion encouraged the maintenance of the desired social order and helped to form a concept of the "we" who acted against the undesirable "them." The rituals of marginalization, therefore, are part of the process of forming group boundaries.

NOTES

1. Bronislaw Geremek, *The Margins of Society in Late Medieval Paris*, trans. Jean Birrell (Cambridge: Cambridge University Press, 1987). First published in Polish in 1971 and in French in 1976.
2. Ibid., see particularly pp. 270–99. Ephraim Mizruchi worked toward a broader definition of marginality for medieval society that could include among the marginals such established groups as monks, apprentices, and Beguines, as well as prostitutes and criminals. His theory is based on a presumption that Europe had too many people to be assimilated into vacancies in the social networks. Medieval society developed institutions of social control that held the surplus in abeyance (that is, they slowed the integration process of the surplus by marginalizing them for a period of years in recognized institutions). See *Regulating Society: Beguines, Bohemians, and Other Marginals* (Chicago: Chicago University Press, 1987). First published (New York: Free Press, 1983). See particularly pp. 8–27.

3. Ronald F. E. Weismann, "Reconstructing Renaissance Sociology: The 'Chicago School' and the Study of Renaissance Society," in *Persons in Groups: Social Behavior as Identity Formation in Medieval and Renaissance Europe*, ed. Richard C. Trexler (Binghampton, N.Y.: Medieval and Renaissance Texts and Studies, 1985), pp. 39–46.

4. Frans B.M. De Waal, "The Relation between Power and Sex in the Simians: Socio-Sexual Appeasement Gestures," in *Gender Rhetorics: Postures of Dominance and Submission in History*, ed. Richard C. Trexler (Binghampton, N.Y.: Medieval and Renaissance Texts and Studies, 1994), pp. 15–32.

5. Excellent studies of royal entries may be found in Janos M. Bak, *Coronations: Medieval and Early Modern Monarchic Ritual* (Berkeley: University of California Press, 1990); and in Barbara A. Hanawalt and Kathryn Reyerson, eds., *City and Spectacle in Medieval Europe* (Minneapolis: University of Minnesota Press, 1994).

6. See Pierre Bourdieu, *Outline of a Theory of Practice*, trans. Richard Nice, (Cambridge: Cambridge University Press, 1977), pp. 90–91, 160–63 for a discussion of social division of space.

7. *Liber Albus: The White Book of the City of London Compiled by John Carpenter and Richard Whitington*, trans. Henry Thomas Riley (London: Richard Griffin and Company, 1861), p. 12. This collection of London's laws, ordinances, and customs was compiled in 1419 by John Carpenter, the Common Clerk, and Richard Whitington, Mayor. The book drew on a number of sources and was compiled for the convenience of city officials.

8. Ruth Bird, *The Turbulent London of Richard II* (London: Longmans, Green, 1949). See also Caroline M. Barron, "Richard II and London 1392–97," in *The Reign of Richard II*, ed. F.R.H. Du Boulay and Caroline M. Barron (London: Athlone Press, 1971), pp. 173–201.

9. *Liber Albus*, pp. 18–20.

10. Charles M. Clode, *The Early History of the Guild of Merchant Taylors of the Fraternity of St. John the Baptist*, I (London: Harrison and Sons, 1888), pp. 21–22.

11. Jean-Claude Schmitt, *La Raison des Gesteur dans l'Occident Médiéval* (Paris: Gallimard, 1990). "The Rationale of Gestures in the West: Third to Thirteenth Centuries," in *The Cultural History of Gesture*, ed. Jan Bremmer and Herman Roodengurg (Ithaca: Cornell University Press, 1991), pp. 59–70. See also Jean-Claude Schmitt, ed., *Gestures*, in *History and Anthropology*, vol. 1, pt. 1 (1984). The limitations of Schmitt's approach to the use of gesture for a more general applicability is that he is mostly concerned with those used in religious rituals, particularly those visually represented in artworks.

12. *Liber Albus*, pp. 21–22.

13. The color of the robes and other dress was of major importance in upholding office. For the cloth fair on St. Bartholomew's eve the aldermen were to meet the mayor and sheriffs at Guildhall chapel in their violet gowns, lined. On Good Friday, on the other hand, the mayor and aldermen were to wear their pewk gowns "without chains and tippets." But on Monday and Tuesday of Easter week the aldermen and sheriffs were to come in furred scarlet gowns with their cloaks, and on horses to the Spital. There they were to put off their cloaks to hear the sermon. On Wednesday in Easter week, they were again to be in violet gowns. Cloths not only made the man, but made the official for the specific occasion. See Clode, *Merchant Taylors*, pp. 26–27.

14. Ibid., pp. 22–23. It became the custom in 1434, after the *Liber Albus* was compiled, for the mayor to return by barge.

15. The priorities of seating are listed in "The Boke of Nurture folowyng Englondis gise by John Russell," in *The Babees' Book: Medieval Manners for the Young*, ed. Frederick J. Furnivall (London: Chatto and Windus, 1923), pp. 70–72. While an earl would be of higher status in ordinary circumstances and correctly assume the first place of honor over a mayor, who is listed below a baron, an abbot, or a chief justice, in London the mayor's rank superseded the ordinary seating rules. Holborn, where the palace was located was not within the walls but was within the jurisdiction (inside the bars).

16. The story is recounted in the chronicles of both Holinshed and Gregory. Gregory's chronicle is quoted in Clode, *Merchant Taylors*, pp. 28–29.

17. The assaults on the mayor's dignity are recorded in the Plea and Memoranda Rolls of the City of London. They range from the actions of obstreperous sheriffs to insults by very lowly citizens and non-citizens. Other officials, such as the sheriffs, were also insulted, and these charges were taken equally seriously.

18. See Reginald R. Sharpe, *London and the Kingdom*, I (London: Longmans, Green, 1894) pp. 221–46 for a narrative of city unrest and political disturbance.

19. *Calendar of Plea and Memoranda Rolls*, 4, ed. Arthur H. Thomas (Cambridge: The University Press, 1932), pp. 158–61, 228–30. Walpole's grievances had a history going back to 1389 when he and other prisoners complained about the distribution of alms. He had put the matter in a bill and had asked that the bill be amended because he had not used a lawyer. He had been given a thorough run around and had even appealed to the Duke of Lancaster. By 1395 when he made his assault on the mayor's dignity, he had some cause to be angry. In the case of a person with a first offense, the mayor would put him in prison but eventually release him on mainprise. The action kept hot heads from disrupting the official dignity (1384, pp. 50–51).

20. *Liber Albus*, pp. 394–95.

21. Corporation of London Record Office, *Letter Book N*, p. 92. This Letter Book is in manuscript and is not published.

22. *Liber Albus*, p. 395.

23. *Calendar of Letters from the Mayor and Corporation of the City of London, A. D. 1350–1370*, ed. Reginald R. Sharpe (London, 1885), p. 125.

24. See Ruth Mazo Karras, *Common Women: Prostitution and Sexuality in Medieval England* (New York: Oxford University Press, 1996) for a full discussion of prostitution and its regulation.

25. See Diane Owen Hughes, "Sumptuary Law and Social Relations in Italy," in *Disputes and Settlements: Law and Human Relations in the West*, ed. John Bossy (Cambridge: Cambridge University Press, 1983), pp. 69–99 for a discussion of distinctions by dress. See also "Earrings for Circumcision: Distinction and Purification in the Italian Renaissance City," in *Persons in Groups: Social Behavior as Identity Formation in Medieval and Renaissance Europe*, ed. Richard C. Trexler (Binghampton, N.Y.: Medieval and Renaissance Texts and Studies, 1985), pp. 155–82.

26. *Liber Albus*, p. 395.

27. See, for instance, the case of Elizabeth Judele, Corporation of London, in *Letter Book L*, unpublished manuscript, p. 169. The church courts also used dress and undress as tools of humiliation and drawing of boundaries. A prostitute convicted in a church court was to lead the Sunday procession dressed only in a smock and carrying a candle. This ritual was to be performed as a penance two to three Sundays. Robert Wunderli, *London Church Courts and Society on the Eve*

of the Reformation (Cambridge, Mass.: Medieval Academy of America, 1981), p. 50.

28. *Calendar of Letter Books of the City of London, Letter Book A*, ed. Reginald R. Sharpe (London: John Edward Francis, 1899), p. 220.

29. *Liber Albus*, p. 396. The symbol for the brawler or scold, of either sex, was a female symbol of the distaff dressed with flax. The usual parade occurred. For other offenses parades with music and imprisonment in the Tun were mandated. The preamble to this whole section, p. 394, describes the need for cleanness and honesty in the city to win the favor of God and thereby preserve the city for the honest people of the wards.

30. *Calendar of Letter Books of the City of London, Letter Book G*, ed. Reginald Sharpe (London: John Edward Francis, 1905), pp. 175, 178, 283.

31. Sylvia Thrupp, *A Short History of the Worshipful Company of Bakers* (London, 1933), p. 42.

32. Arthur H. Thomas, ed., *Calendar of Early Mayor's Court Rolls Preserved among the Archives of the Corporation of the City of London at Guildhall, AD 1298–1307* (Cambridge: The University Press, 1924), p. 67.

33. Walter Prideaux, ed., *Memorials of the Goldsmiths' Company, Being Gleanings From Their Records* (London: Eyre, 1896), p. 38.

34. *Calendar of Plea and Memoranda Rolls of the City of London*, 1, p. 268 (1364).

35. Corporation of London Record Office, MC1/1/142. Two men agreed to drop their suits and drink wine together. Prideaux, *Memorials of the Goldsmiths*, p. 30.

36. Prideaux, *Memorials of the Goldsmiths*, p. 5. For other cases, see pp. 6, 11.

37. *Calendar of Plea and Memoranda Rolls*, 1, pp. 154–55, 206–7.

38. Barbara A. Hanawalt, "At the Margin of Women's Space in Medieval Europe," in *Matrons and Marginal Women in Medieval Europe*, ed. Robert R. Edwards and Vickie Ziegler (Woodbridge: Boydell and Brewer, 1995), pp. 1–17.

3

The Power of Word and Symbol: Conflict Resolution in Late Medieval London

We have long known that in medieval Europe adjudication in court was but one alternative for resolving disputes, for arriving at a determination of guilt or innocence, or for assessing the extent of damages or culpability. We have known that participants in disputes initiated compromises and that officials sometimes preferred to mediate or arbitrate rather than to try cases. What has been elusive are the mechanisms for those alternative means of conflict resolution and the extent to which they were a part of the normal practice of social relations. Usually the records laconically state that there has been a love day or that the parties have paid a fine to have a concord. In contrast, the records of medieval London, both municipal and guild, permit a full analysis of the alternatives to adjudication and the role that compromise or atonement played in resolving conflict when fines and capital or corporal punishment were either inadequate or inappropriate to the offense. While London had a complete legal apparatus including coroners, sheriffs, ward moots, and a variety of mayor's courts, informal arbitration and mediation existed alongside these formal means of dispute resolution. This study begins to explore some of the compelling reasons for the popularity of out-of-court settlements; the types of cases that could most effectively be resolved by these means; and the necessity, in a society that still expected and honored oral traditions, of public symbols and words that indicated an end to the dispute.

Historians of late medieval England have been obsessed with the "efficiency" of royal and local courts in "policing" society and punishing the guilty; as a consequence they have seen the use of informal dispute settlements as a sign of weakness in the court system.[1] As Edward Powell and Michael Clanchy have suggested, modern studies of the development of common law have led to a false assumption that law progressed in a linear fashion and that the use of oaths or arbitration represented aberrations in the steady march of judicial development; such tools were a throwback to the days before courts.[2] Medievalists studying arbitration on the European continent have not been hindered by the overriding emphasis on royal justice and centralized courts, but have also seen arbitration as a replacement for the state.[3] While studies written by Powell and others[4] have illustrated the form of arbitration preferred in England and the ways in which it was used among the gentry, they do not consider the broader implications for the social order involved in the use of arbitration and mediation. These studies still discuss judicial procedure and politics, rather than analyze why arbitration worked and the various forms it could take depending on circumstances. To understand the issues of extra-judicial settlements we must move beyond the political considerations of the gentry and their aristocratic patrons in fifteenth-century England, bastard feudalism, and the War of the Roses, and investigate the role of dispute management in the ordinary contexts of community and business transactions both in medieval England and in a cross-cultural context. A "popular" or "folk" view of conflict resolution existed in England side-by-side with normative law and was effective just as in other societies.[5]

The distinction between formal and informal dispute resolution has engaged considerable attention among anthropologists. Rather than enter into these debates, formal dispute resolution is taken in this essay to be the use of court systems in order to impose a decision on the disputing parties in accordance with established laws. Fines and corporal punishments settle misdemeanors and crimes, while restitution of property settle civil disputes. Negotiated settlements, on the other hand, are those in which the interests of both parties are consulted, either by talk between themselves, or through arbitrators or mediators, in order to reach a closure that is mutually acceptable. While the lines between informal and formal justice can be blurred, this simple distinction is adequate for this study.[6]

Anthropologists who have investigated informal dispute resolution in many different cultures point to conditions that facilitate success. Foremost is the need to recreate a balance between the disputing parties or to restore an equilibrium. But balance cannot be achieved without both parties placing a positive value on the outcome. Not only should the disputants wish to reach an accommodation, but also their society and the culture of peacekeeping within it should place a premium on arriving at an amicable closure without recourse to forced and legalistic decisions. The styles of dispute settlement differ from society to society, but shared values on the efficacy of restoration of balance are essential.[7]

These very basic observations are useful in looking at the particular circumstances of late medieval London. Londoners—city and guild officials and freemen of the city—were very conscious of the need to maintain balance in the city for the sake of peace and order. They stated their shared, cohesive values over and over again in a variety of sources and proclaimed their mandates for the behavior necessary to uphold norms. Two very basic principles underlay their ideas about essential truths for survival of the city and effective peacekeeping among its residents. The city charters from

William I the Conqueror (1066–87) through Henry V (1413–22) had among their clauses "that citizens of London shall not plead without the walls of the City in any plea."[8] If matters of property or other issues arose initially outside the confines of the city, then the citizens could take their cases to the royal courts. But the charter clause meant that citizens and city officials had to place a premium on keeping disagreements within the confines of city jurisdiction or face the possible revocation of their charter, or, at the very least, the intervention of royal authority into their courts and governance.

The threat of royal intervention was a real and present danger to London. English kings had many reasons to seek to suspend London's borough privileges and put Londoners under the direct control of the crown—a threat that arose in almost every reign. Should the king wish to squeeze subsidies for war out of wealthy Londoners (and they were fabulously wealthy), he could threaten to take away London's liberties, as did John I. Should insurrection appear possible in London, the king would again threaten to reduce them to an appendage of the crown, as did Richard II when he moved the capital to York. Loss of independent status was not merely a matter of civic pride, but it also meant a real loss of power to London's ruling class and the possibility of a generalized, heavy burden of taxation.[9] It behooved London's government to retain independence and, as a consequence, it tried to contain within the urban community arguments that could give excuse for royal revocation of liberties. Adjudication might work in some cases, but as we shall see, negotiation and arbitration were essential in others. The city had to have mechanisms to deal with powerful individuals and even simple troublemakers who threatened to short-circuit the city and take their cases to royal justices and even into the king's very own household and hearing. This shared value of containment of squabbles and disputes arose from a fear of far-ranging power struggles and insured that all forms of dispute settlement received official encouragement in the interest of preserving the city's special liberties.

London continually expressed the value of internal harmony in ordinances, guild regulations, and directives for public behavior. The city was organized into wards under the leadership of aldermen. Denizens of the wards were jointly responsible for keeping a night watch and reporting all ward inhabitants and strangers who created nuisances in the way of deposits of foul-smelling muck, buildings on public property, or brothels or disorderly drinking houses.[10] All guilds, be they parish, craft, or trade, had as one of their clauses that the brothers should not go to law against each other, but that they should submit their disputes to the wardens and assembly for arbitration. The Mercers' company ordinance is typical. The members agreed that "for unity, rest and peace to be had within the Fellowship of the Mercery, worship and profit of the same, any variance or discord between members of the fellowship, or between those of the fraternity and strangers or members of another fraternity" should submit the dispute to the wardens.[11] When the king's officials came to the Tower of London to try the pleas of the crown, the city carefully laid out the desired behavior.

> The superior and more discreet persons of the said city ought, and of us-
> age are wont, to meet together at a certain and fitting place, for allaying of
> such strifes, rancours, and discords, as have before arisen in the City; to the
> end that, peace and friendship being thus renewed among them, they may
> be, in will and in deed, as one man and one people, in preserving uninjured
> their persons, their customs, and their liberties.

If an individual broke this united front in facing the king and his representatives, "he is by all to be pronounced, among his fellow-citizens, an enemy
and a public foe." He and even his heirs will be debarred from citizenship
forever: "for it does not stand to reason that for such a person his lordship
the King should take the City and its liberties into his hand, to the griev-
ance and detriment of the whole city."[12]

The success of informal dispute resolution in medieval London, therefore, relied on the positive reinforcement of shared values, agreed-upon normative behavior, and avoidance of litigation,[13] as well as a generalized anxiety among the "superior and more discreet persons" that the pursuit of
acrimonious disputes could make all citizens suffer through the loss of the
city charter. Because so much rode on the successful conclusion of potentially damaging disputes, it was important that the words and symbols of
reconciliation be publicly displayed. Not only the participants in a reconciliation needed outward ceremony to bind their agreement, but the symbolic
exchanges reinforced the urban values of harmony.

Repeated injunctions reinforcing desirable behavior, as any historian
knows, means that slips from the ideal were frequent, thus necessitating rep-
etition of appeals for compliance. Indeed, one of the reasons that it is possible to observe the process of non-adjudicated dispute settlement is that the
cases came into courts when these means failed and the history of the dispute was then recorded. London's various court records often had an executive quality to them in which the mayor and aldermen recorded not only
the outcome of the case but the history of what had led up to it. They also
found it useful to preserve in their records negotiated settlements so that future mayors and aldermen could refer back to them if the need arose. While
not legislating arbitration as did Florence,[14] London's records became something of an archive for dispute settlement and are replete with evidence of
how individuals and officials proceeded to reach consensus. Shared values
of peaceful resolutions did not mean that courts and law were unnecessary,
but records show that within the city arbitration and mediated negotiation
were all employed. The use or the "style" of these measures depended on
the nature of the dispute, the social status of the disputants, and the possibility of extensive disruption from the factious interactions.

ARBITRATION

Arbitration, the settlement of disputes by a person or persons empowered
with entire control over the outcome, was commonly used in disagreements

over the terms of contracts. As a commercial city, Londoners frequently had misunderstandings over purchase and sale of goods, terms of leases, debts, and contracts of service, apprenticeship, and even marriage. Because contracts were often oral or because the parties involved hoped only for an agreeable settlement, not full recovery of goods or rights, arbitration was a useful tool. A businessman, for instance, might realize that the person who owed him goods or money was not in a position to repay it all. Rather than going to court and asking for the full amount, it was more convenient and more satisfying to arrange for a reasonable payment. On the whole, arbitration worked best between parties who could foresee a clear advantage in reaching an early agreement.[15]

Arbitration in London, and in England in general, owed much to the practice of canon law (which in turn derived from Roman law).[16] The laity borrowed its forms from the ecclesiastical procedures. The Franciscans made these even more popular as they moved about the country encouraging "love days" as a way of settling disputes in villages. One could argue, therefore, that far from representing a break with legal tradition, arbitration was a time-honored legal form deriving from Roman law and perpetuating itself through the vagaries of common-law practices. In canon law the parties bound themselves to observe the award of the specified arbitrators and usually posted sums of money to indicate their willingness to abide by the arbitration.[17]

In London numerous cases make the procedure clear. Each party could select one or more arbitrators to represent their claims. The arbitrators had to be acceptable to both sides and the parties to the dispute agreed that the arbitration would be binding, often posting a bond to indicate their willingness to abide by the arbitration. To break any tie, they might also appoint an umpire who was agreeable to both sides. A typical example is the following.

> William Hunte, "pursere," who had been sued both at Westminister by writ and in the Sheriff's Court by John Lubek, saddler, with regard to an apprentice, Richard, seeks a remedy under the following circumstances. He and the above John had agreed and been sworn on the book before the Mayor and Recorder that they would submit to the award of six arbitrators, three being chosen by either party, and that in case the arbitrators should not agree, they would abide by the decision of John de Cauntebrigg as umpire (*nounpier*). The six arbitrators had met at the Church of St. Thomas of Acres on 25 Oct. 38 Edward III (1364) and had failed to agree. The said John's arbitrators then refused to accept either John de Cauntebrigg or any other person as umpire.[18]

Although this arbitration failed in this round, the format is clear. The Mayor officiated at the arbitration of an ongoing dispute in which the form of arbitration was agreed to and the parties swore on the book (the gospels) to abide by the arbitration. While they posted no bonds in this case, the parties had recourse to spiritual enforcement of their oaths and chose a spiritual location for the arbitration. The religious element was a frequent theme in London's arbitration cases.

Guild regulations specified the arbitration process for their members. The wardens selected arbitrators to look into the dispute and had the disputants post bond to abide by the arbitration. The qualification of the arbiters was clearly spelled out in the Merchant Tailors' ordinances. They were to be selected from the "saddest and most discrete of the fraternity" and were to show "no favor or partiality to either party."[19] If the arbitration failed, the wardens were to take such measures as would bring the people to agreement, in other words to move to mediation. The case of Simon Danyel, vintner, and William Sterre, vintner, who disputed over a contract for the sale of four tuns of red wine, is a clear case of the workings of binding arbitration. They put themselves upon the arbitration for "four good men of their mystery (vintner's gild)" and undertook to abide by their decisions. They agreed with the arbitrators that William should deliver a tally for £6 in which Simon is bound to him, and that Simon should deliver a tun of red wine to William. We know about this case because William denied the settlement, and it had to go to the Mayor's Court.[20]

Individuals could appoint their own arbitrators outside the context of a guild. The executors of John Pygeon, a citizen and pie baker, claimed that William Shrympylmessh and his wife, Agnes, gave him rights to tenements and quays enfeoffing him and his heirs. Discord arose between them, and Pygeon sold the property to a third person without enrolling the original deed. When Pygeon died he bequeathed these properties. The executors of his will found themselves in disagreement. "By common assent and accord, they put themselves under judgment, order and determination of John Bryan the younger, chosen by the executors, and of Gilbert Asshurst, woodmonger, chosen on behalf of William Schrympylmessh." The arbitrators agreed that John Pygeon and his wife had claim to the property and that William and his wife had quit claim right. An annuity was to be paid to William and his wife through their arbiter of 100 marks. This action "will dispel and put and end to all said contentions."[21]

Religious settings and ancient symbols of hospitality insured the solemnity of the arbitration. In one case two arbiters for each side were appointed in Guildhall, but they made their agreement in the Church of St. Thomas de Acon in Westcheap. In another case the agreement was made in the chapel of St. Katherine in St. Paul's church. In this agreement the parties "put themselves under the order of the [arbiters], who ordained with the common consent of the said parties that the said William should be non-suited and that the parties should be reconciled and drink wine together. This ordinance was executed and fully agreed upon."[22] The binding symbol of the arbitration thus might include swearing on relics or a gospel and sharing a drink of wine. The symbols reinforced an arbitrated decision and made it a more powerful and public ceremony.

But the religious setting and shared drink also were essential for future relations among participants in the dispute. As the anthropologist Michael Herzfeld has observed of sacred oaths among feuding shepherds, "The oath invests social relations with a theological force." He argues that the religious element "detemporalises a touchy situation: by treating the [oaths] as ritually validated truth, it recasts [the dispute] in terms of Eternity, neutralizing past disputes in favor of present and future harmony." In other words, not only is it necessary for the parties to reach satisfaction in the immediate cause of the dispute, they must also feel that they have returned to trust and equilibrium.[23]

MEDIATION IN WHICH THE MEDIATOR IS MORE POWERFUL THAN THE DISPUTANTS

Not all disputes lent themselves to arbitration. A feud between two guild brothers, in which personal animosities rather than broken contracts were involved, placed the guild wardens in the position of mediators trying to get to the cause of the tensions and arrive at a mutually acceptable arrangement by talking to both parties. The wardens were selected from the most powerful and prestigious members of the guild, so that they were in a position to insist on compliance. Nonetheless, their objective in mediation was achievement of equilibrium between two parties who had entered into an intractable disagreement. Not only the disputants had to find harmony, but the whole of the community had to return to a feeling of amity. Fighting among two guild brothers could create factions that would cause fissures among the guild membership. Imposing closure or a settlement was unlikely to return either the parties or the factions to peace. Thus the same sense of community values that encouraged arbitration led to guild ordinances requiring mediation to preserve harmony in the ranks of members. All guilds had as part of their ordinances a clause similar to that of the Cutlers: "If any contention or injury be stirred up or begun among any folk of the said Fraternity, he who feels himself aggrieved shall come to the two good men elected and shall inform them of his complaint . . . the good men shall endeavor an accord between those who are so at variance."[24]

The mechanism of mediation can be seen in the case of Edward of Bowdon versus Davy Panter, brothers of the Goldsmiths' guild. Edward of Bowdon had been a continuous problem to the Goldsmiths, who had punished him as an apprentice for trying to strangle his mistress and had to put him out of the livery (expel him from the guild) when he was a master because he committed fraud. Only the intervention of the Queen persuaded the guild to take him back. His contentious nature appeared again in 1473 when

> diverse matters of controversy and debate by the subtle suggestion of the ancient enemy of mankind, stirrer and chief mover of strife and contention, were moved and hanging between Edward of Bowdon and David Panter— which matters grew of forward and uncourteous language spoken and uttered by either of them to the other to their rebuke, troubling their neighbors about them and all the fellowship.

The wardens initially tried to stop the fight by the time-honored solution of having them each post £40 to be given to the guild poor-box by the one that first started to fight again.

"Against all humanity, not dreading offense to God," they fell out again "with outrageous, heinous and malicious language and also in assaults and making affrays." Indeed their fighting was so notorious that it came to the attention of the king, and the Goldsmiths had to bribe someone at court to get the case back into their jurisdiction. The two bound themselves for £100 each this time and agreed to allow the wardens to settle the problems between them. The wardens and six former wardens listened to "their complaints and the cause of the matter of their grief, with the answers and replications to the same put in by them . . . in writing." They also examined witnesses. "And after ripe communication and due examination of both the parties with their proofs and witnesses" the wardens concluded that the dispute had started because Bowdon had called Panter a "whoreson, banished Scot" and Panter had called Bowdon "false traitor and false whoreson traitor." Various annoyances followed since one party lived above the other and they shared a common entrance. After investigation, the wardens assured them that both these charges were false. Panter was English by birth, in spite of his north-country accent, and Bowdon was not a traitor.

The wardens proposed a series of solutions to alleviate the animosity between them. In the future neither should stop up the other's gutters or drains, nor cause their wives or servants to do so.

> And because the house of the said Davy is over the shop of the said Edward . . . and the said Davy shall not willfully of malice, he or his servants cast or pour on his floor any water or other liquor to run or drop down into the said Edward's shop, not make a dunning [loud noise] with hewing wood. Nor cast down water or dust out of the window upon the said Edward's stall.

Each was to have a key to the front door and "the door shall not be bolted against the other household." Furthermore, the guild would install in each dwelling a bell hanging in a convenient place so that they could summon the members of the guild if one or the other started the affray again. If a dispute broke out again, the one injured was "to suffer and keep silence, whatever be said or done, except bodily hurt" and report the incident to the warden.

Finally, Edward of Bowden and Davy Panter had to perform the words and symbols of reconciliation. They were to shake hands and desire of each other "good love and brotherhood." Since they had put the wardens and others to expense, including the bribe, and trouble they were to pay £12 each into the common box and each should "submit himself lowly upon [his] knees to the wardens before all the livery and ask pardon and forgiveness." Apparently the mediation worked, for they did not reappear before the wardens. But Davy's north-country accent continued to invite harassment, and a few years later a man was fined for calling him "a false knave and a rough-footed Scot" and throwing a weight at him.[25]

Since mediations involved a return to equilibrium of a larger community, the public recitation of words and performance of symbols of reconciliation such as a shared drink or meal took on an added significance. These were coupled with public notice that the parties had posted a bond to the guild poor box to be forfeit should the parties not abide by the mediation. The Goldsmiths' wardens directed in one case:

> Be it had in mind that whereas divers strifes and debates are and have been between John Adys, goldsmith of London and William Pryence of London, goldsmith ... [who] ... have put themselves ... in the award, rule and ordinance of ... [the four wardens of the goldsmiths] ... of all matters, quarrels, trespasses and debates ... from the beginning of the world unto the 18th day of July ... [1439] ... which wardens award and ordain ... the same 18th day that either of the said John Adys and William Pryence shall give to [the] other a dinner at their leisure and that neither shall take nor withdraw customers from the other nor call chapmen from one shop to another, and that neither shall stir nor labor ... to hire another out of house or shop, and that neither shall give to [the] other words of occasion nor of debate from henceforward upon pain of forfeiture of 100s. to be disposed by the warden ... in the alms of Saint Dunstan.[26]

In other words, the two were to cease trying to hire each other's workers and lure away their customers.

The language used by Goldsmiths to describe their unease with disputes indicates the seriousness of the infractions. The feuds are set in a context of eternity, history, and theology: "from the beginning of the world"; "against all humanity, not dreading offense to God"; moved "by the subtle suggestion of the ancient enemy of mankind, stirrer and chief mover of strife and contention." Their rhetoric lends gravity to what seems to us amusing stories of trade fights, name calling, and nasty pranks. At the base of the warden's concern was maintenance of shared values, guild unity, and the need to keep those fights out of the king's courts.

MEDIATION IN WHICH THE MEDIATOR IS A NEGOTIATOR AMONG ELITES

When powerful individuals or guilds came into conflict, city officials acted as mediators, arriving at agreement through discussion of the opposing sides' goals and arranging a compromise that would contain the dispute and not allow it either to move to the royal court or to turn into a riot. The city had much to fear from urban riots. Not only could they end in bloodshed, but also they gave an excuse to the king to take the city governance into his own hands.[27] When such mediated settlements were reached, they were called "judgments." Nonetheless, arrangements such as these differ substantially from the normal court cases in which the mayor acted as judge and the parties were formally called to the Guildhall to answer charges or present writs.

The negotiators, usually the mayor and aldermen of the city, called representatives of the parties to the dispute and listened to both sides. They then examined them independently or collected further evidence by consulting records of past practice or talking to witnesses. Finally, they would call the representatives of both parties together, perhaps before a full meeting of the mayor, aldermen, and common council in the Guildhall and present their solution, usually conceding something to both sides. Mediated negotiation was the common means for resolving disputes between the guilds, because it did not tie the parties up in lengthy litigation that could provide opportunity for mounting tempers and open conflict. Furthermore, it was flexible enough to handle the wide variety of disagreements that arose between those powerful corporate groups.

In 1477, for instance, the Mercers and the Grocers, two of the most prestigious and wealthy companies dealing in long-distance trade argued over the place they would stand on ceremonial occasions in St. Paul's Cathedral. The Mercers complained that the Grocers, a rather newer company, had "unlovingly and unkindly" taken their place on All Hallows or All Saints Day (November 1) and that this has caused "rancor and great malice, especially by means of uncourteous language on their part."[28] The feast day of All Saints was a major one for the city. The mayor, aldermen, and most powerful guilds made routine processions on set days, and this was one of them. The *Liber Albus*, the city's book of precedents and governance, directed that on this day "the Mayor was wont, together with his household, to proceed after dinner to the church of Saint [Thomas], as also the Aldermen and the people of the Mayor's livery, who met together there, with the substantial men of the several mysteries, arrayed in their respective suits." They then processed to St. Paul's church to hear vespers and processed back again.[29] In other words, the All Saints Day procession was one of those civic spectacles that provided occasion for a display of precedence, power, and male sartorial splendor. Such occasions could determine the guild from which the next mayor and aldermen would be selected, and it indicated to the populace watching the solemn parade, who was most powerful in the city. The Mercers had every reason to feel ill-used by the Grocers.

The Mercers' solution was to go to their alderman and ask him to approach the mayor about meeting with delegations from both guilds. The meeting was not an official one at the Guildhall, but rather the parties met at the southwest end of the Cloister of St. Paul's between 8:00 and 9:00 in the morning of December 24. After much discussion, the mayor pointed out that the Mercers had always stood in that spot and should continue to do so and to be first in municipal processions. The Grocers then requested that they be given a desirable place to stand, and the mayor agreed that they could stand on the steps going up to the choir.[30] Several factors went into the mayor's compromise. He appealed to precedent of long standing—an argument that held particular weight in medieval social constructs—and he settled the dispute during the holy season when messages of peace would be most useful. But the matter had to be resolved that day. On December

25, the Nativity, and December 26, St. Stephen's Day, an even more magnificent procession of the Mayor, Aldermen, Sheriffs and worthies of the city proceeded to St. Paul's, where they met the Dean and Chapter and all took their arranged places for the services.[31] A brawl over where these two powerful guilds stood for mass would have been out of place on such a public and solemn occasion. By taking advantage of the solemnity of the season, the mayor's mediated settlement was much more likely to succeed because it invoked a divine element in its solution. Having been sealed by practice on Christmas Day, it was binding thereafter.

Any dispute between guilds posed threats of widespread disruption. When the Cutlers' guild argued with the more powerful Goldsmiths' guild over the right of working with precious metals, the mayor sought a solution that would satisfy both sides. The Cutlers had all the necessary tools and skills to work with metal and were in the habit of doing silver gilt and inlays with gold and silver on the handles and blades of knives and swords. The Goldsmiths claimed the exclusive right to work in precious metals. After meeting separately and together with the representatives of both parties, the mayor resolved that the Cutlers should be allowed to continue their practice but that the Goldsmiths had the right to inspect their work and assay their gold and silver.[32]

Riots between the guilds, sometimes resulting in murder, could also be handled by mediated negotiation. Ralph Turk, the servant of a fishmonger, was murdered after dinner in August 1340 during a general brawl between the Fishmongers and Skinners. The fight started when the servant of a Skinner assaulted the servant of a Fishmonger outside his shop because of an old argument between them. Guild loyalty ran high and soon the servants and masters of both companies joined the fray. Needless to say each side blamed the other for starting the fight. The sheriff summoned an inquest of "the best, richest and wisest men of the mystery of the Skinners for the following Wednesday, and a like inquest of the mystery of Fishmongers for Thursday next." Although the stories of the event that each side presented diverged, they were agreed on who actually committed the murder, and he, a skinner, was charged.[33] The sheriff had used negotiation to avoid an escalation of the riot.

SUCCESS OF NON-ADJUDICATED DISPUTE RESOLUTION

Modern students of social control regard governments that provide successful alternatives to formal justice with some awe, so that we must look at the reasons for London's success. A number of explanations are present in the environment of London. Anthropologists identify the need for shared values if arbitration, mediation, and negotiation are to work. The society as a whole must agree on the sort of behavior that is acceptable and respond positively to non-judicial solutions, being willing to accept them as binding. Thus well-integrated, traditional societies are more likely to be successful in non-adjudicated conflict resolution than is our modern, pluralistic society. As we have seen, the sense of community among corporate groups such as guilds and even parishes and wards encouraged non-adjudicated dispute settlement.

To form a context and consensus for conflict resolution, a variety of educational processes were necessary. After all, medieval England has been called a litigious and violent society, and so London's widespread use of dispute management techniques demands some attention. The problem was partly one of informing the population about city laws and the civic culture of peaceful settlement of disputes. Medieval cities did not replace their populations, but relied instead on recruits from the countryside, market towns, and younger sons of gentry and nobility. The age of marriage was late in urban areas and the infant mortality high so that the number of people born and raised in the city was low. In 1443, for instance, only 17 percent of the young men who swore apprentice oaths were from London, and in 1315 it was only 25 percent.[34] In addition to the apprentices, a large number of foreigners came to London, as did poorer people from the countryside looking for service positions. The civic culture, therefore, had a large body of strangers to educate and assimilate into their values.

The most common method for acculturating the young men who would become citizens and perhaps guildsmen was through apprenticeship. Service was from seven to ten years and in that time, the apprentice learned not only his craft, but also the city and guild rules of behavior and governance. When he took his oath of apprenticeship, he swore to "conduct himself soberly, justly, piously, well, and honorably, and to be a faithful and good servant according to the use and custom of London." On entering the guild after his apprenticeship, he took an oath to abide by the ordinances and governance of the wardens.[35] Although servants did not take these oaths, they were acculturated in the homes of their masters. Foreigners were strictly limited in their access to trade and living arrangements in the city unless they joined a guild themselves and became free of the city. In this case they too would take the guild oath and agree to abide by the guild rules and norms.

The government of London also emphasized acculturation. As Steve Rappaport has put it, "Londoners lived in a multitude of worlds within worlds: they lived in precincts within wards, households within parishes, they were liverymen within Companies [guilds]." The social groupings were small and the citizens had many opportunities to participate in the governance as beadles, church wardens, etc. While few could aspire to mayor, alderman, or sheriff, many could gain knowledge of the laws.[36] To reinforce the integration of newcomers, the mayor and aldermen required a public reading and discussion of acceptable behavior for the city. In the mid-fourteenth century the mayor directed "that for as much as many citizens, owing to their youth, are not sufficiently instructed in the ancient laws, franchises, and customs of the city," it is agreed that the duties of various officers and ordinances regulating trades be "once or twice a year read in public assembly, and copies delivered to such as desire them." On the event of an affray in 1476 involving the king's officials and people in the city the mayor called together the Common Council, informed them of the king's displeasure, and urged forbearance: "And over this that every person be of courteous demeaning. . . . of language as well in buying as in selling and also in proffering their wares for to sell, and for any nasty or simple word be put forth and spoken, which should cause any rancor of debate by any means."[37]

To reinforce a culture of dispute resolution in medieval London, city fathers fostered an atmosphere of fear of the consequences to personal well-being and civic liberties. Citizens had every reason to arrive at solutions to their disputes because the city fathers had the power to take away their liveries and their citizenship, thus effectively removing their ability to function economically. In the extreme, they could even forbid the miscreant from ever entering the city again.

Power and dominance were in the hands of the city elite. Since the charter of Edward II in 1319 freedom of the city (citizenship) was tied to belonging to one of the mysteries or guilds. The *Liber Albus* underscored the charter by providing a list of civic penalties for those disobeying the guild master:

> If any person . . . be rebellious, contradictory, or fractious, that [the guild masters] may not duly perform their duties, and shall thereof be attained, he shall remain in prison, the first time, ten days, and shall pay unto the Commonalty ten shillings for each contempt; and the second time, he shall remain in prison twenty days, and shall, pay twenty shillings unto the Commonalty.

The third time the penalty was thirty days in prison and thirty shillings, and the fourth time he was to pay forty shillings, and spend forty days in prison.[38] In other words, the city ordinances gave teeth to the royal charter by empowering the city government to punish those who would not submit themselves to the arbitration or mediation of the guild masters. The city government, the mayor, aldermen, and sheriffs, were drawn from the twelve most prominent guilds, so that there was an interdependency between the guilds and the government.

The mayor and his officials held an exalted position within London, but they were answerable for their city's charter and liberties to the crown. The city elite, therefore, took amiss citizens such as the obstreperous Edward of Bowdon who let their petty fights with neighbors come to the attention of the central government. They moved swiftly to bribe officials or negotiate with the royal court when a citizen, contrary to the charter of the city, took a case to the royal courts. Indeed, there was even a place and mechanism for such negotiation. Traditionally, the Justices of Kings' Bench met the mayor at the church of St. Martin le Grand to discuss the problems. This location, on the west side of the city toward Westminster, was a negotiating point. Thus, in 1419 when John Corby, a Cheapside goldsmith, took his grievances against the wardens of his guild to the king's court, the mayor and justices met to discuss the case. The justices agreed to return the problem to the guild, and after the wardens failed in attempts to negotiate a settlement with him, they expelled him from the guild and turned him over to the mayor. The mayor, also failing to negotiate a settlement between him and the wardens, removed his citizenship.[39]

Corby's case is instructive, for if the elite had reason to fear the power of the central government, they made the citizens amply aware of their own clout. Expulsion from one's guild or being denied its cloth (livery) and removal of citizenship effectively undercut the economic position of the miscreant. Only guild membership permitted a person to have the freedom of the city and only citizens could trade. By denying the cloth and freedom of the city, the elite could quickly impoverish a man. It is not surprising, therefore, that in four months Corby humbled himself and crawled back to the Goldsmiths. Before the full assembly in Goldsmiths' Hall he "swore on a book by his own free will" to abide by whatever decrees the wardens might make concerning his trespass thus "to make peace and rest between him and all the Company for ever." When the wardens first revealed these terms Corby had refused to comply, but at the end of the year he made his submission. He lived honorably and peacefully to a ripe old age, when he was relieved of official duties because he was seventy. Another goldsmith was forced to forfeit his membership in the Goldsmiths' guild for his *mals outrages*, but his recalcitrance lasted only fourteen days. He went to St. Peter's Cheap and prayed for mercy, offering the company 10 tuns of wine. He had to pay a pipe of wine and to support a poor member of the company for a year at 12d. alms a week.[40]

Rebellion and insults against any civic authority was swiftly, symbolically, and expensively punished, as is more fully explained in the essay, "Rituals of Inclusion and Exclusion." Roger Torold, a vintner who used opprobrious words against the mayor in front of witnesses, was not released from prison until he paid 100 tuns of wine. Richard Horn, however, was ordered to pay 20 casks of wine for trespass against the mayor and aldermen but by special favor it was reduced to 10 casks, 9 of which would be payable if he was convicted of ill behavior again. Another man pledged himself to give 5 casks of wine at the mayor's pleasure for resisting a sequestration on his goods.[41]

Neither the guild wardens nor the mayor and aldermen appeared to be vindictive in their punishment of the recalcitrant. Their goal was to preserve the dignity and authority of their offices and to reintegrate a citizen into the community, be it the freedom of the city or the livery of the guild. Many of those punished went on to become wardens or even mayors themselves. The goal, therefore, was to provide a punishment that would not cripple the culprit, but would underscore the authority of the offended party so that reconciliation was possible.

Unfortunately, we cannot know how frequently arbitration, mediation, and negotiation were used compared to adjudication.[42] The courts were full of cases tried in the regular fashion, but about a third or more of those never came to judgment. No doubt going to court was one way of forcing the other party to accept arbitration or mediation. But by their nature, we would not have information on the many successful informal settlements or even on private written agreements. The concords we know about come to our attention either because they failed, or because they were made among members of guilds who kept comprehensive records. Further, some sorts of actions were more likely than others to lead to formal justice. Clear violations of city ordinances and laws, unambiguous failure to keep a contract, and felonies would be prosecuted in regular courts. Likewise, some classes of people were more likely to seek an alternative to the courts than others. Those who were integrated into the values and power structure of the city and had reason to fear the consequences of losing trading and citizenship rights were more amenable to reaching concord and conciliation outside court. People who had less to lose in terms of citizenship, such as day laborers and servants, were more likely to appear in courts. Women presented a special problem. While not barred from guilds and citizenship, they did not enter into the full privileges of either. Their debt cases could appear in the mayor's court, but curiously they preferred the archdeacon's court, perhaps because this court readily permitted out-of-court settlements. In dower cases, women used the mayor's court of common pleas, but again many must have settled out of court. In general, women had less reason to appear in the records in either formal or informal judicial situations.

Finally, the words and symbols that indicated final concord or atonement were also part of the educational process. The symbols of private agreement were swearing on relics or the gospels, the clasp of hands with words of friendship, and that most ancient of all symbols, the breaking of bread together. Once a meal, a drink of wine, or bread had been shared together the parties were honor bound not to raise disputes again. The public atonement was done with symbols of humiliation. Recalcitrant guild members asked forgiveness on bended knee. Citizens slandering the mayor and officials presented casks of wine. The ceremonies spoke not only to individual amendment, but to public reinforcement of values.

NOTES

1. John G. Bellamy, in *Crime and Public Order in England in the Later Middle Ages* (London: Routledge and Kegan Paul, 1973), pp. 114–19, saw the use of arbitration as an unfortunate result of the failure of common law. R. L. Storey, in *The End of the House of Lancaster* (London: Barrie & Rockliffe, 1966), pp. 121–22, put the use of arbitration in the context of the breakdown of law and order during the War of the Roses. A desire to investigate the disorders resulting from this series of civil disruptions has continued to influence the interpretation of crime and violence in the fifteenth century. This emphasis on political events at the expense of social or economic ones has distorted the picture of peacekeeping in the fifteenth century.

2. Edward Powell, "Settlement of Disputes by Arbitration in Fifteenth-Century England," *Law and History Review*, 2 (1984): 21–24 has an excellent summary of the historical literature on arbitration. He pointed not only to the work of Bellamy and Story, but also observes that some historians have looked at particular incidents where arbitration was done and the emphasis that this form had in legal training. See also his book, *Kingship, Law, and Society: Criminal Justice in the Reign of Henry V* (Oxford: Clarendon Press, 1989) for more discussion of the use of arbitration. See also Michael Clanchy, "Law and Love in the Middle Ages," in *Disputes and Settlements: Law and Human Relations in the West*, ed. John Bossy (Cambridge: Cambridge University Press, 1983), p. 51. Simon Roberts, in *Order and Dispute: An Introduction to Legal Anthropology* (New York: St. Martin's Press, 1979), pp. 12–13, points out that early anthropologists were also incredulous of primitive societies that could settle their disputes without a court system.

3. Ibid. Power gives a summary of the older works. For more recent studies see Patrick J. Geary, "Vivre en conflit dans une France sans état: Typologie des mécanismes de règlement des conflicts (1050–1200)," *Annales Économies, Sociétés, Civilizations* (1986): 1107–33. See also Wendy Davis and Paul Fouracre, eds., *The Settlement of Disputes in Early Medieval Europe*, (Cambridge: Cambridge University Press, 1986).

4. Ian Rowney, "Arbitration in Gentry Disputes of the Latter Middle Ages," *History*, 67 (1982): 367–76. John B. Post, "Courts, Councils and Arbitrators in Ladbroke Manor Dispute, 1382–1400," in *Medieval Legal Records Edited in Memory of C.A.F. Meekings*, ed. Roy F. Hunnisett and John B. Post (London: H. M. Stationery Off., 1978), pp. 289–339. The approach to arbitration has been largely functionalist and does not stray far from making the forms of arbitration and their conclusions consistent with common law. Philippa C. Maddern, in *Violence and Social Order: East Anglia 1422–1442* (Oxford: Clarendon Press, 1992) has argued that going to law was one way to encourage arbitration.

5. Nicole Castan, "The Arbitration of Disputes under the 'Ancien Régime'," trans. John Bossy, in *Disputes and Settlements: Law and Human Relations in the West*, ed. John Bossy (Cambridge: Cambridge University Press, 1983), pp. 229–60.

6. P. H. Gulliver, *Disputes and Negotiations: A Cross Cultural Perspective* (New York: Academic Press, 1979), pp. 3–34. Simons, *Order and Dispute*, pp. 69–79.

7. Laura Nader, "Styles of Court Procedure: To Make a Balance," in *Case Studies of Law in Non-Western Societies* (Chicago: University of Chicago Press, 1991), pp. 69–91 has made a clear summary statement of this approach. Gulliver, in *Disputes and Negotiations*, pp. 9–11, writes that shared norms are essential for dispute resolution through negotiation.

8. *Liber Albus: The White Book of the City of London Compiled A.D. 1419 by John Carpenter and Richard Whitington*, ed. and trans. Henry T. Riley (London: R. Griffin, 1861), pp. 114–53.

9. Pamela Nightingale, "Capitalists, Crafts and Constitutional Change in Late Fourteenth-Century London," *Past and Present*, 124 (1989): 3–35.

10. *Liber Albus*, pp. 29–37.

11. *Acts of Court of the Mercers' Company*, ed. Laetitia Lyell and Frank D. Watney (Cambridge: The University Press, 1936), p. 43.

12. *Liber Albus*, p. 45.

13. Clanchy, in "Law and Love," pp. 47–56, points out that, while no explicit law in medieval England pointed to arbitration or negotiation, the *Leges Henrici Primi* suggests the use of processual rather than legal means of settling disputes. Simon Roberts, in "The Study of Dispute: Anthropological Perspectives," *Disputes*

and Settlements: Law and Human Relations in the West, ed. John Bossy (Cambridge: Cambridge University Press, 1983), p. 7, has made the argument for the distinction between normative behavior and going to law. When a society has an acceptable understanding of normative conduct that can be translated into explicit recommendations for behavior patterns, going to law is less necessary.

14. Thomas Kuehn, *Law, Family and Women: Toward a Legal Anthropology of Renaissance Italy* (Chicago: University of Chicago Press, 1991), pp. 26–30.

15. Steven White, in " 'Pactum . . . Legem Vincit et Amor Judicium:' The Settlement of Disputes by Compromise in Eleventh-Century Western France," *American Journal of Legal History*, 22 (1978): 281–308, has pointed out that the advantages of an arbitration were that the parties could ask for a generalized settlement of their differences rather than pick on a particular point of law, which would have been characteristic of an in-court settlement.

16. L. Fowler, "Forms of Arbitration," in *Proceedings of the Fourth International Congress of Medieval Cannon Law*, ed. Stephen Kuttner (Monumenta Iuris Canonici, ser. C, 5, 1976), pp. 133–47.

17. For English examples see Edward Powell, "Arbitration and the Law in England in the Late Middle Ages," *Transactions of the Royal Historical Society* 5th ser., 33 (1983): 53–55.

18. *Calendar of Plea and Memoranda Rolls*, 1 ed. Arthur H. Thomas (Cambridge: The University Press, 1926), p. 278 (25 June 1364).

19. Charles M. Clode, *The Early History of the Guild of Merchant Taylors* (London: Harrison and sons, 1888), p. 129.

20. Corporation of London, Mayor's Court 1/2/84. Hereafter referred to as MC. When the guild was unable to bring a case to a successful conclusion, they had recourse to the mayor and aldermen.

21. MC 1/1/5.

22. MC 1/2/157, 1/1/142.

23. Michael Herzfeld, "Pride and Perjury: Time and the Oath in the Mountain Villages of Crete," *Man* (N.S.) 25: 306, 317.

24. Charles Welch, *History of the Cutlers' Company of London*, I (London: Printed privately, 1916), p. 253.

25. Thomas F. Reddaway, *The Early History of the Goldsmith' Company, 1327–1500* (London: Arnold, 1975), pp. 151–53.

26. Ibid., p. 99.

27. Ruth Bird, in *The Turbulent London of Richard II* (London: Longmans, Green, 1949), gives a very good account of the fights among guilds and the disruptions they caused. In Nightingale's "Capitalists, Crafts and Constitutional Change," she discusses the negotiations between the crown and factions in London. See also Gwyn A. Williams, *Medieval London: From Commune to Capital* (London: Athlone Press, 1963), pp. 286–88.

28. *Court of Mercers' Company*, p. 101.

29. *Liber Albus*, pp. 24–25.

30. *Court of Mercers' Company*, p. 101.

31. *Liber Albus*, p. 25.

32. Welch, *Cutlers' Company*, pp. 107–9.

33. *Calendar of Coroners' Rolls of the City of London*, ed. Reginald R. Sharpe (London: R. Clay and Sons, Limited, 1913), pp. 266–69.

34. Steve Rappaport, "Social Structure and Mobility in Sixteenth-Century London, Part I," *The London Journal*, 9 (1983): 119.

35. Clode, *Early History of the Guild of Merchant Taylors*, p. 334.

36. Steve Rappaport, "Social Structure and Mobility in Sixteenth-Century London: Part II," *The London Journal*, 10 (1984): 113.
37. *Letter Book E*, p. 13; *Mercers' Company*, p. 107.
38. *Liber Albus*, pp. 424–25.
39. Reddaway, *Goldsmiths*, p. 97.
40. Walter S. Prideaux, *Memorials of the Goldsmiths' Company Being Gleanings from their Records* (London: Eyre, 1896), pp. 5, 6, 38.
41. *Letter Book F*, p. 53. See also Arthur H. Thomas, ed., *Calendar of Early Mayor's Court Rolls Preserved among the Archives of the Corporation of the City of London at the Guildhall, AD 1298–1307* (Cambridge: The University Press, 1924), pp. 16, 34.
42. Kuehn, in *Law, Family, and Women*, pp. 36–74, has had the advantage of working with Florentine records in which there was a statute for arbitration, and so he has been able to work on a small sample, with the recourse to arbitration. Without such a legal status in London, cases appear as they fail rather than as they succeed.

4

Fur-Collar Crime: The Pattern of Crime among the Fourteenth-Century English Nobility

All baronets are bad; but was he worse than other baronets?

W.S. GILBERT, *RUDDIGORE*

The criminal behavior of the upper classes in society has occasioned social comment for centuries. *Robber barons* is a term that has been applied as readily to the medieval nobles who used their castles to extort money from the countryside as to the railroad magnates of the nineteenth century. Illegal activities among the upper classes have provoked discussion because they are distinct from the crimes of other classes. Usually upper-class criminals commit crimes that are related to their control of wealth and power and that often go unpunished or are inadequately punished because their prominence in politics and the economy makes it difficult for governments to prosecute. The nature of contemporary upper-class crime was sociologically analyzed by Edwin H. Sutherland in his study, *White Collar Crime*.[1] As Sutherland defined it, white-collar crime was "crime committed by a person of respectability and high social status in the course of his occupation."[2] In Sutherland's study the crimes that fell within this group were violations of federal trade laws and fair employment practices and mismanagement of corporation finances. Such areas of criminal activity are obviously not applicable to the upper classes of the Middle Ages but, if allowances are made for differences in occupation between a modern executive and a medieval noble, the concept of white-collar crime may prove useful in forming a more general understanding of the pattern of crime among the elite power groups.

This article was first published in *The Journal of Social History*, 8 (1975): 1–17

In applying this modern criminological concept to a historical setting very different from that which formed the basis of Sutherland's study, we must assess the extent to which the crime pattern of those whose social status, according to the Sumptuary legislation of the fourteenth century, was high enough to wear fur collars is analogous to white-collar crime patterns. In other words, was the fur-collar criminal behavior significantly different from that of the peasant criminal, and was it an outgrowth of his occupation as warrior, estate owner, and political administrator?

Upper-class criminals are unique not only in that their crimes are related to their occupations, but also in that both they and their society do not regard their activities as invariably criminal. This means that the approach governments use in bringing upper-class criminals to justice will differ considerably from that used with ordinary criminals.[3] In addition, the close ties between the upper classes and the government make it very difficult for governments to prosecute the cases at all. Students of medieval history in the English historiographical tradition have on the whole failed to appreciate this unique aspect of the relationship of the kings to their criminal barons. In describing the crimes and outrages of medieval barons, scholars have blamed the nobility for not obeying the laws and kings for not bringing them to justice.[4] These descriptions ignore the fact that kings and barons both assumed that a certain amount of criminal activity was involved in being a noble and that it would be tolerated as long as it did not become excessive. This assumption, and the relationship it fostered between king and nobility, is very similar to that between modern governments and large corporations. Furthermore, as in modern control of corporations, kings could use a number of informal and indirect means to control the illegal activities of their barons without bringing them into common criminal courts. The second part of this chapter, then, will look at the alternatives medieval kings had to direct confrontation with the nobility and their success in regulating crimes of the upper classes.

Before we analyze the criminal behavior of the fur-collar class in late medieval England, both the membership in the class and the term *crime*, as it applied to their activities, must be defined. The distinctive badge of the dress of the nobility was that they and their families were allowed to wear minever fur decoration on their costumes. Edward III's sumptuary legislation regulating the wearing of minever fur drew the line between the noble and the non-noble at the rank of esquires or gentlemen who could claim land and rents yielding £133 6s. 4d. or more per year.[5] However, this definition of nobility was much too narrow to suit the opinion of the day and was violated freely. Furthermore, many an ancient and noble family who did not have such a large income was considered noble by both itself and its contemporaries, even though Edward III would only allow its members to wear squirrel. K.B. McFarlane pointed out that during Edward III's reign the baronage represented only the "upper layer" of a large category of established people of honorable family and ancient wealth who were considered noble by medieval standards.[6] This group, who for the purposes of this book are called the fur-collar class, ranged from the wealthy and ancient gentry to the higher nobility. The distinguishing features of the class were nobility of birth and a particular set of social values. The differences of rank and income within the nobility were reflected in somewhat different patterns of criminal activity.

The crimes that members of this class were likely to commit must be defined because, by and large, they do not fall within the usual medieval category of felonious acts. Felonies were easily delimited in medieval law: homicide, rape, arson, robbery, burglary, larceny, and receiving. Although the nobles might commit these acts against the king's peace, they most often used their position in society to interfere with the course of justice and to extort land and money in a variety of ways. These actions, while often violent, were not always considered to be criminal matters, but rather trespasses. They might be tried by private suit as well as at the king's behest, and they were punishable by fine rather than hanging, which was the punishment for felons. The distinctions between crime and tort were not established in the Middle Ages because, as the legal historian T.F.T. Plucknett observes, "the Middle Ages were more intent on doing what had to be done, than on classifying ways of doing it."[7] In view of the confusion that existed in medieval law, the best solution is to impose a definition from modern criminology. In summing up the definition of crime employed in his study, Sutherland emphasized that a criminal act was one that was socially harmful and for which a state-imposed penalty was legally provided.[8] The illegal actions discussed in this essay fall well within this definition. Corruption of justice, widespread extortion in the countryside, and violent behavior of the lords' gangs were certainly harmful to the state and to society and were punishable through criminal court procedure with penalties imposed upon conviction. As we shall see, however, these cases were often not tried in criminal courts or were pardoned before they ever reached court. Nonetheless, there were legal provisions for trial if such a solution seemed most expedient.

In his study of white-collar crime, Sutherland eliminated the ordinary felonies from his categories of upper-class criminal behavior because acts such as homicide, robbery, and rape were rare among that group, and were not connected with the criminals' occupations. In the Middle Ages, however, warfare was part of the occupation of the upper classes and murder and pillage (robbery and burglary) could be work-related crimes. Furthermore, comparing the involvement of the nobility and the peasantry in ordinary felonies indicates how substantially different their criminal activities were. The most immediately apparent difference is the paucity of nobles in the ordinary criminal court, jail delivery. Only 14 out of about 10,500 felony indictments in the fourteenth century involved members of the nobility.[9] The low number of nobles in this ordinary court is not surprising because they could easily use their influence to avoid prosecution. In the Kent indictments of 1316–17, only four of the seventy-seven people indicted for felony were noble, and all were either acquitted or never tried.[10] In order to indict the weightier criminals of his realm, the king had to rely upon commissions of trailbaston or oyer and terminer, which gave the assize justices special powers to hear and determine cases. But these procedures also reveal that nobles rarely engaged in ordinary felonies.

The absence of nobility in felony cases stems only in part from their ability to quash indictments, for it was more important that their social position gave them little reason to commit ordinary felonies. Homicide patterns illustrate this point very well. The barons and gentry of medieval England were involved in some very notable murders in the fourteenth century, such as the beheading of Piers Gaveston,[11] the sadistic execution of Edward II,[12] and numerous homicides in connection with private warfare and civil wars. These acts, however, ranged in description from treason to vague feudal rights of revenge and private war, to execution of the ruler's orders. Homicides of this sort were distinctly fur-collar crimes because they were directly related to the nobles' political and military functions. Members of the higher nobility had little occasion to stain their hands in ordinary homicide involving disputes with the lower classes, because their household retainers could be ordered to take the necessary steps. (One may see here a clear analogy with the noninvolvement of the modern upper classes in the formal statistics of homicide and other conventional crimes.) For example, after dinner on 13 May 1301 Sir Ralph Porthos of Polebrook sent two of his men to John of Weldon's house in Polebrook to bring him to Sir Ralph's court dead or alive. Porthos's men killed Weldon and brought back ten shillings of his instead. In this murder Sir Ralph was an instigator and receiver but not a murderer.[13] The lower ranks of nobility, such as the Folvilles, were more likely to wield the murder weapons themselves. For instance, Sir John, son of William Grammary and his servant, killed Alexander le Smith at Tadcaster.[14]

Knights were also more likely than the higher nobility to participate personally in occasional robberies, burglaries, and larcenies. Again, this parallels the modern situation where those of lower status in the white-collar classes are more likely to be directly involved in criminal acts. The activities of these lower ranks of the nobility were so bad in 1331 that a special complaint was made in Parliament about the involvement of gentry in criminal bands.[15] Part of the reason for the gentry's criminality may have lain in their worsening economic position. M.M. Postan's research has shown that by the end of the thirteenth century, the gentry were sinking economically.[16] Under these circumstances, some of them may have turned to crime to keep up their standard of living. Robbery certainly paid well for those knights who could muster a gang for that purpose. Sir Robert Rideward and Sir John Oddingseles staged an ambush and robbery of merchants that brought in £40,[17] but this was a small affair compared to the thirty-eight-member gang of Sir John de Colseby and Sir William Bussy, which was able to take goods amounting to £3,000 in various robberies and larcenies.[18] These knights did particularly well in crime considering that the average value of goods stolen by persons tried in jail delivery was £3 4s. Since knights could rely on their estates or upon receivers for their daily bread, they tended to steal items of larger value than did ordinary thieves. For instance, Lord Simon de Monteacute and Lord Ulfrid de Beauchamp came with arms and troops to the Abbot of Glastonbury's woods and carried off 100 trees and killed one of the Abbot's men.[19] Even when stealing victuals they thought in larger terms than those of a peasant. Lord Robert de Mangleye sent four of his men to carry off no mere side of bacon, but five stones of meat.[20]

Among the highest to the lowest level of nobility, receiving was the most common felony. If barons like Lord Robert de Mangleye and Sir Ralph Porthos did not do their own hatchet work, they did shelter and protect their criminal henchmen. When the justices came to Somerset in 1305 to make special inquiries into criminal activities, they found that Lord Simon de Monteacute, Lord Robert son of Payn, Lady Juliana la Brett, and Lord Robert de Brente were all suspected of receiving felons, as were the high churchmen of the region.[21] None of these peers had taken part in the felonies, but they were accused of inciting the deeds and sheltering the culprits, who were often members of their households.

For most of the fur-collar class simple felony was not as profitable as were a number of other illegal activities more closely related to their occupations. As maintainers of armed households, owners of estates, ultimate judges in manorial courts, and members of royal commissions, nobles could make abuse of their powers very profitable. The barons' households often appear in the records in the role of unscrupulous collection agencies. As McFarlane pointed out, the "barons' councils" were necessary to protect the lord's interest with his tenants, but there was often a thin line between collecting legitimate rents and looting the tenants possessions.[22] In a contemporary analogy, Sutherland described this blurring of lines between legal and illegal acts as a failure on the part of the white-collar class to regard their acts as criminal.[23] Two instances of fourteenth-century confusion of function are those of Lord Robert son of Payn and members of his *familia*, who forced Richard Seger of Raunton to pay twenty marks or be evicted from his tenement,[24] and Sir Ralph le Cort, who ordered his household to expel his miller or burn the mill.[25] Both of these cases could have involved tenants who defaulted on rents, and hence the actions of their lords would have been legitimate. In other cases peasants paid with their lives as well as with their property:

> On 3 December [1274] John of Rushall, knight and his esquire Henry of Hastings were entertained at the parson of Melchbourne's house and Henry took provisions necessary for his lord's use from many men in Melchbourne. Those whom they owed money for food and oats came and asked for it. John and Henry said that they had no ready money in Melchbourne and asked them to send a man with them to Cambridge and [said] that they should have the ready money there. They unanimously sent Ellis of Astwood with them. Ellis followed them from Melchbourne to "le Rode" where John and Henry and others unknown of John's household cut his throat.[26]

The nobles of Somerset were indicted for a number of beatings, which often ended with broken bones.[27] The motives for these orders are not always clear, but some may have involved intimidation of tenants as well as collection of goods and money.

The nobility used the techniques of extortion not only on their tenants but also on their neighbors in order to extend both their wealth and their sphere of influence. At the lowest level the extortion of money was a crude protection racket. Armed members of the noble's household would beat and wound a victim (being careful not to raise it to a felony by killing him) and then demand a money payment to buy protection against future assault. Lord Robert son of Payn's *familia* was indicted for extorting from 13s. 4d. to £2 from five victims for a total of £6 9d.[28] The exact profit to the lord from such ventures was even spelled out in one case. Lord Robert son of Payn's men John Gaillard, Thomas Southbourne, and Reginald Talcon, and perhaps others from his household, extorted 70s. from four men. Lord Robert took 30s. and the rest was divided among his men for their pay.[29] Some of the gentry and their gangs won such an evil reputation for extortion that they had only to send a letter that threatened a victim's life, limb, and property in order to extort money. Members of the Coterel gang developed extortion of this kind into a refined technique. They would send a victim threatening letters and one-half of an indented bill. The victim was forced to pay the fee demanded by the bearer of the other half of the bill.[30] In early fourteenth-century Staffordshire John Somery not only forced the whole county to pay protection money to him, but was also able to make the inhabitants seek justice through him.[31] Extortion techniques could be used to gain land as well as money. For example, two brothers in a venerable Somerset family had a dispute over land. Thomas de Hywis took John de Hywis to his home and tied him up until he drew up a charter of enfeoffment for his brother and paid £20.[32]

Another form of extortion was abduction and ransom. The procedure was to waylay wealthy travelers or to attack the victims' homes and drag them off to the lord's castle or other places of safekeeping. The most famous fourteenth-century ransom case is Sir Gilbert de Middleton's abduction of the Beaumonts. Sir Henry Beaumont was traveling to Durham with his brother, the bishop-elect of Durham, and two cardinals who were on a peacemaking mission to northern England. Sir Gilbert and a gang of northern gentry robbed the cardinals and took the Beaumonts to Sir Gilbert's castle at Mitford, where they were released only after they had paid a ransom.[33] Another famous ransoming is that of Sir Richard de Wylughby, a King's Bench justice, by the Folvilles, Coterels, and other Staffordshire gangs. The risks involved in abducting such highly placed people were well worth it—the Wylughby ransom was £866 13s. 4d.[34]

The culpability of the nobility in the abduction and rape of women is not recorded, but the abduction and marriage of a king's heiress was acceptable if the noble paid the king a fine.

Finally, the nobles could make money by using their might and influence to protect and benefit weaker neighbors and thereby extend their own prestige in the county. Lord Adam de la Ford was indicted for receiving and protecting Walter le Moch of Edyngton, a serf of John le Waleys, and for maintaining him against John. Walter paid Lord Adam £1 8s. 8d. for his aid. Apparently this was Lord Adam's pattern, because the indictment goes on to say that he is "a common maintainor and protector."[35] His practice was, indeed, rather common (in the other sense of the word), compared to the actions of some nobles. Lord Robert son of Payn, Lord Henry de Urtiaco, Lord Mathew de Fourneaux, and their men aided Stephen de Beaumont in taking over Maurice de Membury's manor at West Bagborough. The four nobles came with troops and arms and attacked and wounded members of Maurice's household. They each took goods and chattels worth £40 from the manor, and in addition Stephen paid them £40 for their aid.[36]

If the nobles were caught or recognized while committing a criminal act, they had a number of ways to subvert justice and protect themselves and their followers from prosecution. In this they resemble the heads of modern corporations.[37] One option was to intimidate jurors so that they would not bring charges against the magnates and their people. When Robert Gran testified at the assize against Lord John de Mandeville, Lord John sent Nicholas de Karmle and William Parker, who assaulted Robert and broke his arm "as a warning to others."[38] Lord Simon de Monteacute employed his trusty thug Luke le Little and his gang to break the millstones and burn the mills of three jurors who had testified against Matilda Simon of Cerde, a woman under Lord Simon's protection.[39] On another occasion Hugh le Franne, who was accused of robbing a man of two horses, gave Lord Simon 100 sheep to procure an acquittal through jury intimidation.[40] If the jurors would not be persuaded by maltreatment or bribes, then the lords would turn their attention to the justices. Roger, son of Lord Robert de Brent, two of the Hywis brothers, and three other men wounded and maltreated one of the justices of the assize who was holding the sessions at which they were finally indicted.[41] Justices were often persuaded to drop charges by gentler means than physical assault, however. In a very modern-sounding letter a justice wrote to a young noble, "For the love of your father I have hindered charges being brought against you and have prevented execution of indictment actually made."[42] If neither love nor money could stop a case from proceeding, then the noble might try to stop the session altogether. Sir Roger Swynnerton of Staffordshire and his supporters closed the doors of the hall where the county court was being held and threatened to kill the sheriff if he tried to start the session.[43] Another way to halt a case was to prevent a victim from testifying in court and bringing an appeal against the criminal. Sir William Bradshaw appeared at court with sixty armed men and prevented Cecilia le Boteler from bringing an appeal against him.[44] And, finally, there was the unsubtle method of Lord John Fitzwalter of Essex, who sent his men to rescue a client from custody before he could be tried.[45]

How did a person like Sir William Bradshaw persuade sixty people to come in arms to intimidate juries, justices, and witnesses, and where did a baron like Robert son of Payn find thugs who would break bones to provide him with 30s. in extorted money? As in modern corporations, the ba-

sic structure of the organization provided the manpower and division of authority necessary for illegal acts.[46] A medieval baron's household retainers
formed the backbone of both legitimate and illegitimate operations; in the
records they are variously referred to as the lord's *familia* or *meinie*. As Mc-
Farlane described them, the retainers were kept by the lord in addition to
his regular household servants, but they performed similar functions. Indeed, there was no clear distinction between those of gentry and non-
gentry status in the household.[47] The number of retainers a lord was able to
keep in his *meinie* became a status symbol for fourteenth- and fifteenth-
century nobles. Maintaining many men and dressing them in his livery was
not only important for a lord's place in society, but it was also necessary for
the protection of his interests at home and for his service in the wars of the
king.[48] Keeping retainers was expensive, for they had to be paid and housed.
The practice grew up of hiring retainers for special occasions and granting
them liveries for a short period rather than for life. Sometimes the hired retainers were criminal gangs, often led by younger sons of nobility. When Sir
William Stafford got into a dispute he brought in his brother James's criminal gang while the other side employed Sir William Chetulton's outlaws.[49]
A temporary retainer's pay might be part of the spoils, as in the case of the
kidnapping of Sir Richard Wylughby,[50] or it might be a flat sum. One man
in Yorkshire paid two arsonists 6s. 8d. each to burn a mill.[51] Whatever the
source of a noble's armed household, the effect of short-tem retainers was
obvious in later medieval England. As one churchman described these retainers, "no hounds were ever readier for the chase, no hungry falcon for
the bird it has spied than these to do whatsoever their great lords bid them,
if they should want to beat or spoil or kill anyone."[52]

Throughout the fourteenth century considerable concern was expressed
by both the king in statutes and members of the Parliament in petitions regarding the criminal activities of the nobility and their households. A statute
attempting to deal with the problem in the late fourteenth century described
accurately the king's dilemma in curtailing the nobility. After listing the
heinous crimes of the nobles and their households, the statute went on to
complain:

> [they] sometimes come and take the king's liege people in their houses, and
> bring and hold them as prisoners, and at the last put them to fine and ran-
> som as it were in a land of war; and sometime come before the justices in
> their sessions in such guise with great force, whereby the justices be afraid
> and not hardy to do the law; and do many other riots and horrible offences,
> whereby the realm in diverse parts is put in great trouble to the great mis-
> chief and grievance of the people.[53]

This statute was one of many of the king's efforts to quiet the continuous
complaint of the Commons: "May it please our lord the king to charge the
nobility of the land that none such [gang of robbers] be maintained by them,
privately nor openly; but that they help to arrest and take such bad ones."[54]

As in the analogous situation of white-collar crime, fur-collar crime could not be controlled effectively through either the regular gaol-delivery session or the special commissions of trailbaston. In fact, kings did not try to eradicate fur-collar crime, but to regulate it. A look at the final outcome of indictments against the nobility shows how ineffective the regular legal system was in dealing with the problem. All the nobles and members of their *familia* who were indicted for felonies at the Somerset trailbaston session in the summer of 1305 were dismissed with a rap on the knuckles. Simon de Monteacute was pardoned,[55] Robert son of Payn was acquitted, Stephen de Beaumont, Henry de Urtyaco, and Mathew de Forneaux paid fines of £3 4s. each, while the others who had committed extortion, felony, and trespass were fined or were outlawed. A similar pattern was followed in 1351 in Essex with Lord John Fitzwalter's gang. Fitzwalter himself received special treatment, which will be discussed later, while two of his *familia* apparently escaped punishment altogether. A parson among them resigned his living, two were pardoned, three were put in exigend, and two were acquitted. Only one of the group of ruffians who had terrorized Essex for ten years was hanged, and he was the least significant: "As it is saide in olde proverbe—'Pore be hangid by the neck; a riche man bi the purs.' "[56]

If the king could not punish his barons through regular criminal procedure, he had other ways of forcing them to observe his peace. Bellamy has said that Edward II "quite unreasonably . . . called the crimes of Middleton treason."[57] Sir Gilbert de Middleton's robbery of two cardinals and ransom of a bishop-elect and his brother may not seem to fall within the legal definition of treason as seen through the eyes of a twentieth-century expert on medieval treason laws,[58] but there was nothing unreasonable about Edward II's action. It worked. Middleton was brought to London and executed, and his adherents were gradually rounded up and punished. Elevating particularly serious outrages to the level of treason gave the king a legal clout and support from loyal gentry that he could not have mustered through regular criminal procedures. This practical sense of "doing rather than classifying," as Plucknett put it, was also used in the Fitzwalter case. Edward III tried a number of expedients to stop Fitzwalter's criminal activities, including recruiting him for the siege of Calais, before he finally threw him into the Tower of London and confiscated his lands. After Fitzwalter spent about a year in prison, the king pardoned him and then "sold" his estates back to him. Again, this unorthodox solution to the punishment of a felonious noble worked. Fitzwalter lived for ten more years, but he was so busy buying back his estates that he had no time or money to maintain a band of felons. Years of Pipe Rolls benignly enter payments to the king from his "dear and faithful" John Fitzwalter.[59]

For the most part, kings seem to have avoided direct confrontation in the courts because the royal judicial system was likely to back down in the face of threats from the nobility. It was more to the king's advantage to recruit the upper classes to peacekeeping commissions of various sorts where they could use their warring propensities and desire for prestige in royal service. Edward I effectively put a stop to Robert son of Payn's criminal activities and separated him and his *familia* after the 1305 trailbaston session by sending him to Gascony on a commission of oyer and terminer.[60] The use of a peace commission for controlling outlaws was so common that it became part of the folk legend of Robin Hood. When the king finally made him sheriff of Nottingham, Robin Hood became a loyal servant of the government.

Rather than stop a life of crime, however, a peacekeeping commission could just as easily extend a criminal career. The king was not above using one gang to attack and arrest another and would even pay them for it. For instance, Sir William Chetulton joined another gang leader, James Stafford, to capture two robbers.[61] The king took advantage of already existing gang warfare when he gave out a commission: Lord Robert de Wennesley was asked to arrest the Coterels and Folvilles because he had a feud with them that had led, nine months before, to the murder of a relative of the Coterels.[62]

Another course for the king was to remove the nobles and their households from the country entirely by summoning them to serve in foreign wars. It is no accident that the medieval English kings who are given the most credit for good government are also those who waged extensive foreign wars—Edward I and Edward III. After the 1305 indictments, Edward I involved Simon de Monteacute in the war with Scotland.[63] Previously, in 1290, Edward had sent him as constable of Corf castle,[64] less than a year after a commission of oyer and terminer had been sent out to investigate "persons . . . avowing themselves to be of Simon de Monte Acute [who make] assemblies . . . and by day and night commit robberies, homicides, and other trespasses, to the scandal of the said Simon."[65] Since he was pardoned in 1274 for exactly the same acts,[66] it is hard to believe that Lord Simon was not directly responsible for ordering them. Perhaps this was a ruse on the part of Lord Simon when the king confronted him with the crimes—he denied that they were done by his orders and he was to be pitied because they ruined his name. The Folvilles and the Coterels did cease their criminal activities permanently when they were asked to serve in the wars in Scotland and were pardoned for their service.[67] The policy of recruiting nobles for foreign wars was a two-edged sword. While it got them out of the country and sometimes, as in the case of the Folvilles, did end their criminal careers, it encouraged others to build up even larger households during the years of foreign service. As long as they were occupied in France or Scotland fighting for the king, the system of indentured troops worked well. However, when the nobles returned to England with enlarged households to maintain, they often continued living off the land as they had done in France.[68] This meant that crime tended to increase in the countryside after truces with France.[69] The abuses of livery and maintenance, which were only briefly interrupted by periods of foreign service, became increasingly uncontrollable for the English kings.

A strong argument may be made that neither kings nor their nobles thought that arming a household and subverting justice was wrong as long as excess could be avoided.[70] The nobles, as feudal lords, had made their

living as warriors and as dispensers of justice for centuries. Most of the nobles discussed in this essay had fairly extensive estates with a number of
people dependent upon them for day-to-day justice in the cases of land and
property disputes, assaults, and infringements of manorial rules. A lord's
right to govern his manor was accepted by other lords, king, and commoners. For instance, when a knight and his son were brought into jail delivery
for breaking into a man's house and taking his goods, the charges were dismissed when the jurors pointed out that the victim was the knight's serf
who was in arrears on rent.[71] The lords had, until shortly before the fourteenth century, extensive rights in trying cases later reserved for the royal
courts. It was only three decades before the 1305 indictment of Simon de
Monteacute for tampering with justice that Edward I had made his famous
effort in the *quo warranto* proceedings to eliminate the extensive legal rights
of the nobility over felony matters and to extend the king's law throughout
the land.[72] At the time of the proceedings the Earl of Warenne was reported
to have brandished a rusty old sword and protested: "Here, my lords, here
is my warrant. My ancestors came with William the Bastard and conquered
their lands with the sword, and by the sword shall I defend them against
anyone who tries to usurp them."[73]

If the nobility did indeed believe that it was their ancient right to exercise control over justice, then this explains a phenomenon that many observers have found curious: the same men may simultaneously have been
criminals and involved with offices for keeping the king's peace. Plucknett
observed that a number of the knights returned to Parliament in the 1330s
were guilty of homicide, theft, burglary, corruption of justice, and so on.[74]
Lord Robert son of Payn was one of the king's most trusted justices, and
Simon de Monteacute served two kings and rose to the rank of admiral.
These men were loyal and devoted subjects in all ways, except when the
keeping of the peace infringed on matters touching their own rights. No
doubt the fourteenth-century kings accepted their nobles' behavior and
freely pardoned them as long as they were not too disruptive to the countryside and did not directly affront the king as had Sir Gilbert de Middleton. After all, these kings shared the values of the noble classes, and they
themselves had considerable blood on their hands from the murders and
thefts that they had committed in the name of political stability. Self-help
was a well-established part of the legal tradition for all who could make
might right.

> For why? the good old rule
> Sufficed them,—the simple plan
> That they should take who have the power,
> And they should keep who can.[75]

Certain circumstances encouraged the nobles to reassert their latent
rights and to take the law into their own hands. Sir Roger de Leiburn had
been a close friend and supporter of Edward I, but the relationship had

soured, and Sir Roger formed a gang and began to lead a life of crime and trespass in Kent. When he was again the king's favorite several years later, he returned to being a loyal and law-abiding subject.[76] Sir Roger's period of depredations in Kent was partly due to financial reasons. He took property and money to support his position in society. When he returned to favor, the king gave him gifts and revenues from lands that removed this need. Others reacted in the same way. Sir William Aune started his criminal career upon being denied the inheritance of a manor that he thought was rightfully his. When he was given an office and compensation, he curtailed his unlawful acts.[77] Another condition also encouraged crime among local magnates—the absence of one of their number from the county, which seems to have disturbed the balance of power and could lead to raids on the lands of the absent lord. The king tried to protect the lands of those he called out of the country on his service by issuing letters patent putting their lands under royal protection. It was a necessary precaution. For instance, when Maurice de Berkeley was serving the king in the Scottish wars, the mayor and citizens of Bristol broke into his manor at Bedminster, destroyed his property, and wounded his servant.[78]

Even if ancient tradition had not given the lords considerable legal rights, the nature of the society would have made these rights easy to acquire. Medieval society was of necessity based on systems of interpersonal relationships that could act as a buffer in times of trouble. The troubles were many—crop failures, invasions, tax collections, and bands of robbers. With these uncertainties in life, a local strong man was a good person to have as a protector. When we read historical documents that show the lord's thugs going to a mill and breaking the millstones, our sympathies are drawn to the miller. But the lord may have been protecting one of his people from arrest who perhaps deserves some sympathy and certainly some respect for having had the foresight to find herself a protector. The rebels from Kent and Sussex repaid their debt of gratitude to the abbot of Battle Abbey for aid and protection he had given them during the French raids by not destroying his property in the 1381 revolt.[79] In his *Social History of English Law*, Alan Harding points out the analogy between the local county nobility, who were drawn upon for the offices of the county, and modern political bosses running their cities.[80] One of the characteristics of the political boss is that, although he does not necessarily conduct justice and politics within the normal legal system, he does ensure that things run smoothly and that order is maintained. It is beyond the scope of this essay to investigate the extent to which the nobility, having gained control of a county as had Lord John Fitzwalter in Essex, were able to maintain peace in their own fashion.

Our concern in this chapter has been twofold: to investigate the distinctive pattern of crime among the upper classes of late medieval England and the success of the central government in controlling it, and to assess the applicability of Sutherland's modern sociological description of white-collar crime to the criminal activities of elite groups in medieval history. The uniqueness of fur-collar crime is apparent when it is compared to the criminal pattern of the lower classes, the bulk of whose offenses fell into the categories of larceny, burglary, and homicide. The lower classes did practice extortion and corruption of justice, but did not do so on such a grand scale, nor were their actions an extension of their occupations. Although the nobles provided the leadership and the employment for criminal gangs in medieval England, they may not be equated with organized-crime bosses of the mafia type. Since crime was not their sole occupation but rather an outgrowth of their real professions as administrators and warriors, they cannot be classed with professional criminals. Furthermore, their criminal careers tended to be a sporadic rather than a persistent way of life, and their households served many other functions besides criminal ones. The fourteenth-century kings cannot be faulted, as Bellamy has attempted to do, for failing to maintain order among those overmighty subjects, because it is absurd to apply modern standards of efficient administration of justice to the Middle Ages and because, given the limitations of royal authority, the kings were effective in using extralegal means to divert their nobles from criminal careers.[81]

Can this distinct pattern, which belonged neither to the lower classes nor to organized crime, be considered analogous to that of white-collar crime as Sutherland has described it? Certainly the criminal activities of the nobility fit into the broad description of white-collar crime as criminal acts committed by people of high social standing in connection with their occupations. The occupation of the medieval nobleman differed greatly from that of the modern corporate executive, but the noble's criminal opportunities grew out of his legal occupation as administrator of estates and military leader. Furthermore, the very organization used by the nobility to administer and fight formed the basis of their criminal activities, as does the corporate structure in modern white-collar crime. Like modern corporation heads, the members of the noble class shared common assumptions about goals and methods that not only made the illegal use of power acceptable, but also raised the status of persons who used such power in the eyes of their peers.[82] They could rest assured, as does the modern executive, that the bulk of society would not regard their crimes in the same light as those of professional thieves or murderers. Their self-image was not that of a criminal, nor did their society view them as such.[83] Since there was often a thin line between legitimate exercise of authority and crime, many of their illegal acts could be rationalized. Finally, in their relations with law-enforcement agencies, barons and executives pursued the same objectives even if their means of achieving them proved radically different. Both groups resorted to bribes, jury intimidation, and public relations to avoid prosecution. They were also accountable to governments that used special tools rather than the regular police and criminal courts in dealing with their breaches of the law. Special hearings, desist orders, and commissions deal with the modern upper-class offender just as medieval kings sent out special commissions to investigate their barons.[84] The nobles knew then, as executives know now, that a government will overlook many illegal activities unless those activities become excessive and a threat to its power. Although there are many similarities between fur-collar crime and white-collar crime, there is also a major difference. Since the activities of the barons had evolved not only from their monopoly of wealth and power but also from their former legitimate rights to administer the law, their actions, though considered decidedly criminal by the end of the thirteenth century, had at least some tradition of being legal. No corporate executive can claim, as did the Earl of Warenne, purportedly, that he has an ancient warrant from time immemorial to take the law into his own hands.

NOTES

1. Edwin H. Sutherland, *White Collar Crime* (New York: Dryden Press, 1949).
2. Ibid., p. 9.
3. Ibid., pp. 221–25.
4. Michael T. Clanchy, "Law, Government and Society in Medieval England," *History* 59 (1974): 73–78. Clanchy has pointed out in this review article that historians such as John G. Bellamy in *Crime and Public Order in England in the Later Middle Ages* (London: Routledge and Kegan Paul, 1973) tend to be "king's men," and to regard the magnates as "overmighty subjects" whose exercise of individual power was a rebellious and illegitimate attack on the royal authority. Bellamy and others in this tradition seem to have forgotten that fourteenth-century kings and barons thought about rights and obligations in government more in feudal terms than in those of Tudor absolutism. Continental medievalists such as Marc Bloch (*Feudal Society*, trans. L.A. Manyon [Chicago: University of Chicago Press, 1961]) and Otto Brunner (*Land und Herrschaft* [Vienna: R. M. Rohrer, 1965]) have a much greater appreciation of the thin line between the nobles' legitimate and illegitimate exercise of power. Even the two excellent studies of the criminal activities of upper-class gangs in fourteenth-century England have ignored the broader implications of their relationship to the king and his justice (see E.L.G. Stones, "The Folvilles of Ashby-Folville, Leicestershire, and Their Associates in Crime," *Transactions of the Royal Historical Society*, 5th ser., 7 [1957]: 117–36, and John G. Bellamy, "The Coterel Gang: An Anatomy of a Band of Fourteenth-Century Criminals," *English Historical Review*, 79 [1964]: 689–717).
5. The *Statutes of the Realm: Printed by Command of His Majesty George III* (London: Dawsons, 1963), 37 Ed. III, ch. 8–12.
6. Kenneth B. McFarlane, *The Nobility of Later Medieval England* (Oxford: Clarendon Press, 1973), pp. 6–8.
7. Theodore F.T. Plucknett, *A Concise History of Common Law*, 2nd ed. (New York: The Lawyers Co-operative Publishing Co., 1936), p. 374. Following Plucknett's lead, we might look for a rough-and-ready administrative distinction. For instance, we might call "criminal" all cases that jurors considered sufficiently criminal to bring indictments against the suspects. This division, however, would not eliminate confusion, because similar cases may be found in civil pleas. For instance, Elizabeth Furber (*Essex Sessions of the Peace 1351, 1377–89* [Colchester: Essex Archaeological Society, 1953], pp. 44, 56–57) cites one case which was brought into court on a criminal indictment but was changed to a trespass case during the session. Church opinion is no more helpful than that of laymen on

the nature of a criminal act. The only thinker who went further than equating crime with sin was Lucas de Penna, who insisted that criminal intention had to be present for an act to be a crime (Walter Ullman, *The Medieval Idea of Law* [London: Methuen, 1946], pp. 144–49). But here again there is a problem. It is far from clear that the nobility considered their actions to be wrong; instead they viewed them as a legitimate extension of their rights as barons.

8. Sutherland, *White Collar Crime*, p. 31. James F. Stephen, in *A History of Criminal Law*, 1 (London: Macmillan, 1883), p. 3, gives a more detailed definition: "The criminal law is that part of the law which relates to the definition and punishment of acts or omissions which are punished as being (1) attacks upon public order, internal or external; or (2) abuses or obstructions of public authority; or (3) acts injurious to the public in general; or (4) attacks upon the persons of individuals, or upon rights annexed to their persons; or (5) attacks upon the property of individuals or rights connected with, and similar to, rights of property." These five points easily encompass the range of criminal behavior of the nobility.

9. This figure includes only those of the rank of knight or above who were mentioned in the records by their titles. Untitled members of noble families, that is, younger sons, and members of local gentry may appear more regularly, but it has been impossible to check through all the names. A *per capita* estimate of crime rates for nobility and other classes in society is impossible because there are no reliable population estimates for either the whole of the population of England in the fourteenth century or for the number making up each class. Noel Denholm-Young, in *The Country Gentry in the Fourteenth Century* (Oxford: Clarendon Press, 1969), p. 507, has used heraldric rolls of arms to estimate the numbers in the upper classes and finds 160 temporal lords, perhaps 1,400 baronets, and something around 5,000 knights. It has been traditionally assumed that this upper level of society with their families made up about 10 percent of the population. If this is true, then they were very underrepresented in the jail delivery rolls, even if not all of their members were listed by title.

10. Bertha H. Putnam, *Kent Keepers of the Peace, 1316–17* (Kent Archaeological Society XIII, 1933), pp. xxix–xlii.

11. May McKisack, *The Fourteenth Century* (Oxford: Clarendon Press, 1959), pp. 25–26. Gaveston was a favorite of the king, but the barons resented his control over the government.

12. Ibid., p. 94.

13. Charles Gross, *Select Cases from the Coroners' Rolls*, Selden Society, 9 (London, 1895), p. 58.

14. Public Record Office, Just. 27/334. Hereafter referred to as P.R.O. Just.

15. *Rotuli Parliamentorum* et Petitiones et Placita in Parliamento (London: 1832) 2, 64.

16. Michael M. Postan, lecture at University of California, Los Angeles (March 1974).

17. Jean J. Jusserand, *English Wayfaring Life in the Middle Ages* (London: Methuen, 1961), pp. 73–74.

18. P.R.O. Just. 3/74/4 ms. 1–2. See also Just. 3/49/2 m. 4; the gang of Sir John son of John Howard in KB 27/248 m. 10.

19. P.R.O. Just. 1/764 ms. 2, 11.

20. P.R.O. Just. 3/51/3 m. 6d.

21. P.R.O. Just. 1/764 ms. 1–10.

22. McFarlane, *The Nobility*, pp. 213–27.

23. Sutherland, *White Collar Crime*, p. 225. For instance, false advertising is seen as boasting about a product.
24. P.R.O. Just. 1/674 m. 1.
25. Ibid., m. 2.
26. Roy F. Hunnisett, *Bedfordshire Coroners' Rolls* (Bedfordshire Historical Record Society XLI, 1960), p. 82. John de Rushall was acquitted at the eyre.
27. P.R.O. Just. 1/764 m. 1.
28. Ibid., m. 1. In another case (m. 2), Lord Adam de la Ford extorted 40s.
29. Ibid., m. 3d.
30. Bellamy, *Crime*, p. 80.
31. Ibid., p. 22.
32. P.R.O. Just. 1/764 ms. 2d, 3. Lord John Fitzwalter did the same sort of thing in Essex (Furber, *Essex Sessions*, p. 63).
33. A.E. Middleton, *Sir Gilbert Middleton and the Part He Took in the Rebellion in the North of England in 1317* (Newcastle-on-Tyne: Mawson, Swan and Morgan, 1918), pp. 28–29.
34. Stones, "Folvilles," pp. 122–24; Bellamy, "Coterel Gangs," pp. 707–8.
35. P.R.O. Just. 1/764 m. 2.
36. Ibid., ms. 2, 4, 11. Stephen de Beaumont paid a fine of £3 4s. for his part at the trial.
37. Sutherland, *White Collar Crime*, p. 232.
38. P.R.O. Just. 1/764 m. 3.
39. Ibid., m. 1d.
40. Ibid., m. 2.
41. Ibid., m. 3.
42. Putnam, *Kent Keeper*, p. xli. Quoted from *Literae Canturiensis*, vol. 1, pp. 120–23.
43. Bellamy, *Crime*, p. 19.
44. Ibid., p. 20. McFarlane (in *Nobility*, p. 115) has claimed that before 1422 it is hard to find evidence of magnates using armed men to tamper with the courts.
45. Furber, *Essex Sessions*, p. 63.
46. Sutherland, *White Collar Crime*, p. 220.
47. McFarlane, *Nobility*, p. 105.
48. Ibid. See also A. E. Prince, "The Indenture System Under Edward III," in J. G. Edwards, Vivian H. Galbraith, and Ernest F. Jacob, eds., *Historical Essays in Honour of James Tait* (Manchester: Printed for the subscribers, 1933), pp. 283–97.
49. Bellamy, *Crime*, p. 26. The Coterels and Folvilles were at various times in the employ of the canons of Litchfield Cathedral and other religious houses.
50. Stones, "Folvilles," p. 122.
51. P.R.O. Just. 3/76 m. 7.
52. Bellamy, *Crime*, p. 29.
53. *Statutes of the Realm*, 2 Rich. II, I, ch. 6.
54. *Rotuli Parliamentorum*, vol. II, p. 201.
55. *Calendar of Patent Rolls* p. 438, 1301–7 (Nedeln: Kraus Reprint, 1971)
56. Furber, *Essex Sessions*, p. 65.
57. Bellamy, *Crime*, p. 49.
58. John G. Bellamy, *The Law of Treason in England in the Later Middle Ages* (Cambridge: The University Press, 1970).
59. Furber, *Essex Sessions*, p. 65.
60. *Calendar of Patent Rolls* p. 349, 1301–7.
61. Bellamy, *Crime*, p. 84.

62. Ibid. See also the example of Lord William Beckwith, Ibid., p. 26.
63. *Calendar of Patent Rolls* p. 490, 1301–7.
64. *Calendar of Patent Rolls* p. 436, 1292–7.
65. Ibid., p. 383.
66. Ibid., p. 79.
67. Bellamy, *Crime*, p. 84.
68. *Past and Present* ran a conference and subsequent debate on the effects of the Hundred Years' War on society. See Kenneth B. McFarlane, "England and the Hundred Years' War," *Past and Present*, 22 (July 1963): 3–17; and Michael M. Postan, "The Costs of the Hundred Years' War," *Past and Present*, 27 (April 1964): 34–53.
69. Barbara A. Hanawalt, "The Economic Influences on Crime in England, 1300–1348," *American Journal of Legal History*, XIX (October 1974): 281–97.
70. McFarlane, *Nobility*, p. 107. The king introduced sumptuary legislation to limit the size of the *familia*. He obviously accepted the existence of the households but thought that the status of the lord should determine the size of the household.
71. P.R.O. Just. 3/48.
72. Donald W. Sutherland, *Quo Warranto Proceedings in the Reign of Edward I* (Oxford: Clarendon Press, 1963).
73. Ibid., p. 82.
74. Theodore F.T. Plucknett, "Parliament," in J.G. Willard, W.A. Morris, and W.H. Dunham, eds., *The English Government at Work*, 1 (Cambridge: Medieval Academy of America, 1940), pp. 102–3.
75. L.R. Larking, "On the Heart Shrine in Leyburn Church," *Archaeologia Cantiana*, V (1863): 143.
76. Ibid., pp. 142–47.
77. Bellamy, *Crime*, p. 86.
78. P.R.O. Just. 1/764 m. 8.
79. Eleanor Searle and Robert Burghart, "The Defense of England and the Peasants' Revolt," *Viator*, III (1973): 386–87.
80. Alan Harding, *Social History of English Law* (Baltimore: Penguin Books, 1966), p. 70.
81. Bellamy, *Crime*, ch. 4; throughout the book he is critical of the king for not keeping the peace.
82. Sutherland, *White Collar Crime*, pp. 219–20.
83. Ibid., pp. 221–25.
84. Ibid., p. 225.

5

At the Margins of Women's Space in Medieval Europe

Marginals have constituted the newest social group within medieval society to be discussed over the last two decades, beginning with Bronislaw Geremek's study of vagrants and other "low life" who lived in late medieval Paris.[1] With such a prestigious beginning, we might assume that a definition of what constituted marginality among medieval people is by now well established. To Geremek, who was working within a Marxist framework at the time of writing his book, marginals were those people and groups who fell outside the social and economic or the legal and political categories that were acceptable to the mainstream of society. They may have been criminals, but they included bohemians and some clerks, tricksters, con-men, prostitutes, and even urban hermits. Geremek characterized their status by such attributes as having no settled home or family ties and being vagrants. Their place of association was the tavern. In contemporary parlance they were "of no account" or "not of good fame,"[2] that is, they were not a part of the social and economic power structure. Such a definition of marginality contains a built-in Marxist limitation, for it presumes that the only social marginals will be those who are at the bottom of society and regarded as morally reprehensible by the more fortunate classes.

A sociologist, Ephraim Mizruchi, worked toward a broader definition

I thank Judith Bennett for reading drafts of this paper. I have delivered the paper at a number of places before publication and am grateful for comments from audiences at Dickenson College, The College of Wooster, The Institute of Historical Research at the University of London, and the Medieval Academy of America. Fellowship support during the writing of this paper came from the John Simon Guggenheim Foundation and the Wissenschaftskolleg zu Berlin. This essay was first published in *Matrons and Marginal Women in Medieval Europe*, ed. Robert R. Edwards and Vickie Ziegler (Woodbridge: The Boydell Press, 1995), pp. 1–17.

of marginality within medieval society that included such established groups as monks, apprentices, and Beguines, as well as prostitutes and criminals. His theory is based on the presumption that Europe had too many people for all to have been assimilated into vacancies in the social networks. Medieval society developed institutions of social control that held the surplus in abeyance (that is, they slowed the integration process by marginalizing certain groups for a period of years in recognized institutions).[3] One cannot speak comfortably, however, about an excess of population in the century following the onset of plague in 1347. The fifteenth century was a demographic trough. Mizruchi's demographic evidence is from the sixteenth century and is projected back on medieval groups and institutions. Still, his inclusion of a larger variety of groups from different social classes under the marginal rubric is a move in the right direction.

Neither author views women as having a definition of marginality separate from that of men. Their examples of female marginality, prostitutes on the one hand and Beguines on the other, seem to our modern categories at opposite ends of the moral scale. The prostitute is a woman, married or single, who has slid into a transient life, selling her body, and assuming an outcast role in society in general. On the other hand, Beguines were single women who refused to accept such a demeaning role, and who sought instead to preserve their religious and moral integrity by forming communities of single women who led sober, pure lives outside a nunnery. They might eventually marry, or they might devote their earnings to the service of God and the poor throughout their lives. If we followed either Geremek or Mizruchi, we would agree that these were, in their own ways, marginals.

Modern discussions among feminist historians have centered on spheres of power akin to Geremek's definition, which impose limitations on a discussion of marginality. This argument posits that women's sphere of power is domestic while men's is public. Much has been written about patriarchy and the power that both Church and secular law gave to men to restrict women from entering into the public sphere. Women's lack of access to magisterial ranks and higher market economies, and the banning of women from universities, legal practice, and even most branches of medicine other than midwifery are well documented. All of these matters deal with power manipulations over women's access to economic, political, and intellectual spheres. But these categories apply more to the nineteenth century than to the Middle Ages, since women had virtually no access to the public arena in medieval times. Placing marginal women into a discussion of spheres of influence becomes a useless exercise, because *all* women in such a discussion would fall into the excluded category. Within the domestic sphere, the analysis of power relations also does not identify marginal women, since all women lived under patriarchy.

Those leading purveyors of patriarchal ideology, the medieval church hierarchy, regarded both prostitutes and Beguines as marginal women, but prostitutes were a necessary evil, whereas Beguines were an unusual threat as religious women because they were outside traditional male control. Adultery, fornication, or any deviation from the preferred state of virginity or abstinence was unfortunate, but very likely to happen. Rather than having unbridled lust rampant among respectable lay and clerical men, prostitutes provided a convenient, limited locus for lust. Church authorities felt no moral dilemma in owning property on which organized brothels were located and collecting rents from such establishments. As we shall see, the real problem that they saw was in the prostitute who went unregulated into the community at large. Like city officials, they wanted to know and distinguish prostitutes from the rest of the female population. They wanted them geographically contained and officially sanctioned, but did not strenuously object to their trade. On the other hand, the church authorities were very threatened by the pious, semi-secular Beguines. These women were virtually nuns, except for their refusal to live within the confines of monastic space and be directly answerable to a male ecclesiastical structure as were cloistered nuns. Their dwellings were among the poor or in secular households. Again, without an established spatial containment for these women, the male hierarchy was uncomfortable with their presence. Medieval concepts of marginal women, therefore, are not entirely akin to ours, and thus an exploration of what medieval men considered central in women's behavior and the space women could occupy are important to establish prior to a discussion of marginal women.

Centrality and marginality imply boundaries. I will argue, in this chapter, that for medieval women the boundaries marked the physical space that could be occupied by medieval women. This exercise finds less significance in separating respectable women and marginals than in studying the spaces that they occupied. Women such as prostitutes and Beguines, who moved beyond the bounds of prescribed space, became marginals. By limiting the physical spaces that women could occupy and controlling women both within those spaces and outside of them, medieval men defined spatial locations for women that made those who moved beyond those boundaries more clearly marginal.

The questions that arise about women's restricted space help to form a definition of female marginality. Where could women go to conduct their admittedly limited social, political, and economic activities without male protection or censure? What did it mean when a woman stepped over those boundaries into a space beyond the pale—into the marginal area where respectable women could not venture unaccompanied or inappropriately attired (that is, not dressed in the symbols of their legitimate space)? For women to be physically unconstrained in mobility did not mean the same thing when applied to men. When women stepped out of their physical space, they were carrying an additional connotation of marginality. In the best of circumstances, and the Beguines are arguably that, women could not depart from a defined physical space without arousing more suspicion than would men in similar circumstances. A man in the late Middle Ages could be a mendicant friar living outside the walls of a monastic order, but a woman could not. Women who were in established prostitution houses or permissible areas were accepted, but the freelance street walker was not.

Physical boundaries as well as moral and institutional ones are important in defining those who are inside and those who are on the margins, but Geremek, Mizruchi, and modern discussions of gendered power spheres do not refer to gendered space. Women stepping outside physical boundaries and becoming transients (an aspect of Geremek's definition) connoted a moral lapse in itself. An example from the London Goldsmiths' guild tells of the degradation implicit in the removal of a female from the socially accepted space. William Rothely was fined "because he ... against all humanity, sent his maid out of his house and suffered her to lie out two nights so she was fain to borrow money to lie at the Pewter Pot to the dishonor of all the fellowship [of goldsmiths]."[4] By expelling his servant from her protected physical space and forcing her to stay at an inn, Rothely had disgraced himself and his guild. A more extreme example is Joan of Arc, who moved beyond woman's space and dress into the male realm of battlefield and armor. In forming a definition of marginal women, therefore, we must look beyond the usual issues of patriarchal constraints over women's spheres of influence to the actual physical constraints on women's movements.

It is to anthropologists that we owe the observation that women's access to the entire environment was restricted. Pierre Bourdieu observed among the Berbers not only the division of the house into male and female space but also the value judgments associated with this division. This led to a more generalized observation that the power of dominant groups lies, in part, in their ability to control the ordering of space for subservient groups.[5] Daphne Spain has done an extensive survey of household space but has not applied her analysis to preindustrial Europe.[6] Martine Segalen's exploration of the division of male and female space among the French peasants is valuable because she brings her observations to a rural European situation. She notes that there was "a female *house*," and "a male *outside*." When women went outside the house, they did so in the company of other women. Men's space was the fields. Thus, she observed, not only were tasks divided in the peasant communities, but so was the allocation of space.[7] Traditional European society did not have space (outside of some sacred areas such as monasteries) that absolutely excluded either sex. Men did not congregate alone in taverns or temples and women were not kept in women's quarters or harems. Women did work in fields at harvest and men lived in the houses. Nonetheless, strong custom dictated how women could move within the spaces that men dominated. When they broke these rules, as Mary Douglas observed, women became "polluting" and "dangerous."[8] Thus, as we shall see, women who broke the codes limiting their movement outside their allotted physical space were subject to harassment.

Lest we think that spatial limitation on women was only a preindustrial phenomenon, consider the many places that a Victorian woman could not go: whole city districts, taverns, many offices, social clubs, and so on. Consider the comments that women receive today when they enter men's bars or even the physical abuse they may suffer if they enter "male space," such as locker rooms. Modern men would argue, quite correctly, that they too suffer ridicule upon entering "women's space." If some of the boundaries between proper and marginal space for women have been removed over the centuries, they are hardly entirely gone.

DEFINING THE PHYSICAL SPACE:
THE PROPER ARENA FOR MATRONS

For ordinary women early socialization reinforced by moral precepts in advice books and sermons contributed to a spatial identity and an early awareness of the consequences of marginalization. As one would assume, it was not only male preachers who taught women their spatial identity. Children learned very young, at their parents' knees, about gendered space. Medieval coroners' inquests into accidental death clearly show that by the age of two and three more female children died in the house and about the hearth than did male children. The female children identified early with their mother's work pattern and died tipping pots of hot liquid on themselves or getting too near the hearth, while male children followed their fathers outside and drowned in ditches.[9]

Playing upon the mother's role in socialization were such poems as "How the Good Wife Taught Her Daughter," in which the daughter is told that her place is the home and that she should keep her eyes down when she is in the streets. The poem carefully spells out the dangers of public places:

> An wan thou goist in the way, go thou not to faste,
> Braundishe not with thin heed, thi schuldris thou ne caste;
> Haue thou not to manye wordis; to swere be thou not leefe,
> For alle such maners comen to an yuel preef:
> For he that cacchith to him an yuel name,
> It is to him a foule fame,
> Mi leue childe.

Further warnings about behavior out of the house include not getting drunk in taverns, not going house-to-house buying beer after selling your cloth, and not accompanying your lover to places where he might be able to seduce you. Finally, a good daughter would not go to shows like a common strumpet but "wone at hom, daughtir, and loue thi werk myche."[10] Equivalent moral poems for men caution against appearing too frequently in taverns, but they suggest meeting the eyes of others on the street to show a good quality of deportment. Women are encouraged to preserve their private space in cities by keeping their heads down, but men are urged to use the streets as an arena for impressing others.

In Florence, bourgeois girls were more literally isolated, thus giving them an early sense of limited space. At the age of six or seven their fathers enrolled them in convents where they would stay until they were married at about age sixteen or where they would take the nun's veil at about the age of twelve. Boys, on the other hand, remained at home and went to secular schools.[11]

Books of advice for rearing noble girls emphasized carefully guarded seclusion, and, obviously, the bourgeois literature imitated these. While girls should be taught to read, write, and pray in addition to sewing and weaving, isolation was to be reinforced by teaching them silence along with chastity, modesty, and humility. Nothing can be more spatially confining than enforced silence in which the very escape of words puts the speaker in a marginal category. Giles of Rome enjoined lessons in silence and physical seclusion of noble girls. Seclusion was still an important characteristic of women's education in the Renaissance. Vives, the Renaissance expert on educating women, devoted more chapters to guarding and teaching noble girls to limit their social participation than to their literary or household skills.[12] Male advisers of noble women realized that their advisees would have to appear in public even though they did not consider it desirable. If the women had to leave their homes, then they should do so appropriately accompanied and keep their eyes down to insure that they did not participate, by eye contact, in public space.[13]

Moral injunctions had long criticized women who dared to move outside their space. The synod of Nantes in 895, for instance, condemned women who "with barefaced impudence" pleaded in general assemblies and public meetings:

> It is indecent and even reprehensible, even among barbarians, for women to discuss the cases of men. Those who should be discussing their woolen work and weaving with the residents of women's quarters should not usurp the authority of senators in public meetings just as if they were palace officials.[14]

Not content with limiting the space that women were to occupy and their behavior when they moved out of that space, male moralists also imposed regulations on what women could wear. Dress codes are, of course, another way of confining women—in this case within an outer layer of cloth. The nun's veil was the most apparent of the dress codes, but in London and in many cities of Europe, city fathers regulated headdress:

> No women of the town shall henceforth go to market nor into the highway out of her house with a hood furred with budge, whether it be of lamb or of connies, upon pain of forfeiting her hood to the use of the Sheriffs, except dames who wear furred capes with hoods of which bear fur such as they must. . . . Brewsters, nurses, other servants, and women of disreputable character adorn themselves and wear hoods furred with *gros veer* and miniver after the manner of reputable women.[15]

Not only head dress, but a variety of clothing items determined the properly clad woman in public.[16]

The obverse of city regulation for respectable women were the clothing signifiers that cities prescribed for prostitutes. In London a hood of multicolored cloth and in southern France sleeves and head dress distinguished prostitutes. Italy prohibited prostitutes from wearing veils or mantels like respectable women and required them to wear a yellow strip denoting their trade.[17] Perhaps the moralists most preoccupied with women's dress were those advising noble women on proper courtly attire for keeping spatial decorum in public. "Der Waelsche Gast," an early thirteenth-century moral poem, contains a long description indicating how a woman can ride a horse so that her mantel completely enshrouds her: "no part of her body can be discovered." This type of advice was international in character, for it also appears in Robert de Blois's "Le Chastoiement des Dames," among other publications.[18]

Many factors were involved in men's attempts to regulate female dress. In part, they wished to maintain control over the signifiers of social class so that only wives and daughters of the right sort could wear fine furs and appear in public properly escorted. In part, the city fathers felt that prostitutes should wear a sign denoting their trade as a way of maintaining truth in advertising as well as of establishing social distinctions. But the veiling, hooding, and capping of women also served a purpose similar to veiling in Islamic society. Women could walk outside their homes in the privacy of their own space, surrounded by veils or hoods that limited both others' view of them and their own view of the outside world. Like horses with blinders on, they were less likely to stray from the straight and narrow path.

If women's exterior space was regulated, so too might their interior physical space, particularly if they were pursuing a religious life. The ideal of total virginity was described in terms of a space with walls and physical boundaries, a sacred vessel enclosing an object—a jewel or treasure. Jerome put the choice of defending the internal space graphically, as usual: "Go not out from home, nor wish to behold the daughters of a strange country. . . . Diana went out and was ravished." Those virgins who "seek a bridegroom in the highways" will suffer a similar fate. Such a fallen virgin "shall be stripped and her hinderparts shall be bared in her own sight."[19] The language of spiritual virginity, therefore, might also be couched in terms of private space and its loss in terms of exposure in public space.

WAS WOMEN'S SPACE THE MORALISTS' MYTH?

One could argue that the parameters of women's space were all in the minds of moralists and that in real life women did not confine their movements to the house, castle, village, and urban quarter. Historical evidence, however, indicates that women did indeed spend the larger part of their lives within prescribed spaces. Record evidence and literature speak to a general social consciousness about gendered space. My argument reaches beyond the traditions of the ancient and Carolingian world in which some women were confined to the *gynaeceum* either as slaves or serfs for a period of their lives, where they would work together producing cloth. They were carefully protected and had their separate living quarters in the compound with their workshop.[20] Segalen's observations about the space of a peasant woman's sphere of activity receives confirmation from the study of accidental deaths recorded in fourteenth-century English coroners' inquests. Medieval coroners, like modern ones, were charged with investigating all cases of violent death. Thus their duty was to inquire about all homicides, suicides, and misadventures. The inquests can, at their fullest, provide a wealth of detail that gives the reader a sense of being at the scene of the tragedy. The inquests that I used gave the name of the accused; the date, and sometimes the time of the accident; sometimes the age of the victim; and usually the place, activity, and instrument that caused the death.

In rural coroners' inquests, which reflect the life of the peasants, 1,000 adult male and female names were found for whom a clear place of accident could be established; the differences were striking. Only 12 percent of the men compared to 30 percent of the women died in their homes. Private property such as a neighbor's house or close, tavern, manor house, and so on was the place of death of only 6 percent of the men but 9 percent of the women. In public areas within the village such as greens, streets, highways, churches, and markets women again predominated with 22 percent of their accidents there compared to men's 18 percent. But if we look at accidents in fields, marl pits, forests, and so on we find that 38 percent happened to men and only 18 percent to women. Likewise, men had 4 percent more of their accidents in waterways. The aggregate picture is more dramatic than the breakdown into various categories. Women had 61 percent of their accidents within their home and village while men had only 36 percent in this limited area.

Peasant women's daily round of activities within their sphere reflects the reason for such spatial limitation: thirty-seven percent of their activities were related to maintaining and provisioning the household. Those activities included food preparation, laundry, brewing, getting water, starting fires, collecting fruits, and working with domestic animals. The other major activities (30 percent) that involved women in accidents were related to transportation such as walking. For men transportation accidents were the highest (43 percent), and this category included carting, horseback riding, and boating in addition to walking. The pursuits of agriculture and construction, however, show men's greater range of mobility: 19 percent of men compared to 4 percent of women died pursuing agriculture, and 11 percent of men and no women died in construction-related accidents.[21]

To translate the numerical picture of women's as opposed to men's space into a visual picture, imagine a village in late February or March when the plowing for summer crops was in progress. At mid-morning the men and boys of eight and above will be out in the fields. The men will be plowing and the boys goading the ox or taking care of the village herds. The only men in the village will be the priest and perhaps an infirm man or two. It is no wonder that the priests had a reputation for lechery akin to that of the mid-twentieth-century milkman, since they were the only vital males who occupied women's space while all other men were in the fields. Those occupying the village streets, tavern (with the alewife attendant), closes, and houses will be women and small children. Women will be found in the fields when necessity demands it: when there are no boys to goad the ox, when field work such as weeding or harvesting requires all hands to turn out, or when girls replace boys as herders. During the midday meal and after vespers, the streets, greens, and closes will also contain the male population.

The abandonment of house and village space to women during the day was a source of anxiety on the part of peasant males, not simply because the village priest had license to roam freely. Most peasant societies have a version of the tale in which the husband accuses his wife of spending her day gossiping at the tavern rather than working hard like he does in the field. He proposes that they change places for the day. The emphasis on "changing places" rather than roles is significant. Medieval England had its version called the "Ballad of the Tyrannical Husband." The good wife warns him that her day started earlier than his, for she rose to nurse the baby and to start the fire. She then milked the cows and took them to pasture and made butter and cheese while she watched the children and dried their tears. Next she fed the poultry and took the geese to the green. She baked and brewed every fortnight and worked on carding wool, spinning, and beating flax. However, her husband insists that they change places, claiming that her work is easy by comparison to his. Although our manuscript is incomplete, the denouement of the "Ballad" comes when the wife returns from plowing and finds the children crying, the beer spoiled, the cow not milked, and the husband defeated. He returns to the fields and she to the house and village.[22]

Even though peasant women had the daily use of house and village, their legal control over this environment was limited. As a wife, a woman shared the property with her husband, but he had the legal control over it. As a widow she had dower rights to a portion of the land but only for her lifetime, and she could not alienate it. A woman might control some land in her own right by purchase, gift, or inheritance but the quantity tended to be small unless she was an heiress, and in any case her husband gained control on marriage.[23] Thus, domination in terms of usage of space was different from political or legal control of it.

In the commission of crime, women also stayed near their homes. Their crimes were concentrated in burglary, larceny, and receiving of stolen property or known felons. The first two crimes were most likely to be committed against neighbors in the same village, and the last was, of course, a crime committed in their own home. It was the men who committed crimes in the fields, forests, and highways.[24] Likewise, women were more likely to be victims of homicide in their homes or villages rather than in the fields.[25]

If we look at the landscape of Europe today for archaeological evidence of women's use of space, we will find it in the villages rather than in the fields. The ridges and furrows that create a washboard effect on the land, particularly when seen in aerial photographs, are peasant men's legacy, but in deserted villages and in archaeological sites, U-shaped depressions mark the location of a former house floor formed by the sweeping of a housewife's broom.[26]

Noble women were no more immune to spatial limitations than were peasants and serfs. While they might travel extensively, their space and sphere of activity were still limited to the domestic arena. For some noble women the castle was more cell than home. The Duchess of Brunswick told her priest that after her hard life, she expected to go directly to heaven. The priest reacted with disbelief:

> "That would be a marvel. You were born in a fortress and bred in castles and for many years now you have lived with your husband, the Lord Duke, ever in midst of manifold delights, with wine and ale, meat and venison; and yet you expect to fly away to heaven directly you die." She answered, "Beloved father, why should I not now go to heaven? I have lived here in this castle like an anchoress in a cell. What delights or pleasures have I enjoyed here, save that I have made shift to show a happy face to my servants and gentlewomen? I have a hard husband (as you know) who has scarce any care or inclination toward women. Have I not been in this castle even as it were in a cell?"[27]

For the Duchess, the privileged space had not brought happiness but confinement.

For most noble women the routine of the castle or manor house was one of management. The English queens' household books and even those of a more modest establishment such as Dame Alice de Bryene's of Acton Hall in Suffolk show days filled with accounting for household supplies, managing servants, feeding guests and retinue, and perhaps managing estates as well.[28] The sister of Henry III, Eleanor of Montefort, played an active role in her husband's rebellion against her brother, but her political activism consisted of entertaining partisans at the various castles that they controlled. Occasionally, a woman might also be called upon to defend the castle against attack, as did Margaret Paston against those who claimed that her property belonged to them.[29]

If we are to imagine the castle as women's space, as we imagined the village, we will not find the environment devoid of men. Most of the household staff, including servants, grooms, officials, and members of the lord's affinity were present at the castle even if the lord was away.[30] The noblewoman's space would consist of the chamber of the castelaine and the dormitory for the single women in her charge. She would have her female companions and personal servants. The management of the castle would be the concern of the castelaine, but, as with her peasant-woman counterpart, she did not have legal control over it. As long as she had a husband or son, legal disposition over her space was not in her power.

Literary parallels confirm the spatial location of noble women as they do that of peasants. Penny Gold has observed in *The Lady and the Virgin* that the action involving women in the *chançons de geste* always occurs at home. Segments involving men occur in battlefields, courts, or forests, but when the plot features a woman, the action shifts to the castle. In *The Song of William*, for instance, Guiburc plays a heroic role supporting ties of kinship in her family, giving comfort at home, and inspiring her husband and male kin to assert themselves on the battlefield. As Gold points out, "The spatial structure of this epic provides us with a framework for an analysis of the role of women. . . . The male sphere of action and the female sphere of action are clearly separated geographically (with the men, but not the women, present in both spheres)."[31] The real life position of twelfth-century noble French women, as revealed in charters involving gifts of land, indicate that their role was similar to that portrayed in the *chançons de geste.*[32]

Conservative medieval social theorists recognize three social orders: those who worked (peasants), those who fought (nobles), and those who prayed (clergy). Women were classified into those three categories as well. While priesthood was denied to women, those who wanted a life of prayer became nuns and anchorites. These women's geographical space was closely defined—the nunnery and the anchorite's solitary cell. The early advice for claustration of nuns shows the profound concern for isolating women within a defined and secluded place. Caesarius of Arles recommended that "if a girl leaving her parents, desires to renounce the world and enter the holy fold to escape the jaws of the spiritual wolves by the help of God, she must never, up to the time of her death, go out of the monastery." A ninth-century rule, perhaps based on Jerome, was even more graphic: "Let your convent become your tomb, where you will be dead and buried with Christ."[33] Convent life was not a common choice for medieval woman. Entry into a convent required a dowry that was beyond the means of the peasantry. The institutions were, therefore, made up of women of the gentry and noble ranks. At no period was there a large number of nuns. Eileen Power concluded that at its height, around 1350, only 3,500 women occupied the nunneries in England.[34] In other words, conventional nunneries were not the place that society could conveniently shelve, in Mizruchi's terms, an excess female population.

For the nuns, however, the space within the walls was largely their own. The offices of Sacristan, Chambress, and Cellaress were all filled by nuns, as, of course, was that of abbess. All nunneries had to rely on the spiritual services of a priest or chaplain, and the larger ones might also employ men for work around the nunnery. But the cloister, dormitory, refectory, and chapter house were reserved for women to pray, work, and play. Nonetheless, the cloistered area was secured and enforced by bishops or by male-dominated superiors in orders such as Dominicans or Franciscans. Literary parallels again suggest that concepts of women's space entered into the consciousness of medieval people: Chaucer's prioress is accompanied outside her convent with an appropriate escort of a priest and nuns. But even with this escort, Chaucer's Madam Eglentyne is a subject of "worldly" satire.

The anchorite's cell was even more restricted as a physical space than was the nunnery. Anchorites did not necessarily withdraw into the wilderness but lived in cells in parish churches, castles, and even great monasteries such as Westminster. These women hermits (there were men as well) were popular figures and could rely upon the laity and clergy for food, clothing, and a cell in the local church in exchange for prayers for their benefactors. Women who undertook this particularly severe confinement had little or no latitude for movement.[35] Even when they chose an urban environment, their position was marginal in terms of their confinement outside the mainstream. Spatially confined, the worst threat they posed was either local gossip or major visionary experiences (Julian of Norwich). They did not wander about the streets to preach or live outside strictly controlled space.

The urban environment and the urban population were not a part of the original medieval conception of tripartite social organization. The growth of urban centers in the twelfth century and their continued dynamic presence in Europe presented new challenges to classifying social stratification. Artisans fit into the old category of those who worked with their hands, but the merchants who made a profit from investment and could equal or rival in wealth and taste the nobility were a difficult group to classify. Among the novel problems that the new environment presented was a definition of women's space. Women and men were continually mixed together in the urban marketplace, with the home serving as the shop or business headquarters. Men's and women's spaces could not be so easily separated as they were in village and castle. Homicide statistics indicate that, while urban women were more likely to meet with violence in their own homes, more were killed in the street and in other people's homes or taverns than in the rural environment. Furthermore, urban women were more likely to be killed alone, whereas in the country they were more often in the company of a relative.[36]

Even with this greater homogeneity of the sexes, women still moved within a narrower confine of the urban environment than did men. Marriages were, by preference, made within the quarter or neighborhood, partly because people of similar social status or occupation lived in those quarters.[37] The daily round of activities in the London coroners' inquests into accidental deaths also indicates that women's activities were centered in their homes. For women the home and garden area were the major places of death (50 percent), while the streets were the location of 30 percent of their deaths. No women died in shops or workplaces, and only 10 percent died on the wharves or in the river. Men, however, suffered the majority of their fatal accidents in the river or wharf area (30 percent), street (18 percent), and shop and workplace (16 percent), but only 20 percent in the home.[38] Literature, again, provides examples of the uneasiness of males when urban women moved outside the city quarter. Chaucer's Wife of Bath is both a much-traveled and much-ridiculed woman. Her honor is questioned because she travels beyond Bath.

In the religious life, the urban environment also presented new opportunity. As we have observed, Beguines were women who did not have the wealth to join a nunnery but who wanted to live a life of poverty and chastity in urban communities, where they made their meager living by their labor, usually spinning. Italian, French, and Flemish cities were home to these groups of single, pious laywomen who lived uncloistered among the urban poor.[39] Like anchorites, they were marginal because they were outside the normal control of cloister and home, but to the church authorities they were more of a threat because they were outside the spatial control of the cell. These were unconfined women, alone unless they were in the company of other women in urban space.

At the other end of the moral scale, as we have observed, were the prostitutes who plied their trade in the urban environment but were not initially confined to a particular space. These women escaped the strictures of confinement to household and shop and, unlike respectable women, did not keep their eyes down when they were in the street, but openly invited invasion of their physical, bodily space. In this respect they were between respectable women who were not supposed to make eye contact in order to preserve private space and men who were to look about them in order to dominate the public space. Prostitutes looked about them and made eye contact in order to invite invasion of private space. Streets were an arena for a variety of spatial contacts, depending on the gender and profession of the sojourner.

Spatial confinement in medieval society did not necessarily mean safe haven for women. While the allocation of guarded spaces to upper-class women provided security, women who served as slaves or domestic servants found that confined spaces often put them at risk of physical violation and violence without recourse to public intervention. Spatial segregation did not mean security from violence, as homicide figures show. In the case of slaves, they could neither remain chaste because of the abuse of masters nor escape the house because they were forced to remain celibate. Servants, on the other hand, planned to work only for a limited number of years until they had accumulated enough money for a dowry and marriage.[40] Even so, they might be effectively reduced to concubinage or to pay with their bodies as well as their labor for their wages.

Single women also worked as wage laborers and sometimes apprentices in various crafts. They worked at cloth making, silver and gold thread or lace production, and in victualing trades. If the girl were an apprentice, she would live in the same house as her master and work in the adjoining shop. If she were a day laborer, her space would be that of the shop and that of her home. In any case, her work function would be performed in a familial environment. Once married, urban women of the artisanal craft would most likely become part of the production force of their husbands' trade or they would enter the victualing business that could be carried out from their own homes. For upper-class women, those married to the merchant elite, home was the chief center of their lives. Only widows of craftsmen and merchants or, in London, married women acting as *femme sole*, ventured into the broader marketplace or dealt in substantial production. But even here, they were limited to their own cities. They could not accompany their goods to trade fairs or other towns.[41]

In the urban environment, therefore, the home, either natal or that of a master, was the chief place of living and working for urban women. Their relationship to more public places such as churches, streets, markets, guild-halls, and taverns was similar to that of peasant women's relationship to the village. Since the space was shared with men, urban women had more injunctions toward behavior in public that would preserve a space around them. But the homogeneous environment gave more scope to single women such as prostitutes and Beguines.

KEEPING WOMEN IN THEIR SPACE

In taking up once again the issue of space and exercising power over it, we must think again of the arguments of Pierre Bourdieu that domination of space means regulation of those within it. Medieval men consciously strove through a variety of mechanisms to keep women within women's space and to regulate them within that designated area. Since they regarded women as by their very nature unruly, the best way to control them was to enclose them. Male kin, ecclesiastical authorities, and masters all undertook to insure that their female dependents were properly maintained in their homes and were appropriately attired and escorted when they were away from that designated space. Single women were the chief concern of the official male establishment because married women were under the regulation of their husbands, who would presumably take measures to restrict their wives and daughters. Nuns, Beguines, and prostitutes, however, posed a threat to the male establishment, and so they had to be controlled.

Regulations were an obvious way to curtail women's access to greater public space, but moral injunctions, ridicule, and outright attacks were used as well. Women who strayed from their designated space might be subject to sexual assault because they were neither under the protection of a responsible male nor in their accustomed space. Again, lest we think that these injunctions on women's mobility are outmoded today, consider the risks a women encounters in entering an all-male pool hall in modern America.

Female challenges to male spatial domination occurred continually throughout the Middle Ages. Every new monastic movement brought a flood of women anxious to take vows. Charismatic preachers converted pious women to their cause. The Premonstratensian and Cistercian orders found themselves embarrassed by the large number of women who wanted to join their order. Their response was to limit the number accepted and to enclose them severely. The revolutionary mendicant order of Francis of Assisi also attracted women, but Innocent III was quick to insure that they would be under strict claustration rather than begging as did the Friars. Thus the Poor Clares became a convent group like other nuns.[42] Beguines, as we have seen, posed a separate problem because they resisted claustration. It took a combination of a papal prohibition against the uncloistered or vagabond religious persons issued by Boniface VIII, denunciations by bishops and synods, and charges of heresy to discourage the movement or to attach women to the Dominican order.[43]

Prostitutes, likewise, came under spatial confinement. The city fathers relegated those independent, single, loose women to houses or quarters so that they could be regulated. In London they were forced to practice their trade in their stews across the river from the city in Southwark.[44] On the Continent, urban centers undertook to run houses of prostitution and regulate and tax the women. Sometimes these houses of prostitution even went by the name of "nunneries," but for the most part they were bathhouses.[45]

When women did move out of their space, they had to do so with proper escort or risk humiliation or even rape. The moralist constantly warned that if women went out alone they would lose their honor.[46] Margery Kempe, a bourgeois Englishwoman with a penchant for pilgrimage, feared rape. She did not go on pilgrimages alone, but rather in the company of her husband or with companions who made her respectable. Knowing the taboo and risks of women traveling alone, she would not let her daughter-in-law return to Germany alone, but rather accompanied her there. Returning to England alone as a matron, she feared that she would be raped along the way. She joined a company going to Aachen and was explicitly asked "Why, lady, don't you have any man to go with you?"[47] Women who moved out of their space were subject to gang rape in late medieval France, and even the friars seemed, in their sermons against women who wore "lewd" clothing in the streets, to encourage rape as a punishment.[48]

Although medieval society had many ways to define women as respectable matrons or as marginals, one of the simplest but most overlooked by modern historians was the physical boundaries erected around women. The space that women could occupy with freedom of movement was the home, the castle, the nunnery, the village, the city quarter. If they moved outside these areas they did so with proper dress, demeanor, and escort or they risked compromising their honor or their persons. Spatial confinement was not an unconscious aspect of medieval society, but rather a theme that appeared in all types of medieval literature. Once the space of honorable women was defined and its centrality well established, marginal women could be easily defined as those who wandered outside its confines. While I would not argue that women's marginality could be solely defined by the space that they occupied, I am suggesting that space was very gendered in the Middle Ages and that one factor in reaching a definition of marginality for medieval women is gender-prescribed space and the fate of women at its boundaries.

NOTES

1. Bronislaw Geremek, *The Margins of Society in Late Medieval Paris*, trans. Jean Birrell (Cambridge: Cambridge University Press, 1976). First published in Polish in 1971 and in French in 1976.

2. Ibid., see particularly pp. 270–99.
3. Ephraim H. Mizruchi, *Regulating Society: Beguines, Bohemians, and Other Marginals* (Chicago: University of Chicago Press, 1987). First published (New York: Free Press, 1983. See particularly pp. 8–27.
4. Thomas F. Reddaway, *The Early History of the Goldsmith's Company, 1327–1509* (London: Edward Arnold, 1975), p. 151.
5. Pierre Bourdieu, *Outline of a Theory of Practice* (Cambridge: Cambridge University Press, 1977), pp. 90–91, 160–63.
6. Daphne Spain, *Gendered Spaces* (Chapel Hill: University of North Carolina Press, 1992).
7. Martine Segalen, *Mari et Femme dans la Société Paysanne* (Paris: Flammarion, 1980). In her *Historical Anthropology of the Family*, trans. J. C. Whitehouse and Sarah Matthews (Cambridge: Cambridge University Press, 1986), pp. 205–12, 218–19, she extends the observation to other preindustrial societies.
8. Mary Douglas, in *Purity and Danger* (London: Routledge and Kegan Paul, 1966), pp. 140–58, discusses the interplay between men and women and their society's ideas about pollution. Victor Turner, in *The Ritual Process: Structure and Anti-Structure* (New York: Aldine Publishing Company, 1969), 109–11, has spoken about the perceived danger of the weak in societies.
9. Barbara A. Hanawalt, *The Ties That Bound: Peasant Families in Medieval England* (New York: Oxford University Press, 1986), pp. 180–82.
10. *The Babees Book* and *The Bokes of Nurture*, ed. Frederick J. Furnivall (Early English Text Society, 32, 1868), pp. 36–47.
11. Christiane Klapisch-Zuber, *Women, Family, and Ritual in Renaissance Italy*, trans. Lydia Cochraine (Chicago: University of Chicago Press, 1985), p. 109.
12. Vincent of Beauvais, *De Eruditione Filiorum Nobilium*, ed. Arpad Steiner (Cambridge, Mass.: Medieval Academy of America Publications, xxxii, 1938), pp. 172–219. See also Giles of Rome, *De Regimine Principum* (Augsburg, 1473), book ii, part ii, chapters 19–21. All of these are quoted in Nicholas Orme, *From Childhood to Chivalry: The Education of the English Kings and Aristocracy 1066–1530* (London: Methuen, 1984), pp. 106–7, 235. See also Ruth Kelso, *Doctrine for the Lady of the Renaissance* (Urbana: University of Illinois Press, 1956), p. 53 for material containing the recommendation that a young girl remain in her father's house and not go out into the world.
13. Alice A. Hentsch, ed., *De la Littérature Didactique du Moyen Âge S'adressant Specialment aux Femmes* (Geneva: Slatkine Reprints, 1975). See p. 91 (Matfre Ermengau, 1288), p. 105 (Francesco da Barberino, 1309), p. 173 ("Castigos y Doctrinas que un Sabio da Va a Sus Hijas," fifteenth century).
14. Suzanne Fonay Wemple, *Women in Frankish Society: Marriage and the Cloister 500 to 900* (Philadelphia: University of Pennsylvania Press, 1985), pp. 105–6.
15. *Calendar of Letter Books Preserved among the Archives of the Corporation of the City of London, 1275–1487, Letter Book A*, ed. Reginald R. Sharpe (London: John Edward Francis, 1889), p. 220.
16. Diane Owen Hughes, "Distinguishing Signs: Ear-rings, Jews and Franciscan Rhetoric in the Italian Renaissance City," *Past and Present*, 112 (1986): 3–59.
17. Ruth Mazo Karras, "The Regulation of Brothels in Later Medieval England," *Signs*, 14 (1989): 421; Leah Otis, *Prostitution in Medieval Society: The History of an Urban Institution in Languedoc* (Chicago: University of Chicago Press, 1985), p. 80; Jacques Rossiaud, *Medieval Prostitution*, trans. Llydia G. Cochrane (Oxford: Basil Blackwell, 1988), pp. 64–65; and Hughes, ibid, pp. 29–30.

18. See Hentsch, ed. *De la Littérature Didactique*, pp. 52–53, 75–77 and Hentsch's entire collection of didactic literature for women.
19. Jane Tibbets Schulenburg, "The Heroics of Virginity: Brides of Christ and Sacrificial Mutilation," in *Women in the Middle Ages and the Renaissance: Literary and Historical Perspectives*, ed. Mary Beth Rose (Syracuse, N.Y.: Syracuse University Press, 1986), pp. 32–33.
20. David Herlihy, *Opera Muliebria: Women and Work in Medieval Europe* (New York: McGraw-Hill Publishing Company, 1989), pp. 34–38.
21. Hanawalt, *The Ties That Bound*, see tables, p. 271.
22. *Reliquiae Antiquae: Songs and Carols*, 2, ed. Thomas Wright and James O. Halliwell (London: Percy Society, 1841), pp. 196–99.
23. Judith M. Bennett, *Women in the Medieval English Countryside: Gender and Household in Brigstock before the Plague* (New York: Oxford University Press, 1987), ch. 2.
24. Barbara A. Hanawalt, *Crime and Conflict in Medieval Communities, 1300–1348* (Cambridge, Mass.: Harvard University Press, 1979), pp. 120–22, 168–70.
25. In general women were not cited as victims of property crimes because their property, unless they were single or widows, belonged to their husbands. For the pattern on homicide see James B. Given, *Society and Homicide in Thirteenth-Century England* (Palo Alto, Calif.: Stanford University Press, 1977), p. 169.
26. Guy Beresford, *The Medieval Clay-Land Village: Excavations at Glotho and Barton Blont* (London: The Society for Medieval Archaeology Monograph Series, 1975), pp. 27–29.
27. Johannes Busch, *Liber de Reformatione Monasteriorum*, ed. Karl Grube, Geschichtsquellen der Provinz Sachsen (Halle, 1886), p. 779, as quoted by Eileen Power, *Medieval Women* (Cambridge: Cambridge University Press, 1975), p. 36.
28. *The Household Book of Dame Alice de Bryene of Acton Hall Suffolk, Sept. 1412–Sept. 1413*, trans. Marian K. Dale (Ipswich: Suffolk Institute of Archaeology and Natural History, 1931). See also Margaret Wade Labarge, *A Baronial Household of the Thirteenth Century* (Totowa, N.J.: Barnes and Noble, 1965) for a description of the house of Eleanor de Montefort.
29. Labarge, *Baronial Household*; Power, *Medieval Women*, p. 45.
30. Kate Mertes, *The English Noble Household, 1250–1600* (Oxford: Basil Blackwell, 1988), pp. 56–59.
31. See Penny Schine Gold, *The Lady and the Virgin: Image, Attitude, and Experience in Twelfth-Century France* (Chicago: University of Chicago Press, 1985), pp. 5, 10, 14–15.
32. Ibid., ch. 4.
33. Schulenburg, "Heroics of Virginity," p. 42.
34. Power, *Medieval Women*, pp. 89–96.
35. See Anne K. Warren, *The Anchorites of Medieval England* (Berkeley: University of California Press, 1985) for a good discussion of the institution of anchorites.
36. Given, *Thirteenth-Century Homicide*, pp. 179–83.
37. Klapisch-Zuber, in *Women, Family, and Ritual in Renaissance Italy*, p. 81, shows that marriages were usually among the *gonfalone*, a subdivision of the quarter, in Florence unless the family was undergoing social mobility either up or down.
38. The total sample size is 267 accidental deaths from 1275 to 1341. Cases appear in *Calendar of Coroners' Rolls of the City of London, A.D. 1300–1378*, ed. Reginald R. Sharpe (London: Richard Clay and Sons, 1913); Public Record Office Just.

2/94-A; and *Calendar of Letter Books of the City of London, Letter Book B*, ed. Reginald R. Sharpe (London: John Edward Francis, 1900), pp. 256–80.

39. Brenda M. Bolton, "Mulieres Sanctae," in *Women in Medieval Society*, ed. Susan Mosher Stuard (Philadelphia: University of Pennsylvania Press, 1976), pp. 141–56. Ernest W. McDonnel, *The Beguines and Beghards in Medieval Culture* (New Brunswick, N.J.: Rutgers University Press, 1954).

40. Christiane Klapisch-Zuber, "Women Servants in Florence during the Fourteenth and Fifteenth Centuries," in *Women and Work in Preindustrial Europe*, ed. Barbara A. Hanawalt (Bloomington, Ind.: Indiana University Press, 1986), pp. 56–80. See also Susan Mosher Stuard, "To Town to Serve: Urban Domestic Slavery in Medieval Ragusa," pp. 39–55 in the same collection of essays.

41. Kathryn L. Reyerson, "Women in Business in Medieval Montpellier," pp. 117–44; Maryanne Kowaleski, "Women's Work in a Market Town: Exeter in the Late Fourteenth Century," pp. 145–60; and Martha C. Howell, "Women, the Family Economy, and the Structures of Market Production in Cities of Northern Europe during the Late Middle Ages," pp. 198–222 in *Women and Work in Preindustrial Europe*, ed. Barbara A. Hanawalt (Bloomington, Ind.: University of Indiana Press, 1986).

42. Bolton, "Mulieres Sanctae," pp. 144–51.

43. McDonnell, *Beguines and Beghards*, pp. 505–33.

44 Karras, "The Regulation of Brothels in Later Medieval England," pp. 399–433.

45. See Otis, *Prostitution in Medieval Society* and Rossiaud, *Medieval Prostitution* for examples of work done on medieval prostitution.

46. See Hentsch, *De la Literature Didactique*, p. 132 ("Le Chevalier de la Tour Landry, 1346), among others.

47. *The Book of Margery Kempe*, trans Barry A. Windeatt (Harmondsworth: Penguine, 1985), pp. 271–81.

48. Roussiaud, *Medieval Prostitution*, pp. 10–26, 151–52.

6

Separation Anxieties in Late Medieval London: Gender in "The Wright's Chaste Wife"

For centuries, the occupations of soldier, sailor, merchant, architect, and builder have required long periods of separation from wives and families. Those situations have produced a variety of anxieties. Since those occupations were all dangerous, a wife might fear losing both a husband and a means of support. Perhaps even worse was the possibility that a husband would simply be unaccounted for because no one reported the sinking of the ship on which he sailed or because he had been taken prisoner. If her widowhood were in doubt, a wife would not have the legal right to collect the dower from her husband's estate, and she might have to carry on her husband's business even if she was ill-equipped to do so. Other times she might be responsible for raising a large ransom to get her husband out of prison or for paying his debts so that he could come home. Husbands worried about the deterioration of their businesses, the training of their apprentices, and the rearing of their children while they were gone. But these financial and practical considerations were not the stuff of medieval stories that dealt with separation anxieties. Rather, both men and women wrote and spoke about the sexual continence of their conjugal partners during absences. While a husband was away, his wife might have lovers or he himself might have a family in another port or city. Perhaps the expressed anxieties over unfaithfulness masked deeper anxieties about the real risks that separation entailed. Narrative tales that spoke of the constancy of love and the cleverness of women in preserving chastity, and even the ribald recounting of the worst fears in *fabliaux* eased the tension caused by fear of calamities far worse

I wish to thank Ruth Bottigheimer and Inger Lövkrona for reading the manuscript and for making valuable suggestions. This article was previously published in *Medieval Perspectives*, 11 (1996), pp. 23–41.

than unfaithfulness. This paper explores one of these tales, "The Wright's Chaste Wife," and examines the fictional and real experiences of separation. This particular tale, I argue, is preserved in the female voice and recounts the wife's triumphs over assaults on her chastity while the wright is away.

The use of folkloric materials for the study of social and cultural history has enjoyed some vogue in recent articles, particularly those of Robert Darnton, such as "Peasants Tell Tales," and Eugene Weber, "Fairies and Hard Facts."[1] But the problem with these studies is that they try to place tales collected in the late nineteenth and early twentieth centuries into the eighteenth century or even earlier in an attempt to create a *mentalité* for the early modern period. Weber writes that "the popular stories that we describe as fairy tales can tell us a great deal about real conditions." And Darnton has them play two roles: "Folktales are historical documents," and "The stories belonged to a fund of popular culture, which peasants hoarded over the centuries with remarkably little loss." When folk stories have gone through so many filters, reading them as "voices of the people" or historical "facts" becomes a dubious exercise.[2] Instead, I build one argument about separation anxieties that uses historical evidence and another, separate one, from a fifteenth-century folk narrative that presents an alternative, even subversive response to the same anxieties. The arguments run somewhat parallel, and their conclusions show a common thread of anxiety.

The tradition of separation tales has been traced back to a sixth-century Sanskrit version. Persian and Arabic analogues, including one in *The Thousand and One Nights*, preceded the first western example, which appears in the *Gesta Romanorum*. The story is a simple one. A husband is about to leave his new, young wife to take a job or engage in trade in a faraway place. He worries that his wife will be unfaithful (in the Indian version they worry about each other) and is given a wreath or garland that will not fade or wither as long as the wife is chaste. In some versions he is given a shirt that will not stain. The traveler's ever-fresh display of flowers or perpetually unstained shirt arouses curiosity among the men who hear the story and they, of course, decide to test the chastity of the wife. She manages to dupe them by a variety of ruses and then enclose them in chests, cabinets, or a room. She thereby preserves her chastity, increases her wealth from gifts they offer, and saves her marriage. When her husband returns, they enjoy ridiculing the suitors.[3]

The story is a very different one from the usual *fabliaux* of medieval Europe, although certain elements are the same. The *fabliaux* emphasize not only the anxieties of merchants and other itinerant businessmen over their wives' chastity but also the cleverness of the wives. But the majority of *fabliaux* tell stories of illicit love affairs and adultery rather than of sexual integrity. Both the Shipman and the Merchant in the *Canterbury Tales* choose such tales of infidelity on the part of wives. "The Wright's Chaste Wife," however, preserves the original Indian/oriental version.[4] Boccaccio's analogue has some elements of the story, but it involves a widow who dislikes both of her lovers and manages to get rid of them (Day 9, novel 1). Chaucer's

Franklin tells a tale of a chaste wife but with entirely different elements, being a story of male magic rather than of female strategy. Itinerant businessmen and soldiers undoubtedly knew both the chaste wife and the ribald
wife stories. It is possible, however, that women also told these stories as
they worked at their spinning and favored the "chaste wife" versions.[5]

Both men and women also understood and gossiped about the stories
of real, not fictional chaste wives, such as those that appear in the legal
records of fourteenth- and fifteenth-century London. These court cases indicate the problems encountered by both men and women entailed by the
long separations entailed by the husband's line of work. Analysis of these
cases appears in the first part of this chapter. The second part looks more
closely at Adam de Cobsam's 1462 version of the poem as a female narrative. In this analysis the types of ruses, the space in which they occur, the
female symbols the wife uses to humiliate the men, and the wright's scant,
passive role in the narrative action are adduced to argue the presence of a
strong female voice, even if a woman is not the immediate redactor of our
version.

HISTORICAL INSTANCES OF SEPARATION

The wright or carpenter of our story is well known for his skill in his craft
and well liked as a friend in the community (10–24). All he lacks in life is
"a wyfe for to wedde and haue/That myght hys goodes kepe and saue"
(28–29). He hears of a maid who is both "stabyll and trewe, /Meke of man-
ers, and feyr of hewe" (34–35). Her mother is a poor widow and has only a
garland of white roses to give as a dowry. But this garland is a magical one
that will never fade as long as his wife is true to him (34–66). Having secured a wife, he realizes that he will have to go back to work. Fortunately,
the lord of the town wants a hall built and sends for the wright to do the
work, which will take a month or two. The lord asks if he wishes to have
his wife accompany him, but the wright declines the offer since he has made
arrangements to insure her chastity (103–11).

The custom of leaving their wives at home to manage affairs, "kepe and
save," was strongly ingrained in London merchants and craftsmen. Those
going abroad or even into the provinces might arrange for kin or a business
factor to act for them, but often the best expedient was to put their wives in
charge of matters in London. London men were accustomed to trusting their
wives to act as their executors and as guardians of their children should they
die, so that to have them carry on the business during their absence was a
matter of routine.[6] Thus Joan, "wife and attorney of John Olney, woolmon-
ger," sued to recover a debt owed to him, but the man she was suing was
going abroad on the king's service and had a writ of protection from such
actions. Women also appeared as using the ploy of the writ of protection for
their husbands as did Ellen, wife of Nicholas Mate, in a suit of debt brought
by Elizabeth atte Hawe.[7]

A wife, left to handle her husband's affairs while he was away on business, had to be very shrewd in her arrangements, or she could end up being duped or bullied. In court cases, the women who could not cope appear with regularity. Managing apprentices was difficult for women who were not really in the trade. Thus, an apprentice to John Morem claimed that his master was in prison and his mistress was unable to train him. Another apprentice complained that his master was imprisoned for eight weeks in Calais and that the mistress could teach him nothing.[8] But far worse problems arose for women left on their own. William Martyn and his wife had hired a brew house on Flete Street from John Colman. The assumption seemed to have been that Maude, William's wife, would manage it while he was away. John was supposed to roof the house but did not, so William and Maude sued him. They were losing money because no guests would "lie in beds through [because of] rain." While William Martyn was away, John Colman and two servants went to his house where his wife Maude lived with two servants. They threatened William's servants so that they would not work and repeated their assault several weeks later. In her husband's absence, Maude "requested that the defendant find surety of peace against [her] and her servants, because the said William is abroad in the service of the Prince, and in his absence the said Maude has no aid."[9] Another woman complained that a man brought a suit against her, knowing that her husband was in Bristol.[10] An absent husband, in these women's experience, provided the opportunity for men to take advantage of them.

The unsettled political conditions between France and England during the Hundred Years' War meant that the wife might be called upon to organize her husband's rescue from imprisonment, an active role that appears in an Arabian analogue in which a woman liberates her husband from jail.[11] The fourteenth and fifteenth centuries saw the many phases of the Hundred Years' War in which merchants might be arbitrarily imprisoned by belligerents expecting ransom, and all merchants feared pirates as much as they feared shipwreck. Ransoms were a common means of earning extra money in this period, and it was often the wife who had to raise the sums to release her husband. Joan, wife of John Pound, a citizen of London, sought the help of the Mayor of London in getting her husband released. The mayor sent letters to the "Burgomasters, Echevins, and Counselors" of Gent, Bruges, and Ypres explaining that John Pound had freighted a ship to Sluys with goods of the value of £50, which he had bought at the Fair of Antwerp. On the voyage home, Joan claimed, Arnold Jonesson, captain of the castle of Savetyngee, captured the ship and "carried the said John and the goods to the castle, where he still detained them." Beatrice, wife of Reginald Fuller, a tailor, paid William Knott, also a tailor, 8 marks in the presence of London's Recorder and an Alderman. She asked him to obtain the release of her husband and John Goldesmore, a fuller, who had been captured by Frenchmen and were in prison in Bologne. Reginald had already been liberated by John de Burer of Bologne so that he could raise £13 6s. 6d., which was the amount of the ransom. The ransom had been reduced to £5 4s. so that Reginald was free, but William Knotte was to secure the release of John Gold-esmore or return the money.[12]

Communication between husband and wife when the man was abroad was often by messages passed by word of mouth or, less frequently, by personal letters. Other merchants and seamen would bring back word of a husband's whereabouts and how he was doing. But messages often went astray, and the wife did not always know where her husband was or if he were alive. When one apprentice complained that his master left the kingdom a long time ago, the wife of the master told the mayor that she had heard nothing about where he was.[13]

Separations were fraught with uncertainty, and the anxieties over them, as we have observed, took the form of worry about conjugal faithfulness. A beautiful, younger wife was perceived as being particularly vulnerable. The wright of our tale thinks all of this through before he leaves his new bride to manage his affairs. He adds a tower to his house with a conjugal chamber and, below it, a secure dungeon that none could escape from "even if they were kings or emperors." In the middle of the chamber he places a trapdoor that will open at a mere touch and discharge the person into the pit (79–99):

> For hys wyfe he made that place,
> That no man schuld beseke her of grace,
> Nor her to begyle.
>
> (100–102)

The wright is more concerned with protecting his wife from unwanted attention than with planning for the uncertainty of his own return.

During a prolonged separation, however, a wife might not wait for her husband to return before remarrying. These cases are a bit like "The Return of Martin Guerre," except that there is no duplicity on the part of the second husband. Harry Peterson, one of the king's workmen of his "gonnes," [guns] complained that about fifteen years earlier he had married a woman of Brabant, had brought her to London, where they lived together as man and wife for four years and more, and had had a child with her. After that he was away for ten years in the wars of the "king of the Romans [German emperor]." He had left his wife behind in the charge of her brother. While he was gone she took another husband, "but now he has come home and wanted to take up their marriage again." She refused, preferring to stay with her new husband. The church court took her side, so Harry petitioned the Lord Chancellor to intervene because he was "weary and impoverished over the matter."[14]

The wife might, however, receive false word that her husband was dead and decide to remarry. John Ketyng went off to Ireland with a servant, William. Time passed and servant William returned wearing the gown, doublet, and hose that John Ketyng had worn when he left London, saying to John's wife and neighbors that John was dead. On this evidence the ecclesiastical authorities stepped in, and the summoner asked the wife to come before the commissary court to probate John's will. She was then declared a widow and all her neighbors viewed her as such. A suitor soon appeared,

John Talbot, who asked her to marry him. She accepted and the banns were read on three "solemn days." No one came forward to claim a prior contract, so they married. He moved into John Ketyng's house with her. But John Ketyng was *not* dead, and he entered his house and took away his goods as well as those belonging to Talbot, amounting to £30. He also brought an action against Talbot and had him put in jail.[15]

Often enough, of course, the husband really was dead. Alice, widow of William Rolf, a shipman, took a letter from the Mayor of London around to ports where her husband traded, asking "for love's sake to give up the goods and chattels" of Rolf since he was lately drowned at sea.[16]

The wright's concerns and those of the duped husband in the *fabliaux* are also mirrored in the court cases. John de Walkern, a citizen of London, complained that while he was journeying on a pilgrimage to Rome, his wife, Lucy, had removed his goods and chattels from the city. When he returned he went "from country court to county court and from town to town until he discovered a portion of the goods at Lynn." No mention was made of Lucy and her whereabouts. Another case relates that Richard, son of John le Mareschall of Smithfield, was charged with abducting the wife of Stephen Hereford. The neighbors all knew about the affair because Richard had been at the house frequently. When Stephen was away at Winchester Fair, Richard was at his house all the time, and friends and neighbors of Stephen determined to put a stop to it. They searched the house for Richard, but could not find him. Finally, they directed the adulterous wife to open a chest closed with iron, and therein they found Richard. Richard left London for Waltham and did not see the wife again. When she learned that her husband was returning, the wife left home with some goods. Finally, she got the ecclesiastical court to force Stephen into a reconciliation with her.[17]

Wives, too, worried about the fidelity of their husbands. In the Indian version of the separation tale, both the husband and the wife get a lotus flower to keep to show their chastity.[18] When husbands were home, servant girls, who were present in very many households, could prove too tempting to resist,[19] but when traveling, husbands might establish more permanent relationships. Such relationships were fraught with problems for wives. Elizabeth, wife of Thomas Mountague of London, complained that her husband continued in an adulterous relationship with a woman of Stratford atte Bow at the manor of Oldeford, and that the affair was imperiling his soul and also destroying the livelihood of Elizabeth because he was spending all their money on the mistress. Should a bastard be the result of one of these unions, inheritances were endangered. Roger Thorney, a London mercer, was acting for a fellow merchant who died intestate on ship. The deceased merchant's goods were duly sequestered when the ship docked, but matters got complicated when "one Edward, an evil disposed person being a bastard and a Fleming born at Bruges in Flanders, which calleth himself bastard son" of the late John Pykering, claimed a debt against the estate.[20] Wills are full of evidence of these far-flung families. Geoffrey Bonere, a paternoster maker, left bequests to his illegitimate daughter in Flanders. Thomas Gippyng (alias Lincoln) was a draper from London who spent considerable time in Lincolnshire on business. He had a legitimate wife in London, but he left the residue of his estate to his two bastard daughters and his bedding to Juliana Pleydon of Lincoln, who was, presumably, their mother.[21]

GENDER IN "THE WRIGHT'S CHASTE WIFE"

The anxieties caused by separation of husband and wife are clear in courts and wills; the narrators are both male and female; and the traumas of separation were financial as well as sexual in nature. Knowing the historical context of conjugal separation anxieties, we can return to the question of the narrator and audience of our tale. Classification of the folktale by themes in "The Wright's Chaste Wife" emphasizes the entrapped suitors ("Deceptions," K 1218.1–1218.1.3) as well as, within the "Chastity" Index, shirts that never stain (*Gesta Romanorum* version) and wreaths, nosegays, and other flowers that do not wilt (H431.1, H432–432.4).[22] Classification of the folktale, therefore, gives pride of place to the duped suitors rather than to the women who outsmart them, and to magical objects rather than to female wit. The male bias of the folklore indices has increasingly received notice.[23] Class has fared better than gender in consideration of the analogues. Bédier points out that "Constant du Hamel," the French analogue, represents an inversion of class because the wife of a villain outwits the three tyrants of the village: the prévôt, the lord's forester, and the priest.[24] The class element is also present in "The Wright's Chaste Wife." The wright is described as a "good yeman," while the suitors are the lord of the town, his steward, and a church proctor.

The manuscript of our version is bound in a volume (Lambeth Palace Archive 306 dating from 1460–70) that is a curious mixture, in different handwriting, of political events, diaries, recipes and remedies, and literature such as "A treytys of one Gyngelayne-bastard son of Sir Gaweyne," "The Hymn to the Virgin" and several other poems on virginity, "St. Gregoris Trentall," "Complaynt of Christ" (including William Lichfield's version), Lydgate's "Hors, the shepe, and the gosse," and "The Stacyons of Rome."[25] In other words, "The Wright's Chaste Wife" appears to be part of a general household volume and was included perhaps for its didactic qualities and its entertainment value. Given the presence of a poem about London and the descriptions of political events, it is possible that the manuscript was associated with a family with close London connections.

The portions of the poem on which the author, Cobsam, puts his strongest imprint are the beginning and the end. The first nine lines are addressed to "my souereyns in towre and hall," requesting them to listen and hear the story of a "wryght." Cobsam does not interject himself into the poem again until the story is complete, and then he inserts his name: "Thys seyd Adam of Cobsam" (l. 620). The poem ends with praise for good women and a blessing on faithful wives and true lovers.[26] Cobsam, therefore, seems to have rendered the tale into verse, leaving the story much as it was. His own voice is only that of the framer of the tale. But what was his source? Could it have been a female storyteller's tale?

In the case of "chaste wife" tales, the Indian analogues and poems of separation are presented as tales told in the female voice. They represent the lament of the young bride for her departed husband and tell stories of clever wives who dupe their suitors in their house and even move out into the world to rescue their husbands from prison or punishment.[27] These versions presume a strong female voice, even though the *Kathá Sarit Ságara* is a compendium of tales put together by a man, as is *A Thousand and One Nights*, whose storyteller is Scheherazade.

Folklore analysis, the social history of medieval women, and the text itself provide clues for establishing the female voice. I begin with the metaphor of spinning because the activity plays a dominant role in the tale, because it is closely associated with women, and because "spinning tales" and "telling yarns" have long been part of our language for describing storytelling. Karen Rowe has traced the history of female storytellers from ancient Greece as literal weavers of their tales in fabric pictures. She argues that "women as storytellers have woven or spun their yarns, speaking at one level to a total culture, but at another to a sisterhood of readers [or listeners] who will understand the hidden language, the secret revelations of the tale." Men appropriate these tales and, in turn, weave them into their "superior" literature.[28] Marina Warner notes that

> the fiction is that there are three Fates, who spin a woolen thread on a distaff, or a spindle, and with their fingers on account of the threefold nature of time: the past, which is already spun and wound onto the spindle; the present, which is drawn between the spinner's fingers; and the future, which lies in the wool twined on the distaff, and which must still be drawn out by the spinner's fingers onto the spindle, as the present is drawn into the past.[29]

Rowe goes on to speak of documented nineteenth-century scenes of women sitting with their children (including young boys) after a meal doing their spinning, mending, and sewing and telling stories to each other. In doing so, they instilled cultural values in the listening children and defined behavior that would be rewarded or punished.[30] In the case of "The Wright's Chaste Wife," the moral lessons are obvious and designed to empower the little girls and intimidate the little boys in the audience. Marina Warner has described the didactic quality of folktales aptly:

> The pedagogical function of the wonder story deepens the sympathy between the social category women occupy and the fairy tale. Fairy tales exchange knowledge between an older voice of experience and a younger audience, they present pictures of perils and possibilities that lie ahead, they use terror to set limits on choice and offer consolation to the wronged, they draw social outlines around boys and girls, fathers and mothers, the rich and the poor, the rulers and the ruled, they point out the evildoers and garland the virtuous, they stand up to adversity with dreams of vengeance, power and vindication.[31]

Elsewhere throughout the book, Warner presents the males' negative analysis of women in this teaching capacity, which defines it as gossip rather than as useful pedagogy.

The location of the action in narratives provides important clues to female authorship. Ria Lemaire has offered the beginnings of a semiotic analysis of public and private space in women's narratives of unhappy marriages. Those written by women and in their voice show women going out of their houses to meet lovers in woods, by lakes, and generally in public space. When the poems were taken over by men, the assignations with lovers are first in walled gardens and finally, by the fifteenth century, in houses. The clergy also had a version of spiritual assignations that occurred in the cloisters of nunneries. In other words, as the female voice became more and more muted, the action became more spatially restricted, moving from public to domestic space.[32] In the earlier Indian and Arabian analogues, as we have noted, the women go into the marketplace or even to the town where their husbands are trading.

Our poem, however, takes place entirely in the house, as one would expect in a fifteenth-century setting. But it is a space entirely dominated by the wife, since the husband is away. Only the passive devices of the tower and trap door remain of his influence in her domestic arrangements. The space of the house was, in medieval tradition and practice, closely associated with women because their tasks were largely performed there, while men performed the work of merchant, soldier, or peasant largely outside the home. Only crafts associated with shops, such as shoemakers, tailors, goldsmiths, and so on, shared the domestic space of the house with women.[33] Since a carpenter worked on structures away from home, his wife was alone in the space that women traditionally occupied while he was at work. Her husband's absence gave her the type of power that we have seen London women hold when their husbands were away.

Another element of the poem takes us back to women's work, weaving, and gender inversions. When the lord notices the unfading garland of his carpenter, he determines that he will test the chastity of the carpenter's wife. Going to the wright's house, he propositions the wife with an offer of 40 m. (£26 13s. 4d.) She at first refuses, saying that she will not disappoint her husband, who will know because of the garland. Finally she consents, but asks for the money in advance. She leads him up the tower stairs, where he trips and falls through the trap door into the prison. He begs to be let out and then threatens her. She remains unmoved saying, "whyle I am here and thou art there" there is nothing to fear (200–201). She goes about her work. The next day, he begins to beg for food and drink. She tells him he will have to "swete or swynke" for his food. His task is to beat the flax to separate the fibers:

> "For I haue both hempe and lyne,
> And a betyngstock full fyne,
> And a swyngyll good and grete;
> If thou wylt work, tem me sone."
>
> (214–17)

He readily agrees to work for her at this essentially female task.

The steward, missing his lord, asks the wright about the lord's whereabouts. He notices the garland, hears the story of its magic, and sets out to try his luck. He offers 20 m. (£13 6s. 6d.), which the wife pockets before she takes him up to the bedroom above the prison. Again, the suitor falls through the trap door. The lord has finished his day's labor and is beginning to take pride in his work, saying that it is "full clere, and no thing thycke," although he confesses that it is "gret payne" (338–39). He is rewarded with a meal. The steward, meanwhile, threatens to break the wife's head, but his lord points to the impossibility of getting out and suggests that he "rubbe, rele, and spynne" (349). The steward swears that he will starve first, but the lord refuses to give up any of his own hard-earned supper. So the steward is reduced to asking her for work, and she supplies a "swyngellyng stocke" for him to sit on and a "swyngell" to spin with:

> The wife threw hym a swyngelyng stocke,
> Hys mete therwyth to wyn;
> Sche brought a swyngyll att the last,
> "Good syres," sche seyd, "swyngylle on fast;
> For no thing that ye blynne."
>
> (386–93)

He is not happy, but he is fed. And he tells the lord, "Sey, seye, swyngyll better yf ye may,/ Hytt wyll be the better to spynne" (395–96).

Finally, the proctor of the parish church notices the garland and goes to offer his 20 m. (£13 6s. 6d.) to the wife. He meets the same fate. He is amazed to see the lord and steward working away at the spinning and swears he will never have a spindle in his hand, since he has learned from childhood what that means:

> The proctoure seyd, "what do ye in this yne
> For to bete thys wyfees lyne?
> For Ihesus loue, ffull of myght,"
> The proctoure seyd ryght as he thought,
> "For me yt schall be euyll wrought
> And I may see aryght
> For I lernyd neuer in lond
> For to haue a swyngell in hond
> By day no be nyght."
>
> (469–77)

It is instructive that the priest, whose role is to be celibate and, therefore, whose sexual identity is less socially assured than that of the lord and steward, is the one who objects explicitly to the assumption of female symbols. The steward has no sympathy, saying, we are "as good as thou" (479). The proctor succumbs and the wife throws down a "rocke" (distaff). The wife bids him to work fast if he wants food:

> "Yes, dame," he seyd, "so haue I hele,
> I schall yt worke both feyre & welle
> As ye haue taute me."
>
> (511–13)

The lord, an expert by now, criticizes his thread as being too thick: "thou spynnest to grete,/Therefor thou schalt haue no mete" (517–18).

The wright finally returns and hears a din coming from his new tower.

> One of hem knockyd lyne,
> A-nothyr swyngelyd good and fyne
> By-fore the swyngyll tre,
> The thyrde did rele and spynne,
> Mete and drynke ther-wyth to wynne.
>
> (526–30)

He asks his wife what all of this is about, and she replies that the workmen have come to help them in their need. The wright is appalled to discover his lord surrounded by flax and performing demeaning, women's labor. The wright asks what he is doing there, and the lord apologizes and says that it was his own fault. Still, the wright expresses distress at seeing his lord "among thys flex and hempe" (554).

The sexual inversion of forcing men to perform the quintessential women's task of preparing and spinning flax is obvious. The lord, in beating the flax, is at least doing a task that men sometimes did, but the others are doing female labor. More aggravating than the work for the men is being caught with the symbols of female roles. In the Middle Ages the instruments that are mentioned, particularly the distaff, were the women's symbols, while swords, staffs, plows, and flails were the men's symbols. The wife has humiliated the suitors by forcing them into female roles. The humor of such role reversal was, no doubt, more amusing to a female audience than to a male one, and suggests that women were the weavers of the tale. Males might well have felt the punishment was too threatening.

The sexual inversion in the English variation is much at variance with the earlier analogues and the French version, in which the suitors are humiliated by being stripped, painted with lamp-black, dressed up in ludicrous costumes, tarred and feathered, and forced to do silly dances in public or parade home in their costumes. The husband and wife join equally in laughing at her victims. No hint of gender inversions is present. "The Wright's Chaste Wife" stands out because it emphasizes men's humiliation over being both employed in women's work and confined in women's space. The space in which such a story might be told is domestic and the tellers would be spinning or doing other work with fabrics. Ruth Bottigheimer has pointed out that in the German tradition the *Spinnstube* was the setting for much of the tale-telling so that the women could keep awake in the evenings as they worked. Informants who knew of this tradition supplied the brothers Grimm with many of their stories.[34]

Not only do the symbols of sexual inversion suggest the female voice, but the participation of the wright's wife in the story's dialogues does as well. Bottigheimer has pointed to the silencing of women in men's versions of folk tales. In some they have no direct discourse in the story, and in others they are simply forbidden to speak for years on end.[35] The wright's wife is a figure who uses direct discourse, but the wright's lines are confined to three stock repetitions of the power of his garland to the suitors and a speech with his lord in the cellar. His wife, by contrast, does most of the speaking to the suitors, to her husband, and to the wife of the lord. Furthermore, her discourse has some remarkable qualities. In the first encounters with her suitors she is as meek as she is in the description of her in the opening passages. She inquires after her husband and refuses her suitors' attentions because of her loyalty and because of the garland. But she swiftly takes the upper hand in the conversations by requiring payment before the act and ushering the suitors upstairs ahead of her—her hand rules the doors of her house. Once the suitors have fallen through into the cellar/prison, she is in complete command: laughing at their threats to do her bodily injury, refusing to release them until her husband comes home, and insisting that they produce quality thread for her before feeding them. She proves a stern taskmaster, saying that food and drink will be withheld if the quality of the work is not good.

Another element in favor of a woman's voice in the wright's wife's conversations with her suitors is her commentary on her own role as a woman. When the proctor finally agrees to spin, she comments that "whan I was mayde att home,/Other werke cowde I do none" because her life was taken up with spinning (505–7). She forces them to perform not only female tasks, but those appropriate for an adolescent girl rather than the more responsible chores of adult women. She makes an age inversion as well as a sexual one and sets herself up as the men's superior within the house.

Her complete command of the domestic scene is manifested when her husband comes home and finds his lord doing his wife's work. He apologizes and "bids" her to let his lord out of the cellar. She, however, gives him a saucy answer: "Nay, then sorowe come on my snowte/If they passe hens to-daye." She wants to wait until the lord's wife comes to see what the three men intended to do to her and how she handled the situation (560–64). Apparently, the wright's command over the keys and doors of his own house is weak. In fact, women did control the keys to the strong boxes in the house; another symbol of medieval women, sometimes seen on effigies, was a key ring.

The final female element in the narrative is the collusion between the two women of different social classes: gender is more powerful than class in this poem. The lord's wife looks in the pit and asks how the three got there. The carpenter's wife tells the story, and the lady says that she has a lot to do in her own home, "Mo than two or thre" (596–97). She wants her husband to come home, even if he does nothing to help her.

> The lady lawghed and made good game,
> When they came owte all in-same
> From the swyngyll tre.

(601–603)

The two women collude in their mockery of the men who have been forced to assume female roles. As a final punishment for the suitors, the lady tells the wife to keep all the money. The narrative, therefore, is one of women subverting their normally subordinate role. The wright's wife has effectively turned the tables on male dominance, and the lord's wife forgoes class identity for the stronger one of gender role bonds.

"The Wright's Chaste Wife" is a story of separation anxieties, but it is one in which the female voice is strongly present. Although Cobsam appropriated the tale, he left in elements that argue women's strength and authority. The story is one of a woman triumphing over the anxieties of separation by the use of her authority as the housewife, her powers of attorney while her husband is gone, and her wit. The class inversions play only a minor role compared to the gender and authority inversions in the poem. The wife manages to delegate the onerous part of her traditional role of thread-making to the men, and to save for herself the weaving of a narrative around their folly.

Turning back to the questions of the use of history and folktales, we must investigate the advantages of looking at contemporary but parallel expressions of separation anxieties. Real women speak of loneliness, of uncertainty about their husbands' fates, and of the problems of managing a business in a man's world. They speak of their limitations in power in the legal world and in space in terms of their own inability to move freely to solve their problems. The folktale version introduces a magical device that does not empower the wife, but serves instead as a watchdog on her behavior. The addition of the tower and dungeon is another watchdog set up by her husband rather than by the magic of her mother. The wright's wife outwits the magic of the mother, the mechanics of the husband, and the machinations of the suitors to take the situation into her own control. She subverts the dominant male power structure to her own ends. For her, the usual limitations of women's space are not a problem because she uses the domestic environment to her own advantage. Going into a man's world is not at issue; instead, she forces men into the women's world of work. She knows her success, revels in it, and enjoys a laugh that echoes across class lines. Where do the parallel lines of real experience and of women's fantasies intersect? Anxieties over separation are a common thread in both types of narratives. But we cannot argue that the tale is a reflection of historical reality. We cannot even know if it empowered successful women through its lessons, or if men who knew the tale found consolation and hope in their wives' competence and constancy during their absence. Since the tale is preserved in a household book, we can assume that it served as entertainment and instruction for both the men and women in the house. It is recorded in a miscellany rather than among narratives of sexual infidelity or misogynistic tales. We can assume that the tale was popular, that it was told as women of all classes did their spinning and young boys sat at their knees listening, and that it provided an alternative, subversive possibility to the reality of life.

NOTES

1. Robert Darnton, "Peasants Tell Tales," in *The Great Cat Massacre and Other Episodes in French Cultural History* (New York: Basic Books, 1984), pp. 9–72; Eugene Weber, "Fairies and Hard Facts: The Reality of Folk Tales," *Journal of the History of Ideas*, 43 (1981): 347–78.

2. See Weber, "Fairies and Hard Facts," p. 96; and Darnton, "Peasants Tell Tales," pp. 13, 17. Ruth B. Bottigheimer, in "Fairy Tales, Folk Narrative Research and History," *Social History*, 14 (1989): 346–57, presents an excellent critique of historians' use of folklore conventions as historical evidence.

3. *The Wright's Chaste Wife; a Merry Tale by Adam of Cobsam*, Early English Text Society, ed. Frederick J. Furnivall, os. 12, (New York: Greenwood Press, 1969). Further references to this poem will appear within the text. A history of the analogues appears in a supplement to the tale written by W. A. Clouston, pp. 25–39. The separation poems from India form a major genre of lyrical poems in the female voice. Tales in the Barahmasa tradition are the origins of the stories from which "The Wright's Chaste Wife" derives. See, for instance, Charlotte Vaudeville, *Barahmasa in Indian Literatures: Songs of the Twelve Months in Indo-Aryan Literatures* (Delhi: Motilal Banarsidass, 1986).

4. The Indian version appears in *The Ocean of Story Being C. H. Tawney's Translation or Somadeva's Kathá Sarit Ságara*, 1, ed. N. M. Penzer (London: Charles J. Sawyer, 1924), pp. 158–62 as the story of the merchant Guhasena and his wife Devasmita. In a long note, Penzer traces the analogues and speaks of wives' gradual corruption as the story migrated west. He places the story in the "entrapped suitors" motif, pp. 42–44. Joseph Bédier, in *Les Fabliaux: Études de Littérature Populaire et d'Histoire Littéraire du Moyen Âge*, 16th ed. (Paris: Champion, 1982), p. 146, places the French version, "Constant du Hamel," in the oriental tradition, although he only traces it back to the Arabic version in *A Thousand and One Nights*.

5. Marina Warner, *From the Beast to the Blonde: On Fairy Tales and Their Tellers* (London: Chatto and Windus, 1994).

6. Barbara A. Hanawalt, *Growing Up in Medieval London: the Experience of Childhood in History* (New York: Oxford University Press, 1993), pp. 89–97.

7. *Calendar of Plea and Memoranda Rolls of the City of London*, ed. Arthur H. Thomas, 3 (Cambridge: Cambridge University Press, 1929), p. 43 (14 July 1383); and ibid., 2 (Cambridge: Cambridge University Press, 1926), p. 147 (18 August 1327).

8. *Calendar of Plea and Memoranda Rolls*, 3, pp. 120–21, ibid., (10 May 1386); 3, p. 69.

9. Corporation of London, Mayor's Court Original Bills 1/1/56.

10. Public Record Office C1/46/47. Hereafter cited as P.R.O.

11. *Ocean of Story*, p. 43. The story is called "The Lady and Her Five Suitors." She goes to visit officials to get her husband released from prison. The price is supposed to be a night with her, but she locks them in a specially designed piece of furniture. See also Clouston, *Wright's Chaste Wife*, p. 29.

12. *Calendar of Plea and Memoranda Rolls*, 2 (Cambridge: Cambridge University Press, 1926), p. 270, (1380), ibid., 2 (1370), p. 125.

13. *Calendar of Plea and Memoranda Rolls*, 2, p. 195 (1375).

14. P.R.O. C1/105/51.

15. P.R.O. C1/172/1.

16. *Calendar Letters from the Mayor and Corporation of the City of London, 1350–1370*, ed. Reginald R. Sharpe (London: John Edward Francis, 1885), p. 88, letter 192.

17. *Calendar Letters from the Mayor*, p. 5, letter 8. See also Ralph B. Pugh, ed., *Calen-*

dar of London Trailbaston Trials under Commissions of 1305 and 1306 (London: Her Majesty's Stationers Office, 1975), p. 84.

18. See *Ocean of Story*, Book II, ch. 13, in which Siva gives each of them a lotus to keep while they are separated, which will fade if they are not faithful.

19. Hanawalt, *Growing Up in Medieval London*, pp. 187–90.

20. P.R.O. C1/4/116, C1/229/19.

21. *Calendar of Wills Proved and Enrolled in the Court of Husting, London, 1258–1688*, 2, ed. Reginald R. Sharpe. (London: John Edward Francis, 1890), pp. 132 (1369), 564.

22. Antti Aarne and Stith Thompson, *The Types of the Folktale: A Classification and Bibliography*, 2nd ed. (Helsinki: Suomalainen Tiedeakatemia, 1964).

23. Torborg Lundell, "Gender-Related Biases in the Type and Motif Indexes of Aarne and Thompson," *Fairy Tales and Society: Illusion, Allusion, and Paradigm*, ed. Ruth B. Bottigheimer (Philadelphia, University of Pennsylvania Press, 1986), pp. 149–63. Lundell does not use the example of *The Wright's Chaste Wife* in this study, but it is also a case of the male biases in classification.

24. Bédier, *Les Fabliaux*, p. 331.

25. *A Descriptive Catalogue of Manuscripts in the Library of Lambeth Palace*, compiled by Montague Rhodes James and Claude Jenkins (Cambridge: Cambridge University Press, 1930), pp. 421–26, lists the contents (which I have checked against the manuscript) as: "Chronycullys of Englonde"; Lydgate's Verses on the Kings of England; names of keepers and bailiffs and a variety of diaries, etc., from 1563–64; recipes, herbs, proverbs on household economy; "A treytys of one Gyngelayne"; a tale; "Seint Gregoris Trentall"; receipts; "Lyve of Sint Eustas"; receiving of Edward IV at Bristol; songs; retinue of Edward III at Calais; note on Granada, "The parlis dayes of the monthis"; Lydgate's "the Hors, the shepe, and the goose"; "The Complaynt of Christ"; William Lychfelde's "Complaint of God"; "The Stacyons of Rome"; keeping of hawks; "The Wright's chaste wife"; recipes; printed pages from Caxton, "life of St. Wenefryde."

26. A curious addition that helps date the poem is a piece of political propaganda in support of Edward IV at the very end that explains that the garland was made

> Of flourys most of honoure,
> Of roses whyte that wyll nott fade,
> Whych floure all ynglond doth glade,
> Wyth trewloues medelyd in syght;
> Vn-to the whych floure I-wys
> The loue of god and the comenys
> Subdued bene of ryght.
>
> (666–72)

27. See Vaudeville, *Barahmasa in Indian Literature*, p. 8; Friedhelm Hardy, *Viraha-Bhakti: The Early History of Krsna Devotion in South India* (Delhi: Oxford University Press, 1983), pp. 52, 59, 63, 370, 398; and David A. Kolff, *Naukar, Rajput and Sepoy: The Ethno-history of the Military Labour Market in Hindustan, 1450–1850* (Cambridge: Cambridge University Press, 1990), pp. 74–77.

28. Karen E. Rowe, "To Spin a Yarn: The Female Voice in Folklore and Fairy Tale," *Fairy Tales and Society*, ed. Ruth B. Bottigheimer, pp. 57–58.

29. Warner, *From the Beast to the Blond*, p. 15.

30. Rowe, "The Female Voice," pp. 62–68.

31. Warner, *From the Beast to the Blond*, p. 23.

32. Ria Lemaire, "The Semiotics of Private and Public: Matrimonial Systems and Discourse," in *Female Power in the Middle Ages: Proceedings from the Second St. Gertrud Symposium, Copenhagen 1986*, ed. Karen Glente and Lisa Wenther Jensen (Copenhagen: C. A. Reitzel, 1989), pp. 77–104. See also Lemaire's *Passions et Positions: Contribution à une Sémiotique du Sujet dans la Poésie Lyrique Médiévale en Langues Romanes* (Amsterdam: Rodopi, 1988).

33. For a more complete discussion see Barbara A. Hanawalt, "At the Margins of Women's Space in Medieval Europe," *Matrons and Marginal Women in Medieval Society*, ed. Robert R. Edwards and Vickie Ziegler (Woodbridge, Conn.: Boydel Press, 1995), pp. 1–17.

33. Ruth B. Bottigheimer, "Tale Spinners: Submerged Voices in Grimms' Fairy Tales," *New German Critique*, 27 (1982): 144–50.

34. Ruth B. Bottigheimer, "Silenced Women in the Grimms' Tales: The 'Fit' between Fairy Tales and Society in their Historical Context," *Fairy Tales and Society*, ed. Ruth B. Bottigheimer, pp. 115–31.

7

The Host, the Law, and the Ambiguous Space of Medieval London Taverns

The most notable depiction of an innkeeper/taverner in Middle-English literature appears in *The Canterbury Tales* in the character of the Host. Harry Bailly's Tabard Inn, where the pilgrims gather, suggests an institution that is replete with ambiguity and contradictory images. In the *Prologue* the Tabard is described as a "gentyle tavern" rather than one of the sordid ones that were common in London and Southwark. Its clientele is a very varied one that represents regular and secular clergy, nuns, rural laity ranging in social degree from knight to plowman, and a large contingent of Londoners of different ranks and occupations. Not only the variety of social classes represented but also the gender mix is somewhat surprising for medieval society: a woman (the Wife of Bath) traveling alone, a Prioress who is appropriately accompanied but suspect, because she is staying at an inn rather than one of the well-endowed nunneries of London. The Monk, likewise, could have found lodging in a monastery. Were they all eager for an early start or was Harry's place recommended for its fine wines, ales, and cuisine? The Tabard was certainly well-known for its food, both historically and in *The Tales*.[1] The space within the inn also defies the conventional ordering of society in that Harry's wife, Harry eventually confesses, dominates the domestic power relations and challenges his manhood. His position as guide and the acceptance of his role by his social superiors among the pilgrims is also of interest: no one, except the Cook, disagrees with his self-designation as "judge," "governor," "referee," and punisher of "rebels" against his rule. I argue here that Harry Bailly's character and that of his inn may be understood more fully when seen in the context of London inns, their regulation, and the power invested in inn and tavern keepers.[2] While modern readers often see the Host only as a buffoon, a medieval audience would certainly have known the official role of innkeepers and would have understood that encouraging mirth is but one technique for diffusing the

hostilities and fights that arise in a drinking establishment and, by extension, on a pilgrimage. Certainly, a personal knowledge of innkeepers and
taverners had considerable bearing on the language Chaucer used to describe Harry Bailly.

Taverns and inns were among the most complex institutions of medieval
social life and social regulation because they occupied contradictory roles
both in reality and in the mentality of the age. Their very interior spaces
were ambiguous territories. On the one hand, guests were invited to share
domestic and primarily female space—the main living area or hall, where
food and drink were served, and the bedchambers. On the other hand, the
men and women who congregated in breweries, ale houses, taverns, and
inns were held in general suspicion as potentially disorderly. Another ambiguity was that inns and taverns were the resort of ordinary villagers, citizens, and servants, as well as of foreigners, transient English, unspeakable
Scots, and a general rabble of rootless people. Within both the local and
foreign categories were honest peasants and artisans, respectable merchants and their factors, pilgrims, clerics of various sorts, royal officials, nobles, knights, robbers, prostitutes, and con men. Mingling with all these
people were authors such as Geoffrey Chaucer, William Langland, and
Thomas Hoccleve, who recorded their impressions of taverns and inns. Over
all this tumult of people—a hall full of folk—reigned the taverner or
innkeeper.

To speak of a drinking establishment as domestic, female space requires
an explanation. As we saw in chapter 4, "At the Margins of Women's Space,"
the sexual division of labor and thus of space was pronounced. The production and consumption of alcohol, however, stands out as an economic
and social site at which traditional distinctions were blurred. In the countryside, brewing and running a tavern were extensions of domestic labor
and domestic space, with women making and buying ale for home consumption. But the brewer's house was also a social gathering place fre-
quented by both women and men. In cities, where brewing was more
professional and more male-dominated, taverns were, like their nineteenth-
century descendants, a recreational area away from the cramped rooming
quarters of a town or city and a resting place for travelers and foreigners.
Taverns and inns retained many features of the home atmosphere, but
women associated with them had a very bad reputation—offering sex as
well as other domestic comforts. The domestic space of the tavern or inn
tainted the women who worked or routinely visited there.

Presiding over the ambiguous space was the taverner or innkeeper (male
or female), who was empowered by statute law and London ordinances to
act as *paterfamilias* or *materfamilias* over both the household and the guests.
(*Familia* was still defined in the Roman sense as comprising the servants and
guests as well as kin in a domestic environment.) Taverners were thereby
required to assume legal responsibility for the good and honest behavior of
guests, employees, and kin. The position was both quasi-legal and quasi-
familial in that it required both discipline and nurturing protection. In the

London records taverners and innkeepers are the only people who are *consistently* referred to by the title *paterfamilias* and the corresponding *materfamilias*. But the host's position required a difficult balance. Guests had different needs and different relationships to the law, and taverners or innkeepers wanted to make the most profit they could by accommodating them all. Some otherwise respectable travelers or citizens encouraged taverners to act illegally as procurers of prostitutes. Others wanted them to arrange for fencing stolen goods.

Finally, within the limited space of the tavern or inn (within its hall, drinking area, and chambers), the taverner or innkeeper had to maintain the medieval social hierarchy, serving each guest according to his or her degree. Seating at the table followed the social status of the guests, and terms of address mirrored these people's place in society. The small domain of the inn or tavern maintained a semblance of the external world order even though society generally perceived it as potentially chaotic. Respectability, compliance with the law, and suitable service to customers rested with the owner of the establishment. Harry Bailly's role was as complex as the space over which he presided.[3]

THE PERMEABLE DOMESTIC SPACE IN INNS AND TAVERNS

An understanding of the structure of inns and taverns and the role of women in them will help to explain the gender ambiguity of those spaces. Although large quantities of wine were imported and drunk in both private homes and taverns, ale and later beer were the most common drinks and women the usual brewers. While most housewives had the equipment to make ale—pots, ladles, and straining cloths—the process was time-consuming and required careful attention. Malt was easily ruined by mold or heat and ale soured and went off quickly, so that brewing had to be done frequently and usually in large-enough quantities to make the laborious process worth the effort. Many households, therefore, purchased ale or beer either from neighbors who specialized in its production, from regraters who purchased beer for resale in the urban streets, or from taverns.[4] In the countryside, some peasant families invested in larger, leaden vats so that the wives could supplement their agricultural income by selling ale or beer. The homes of these brewsters became both taverns and shops and were thus extensions of domestic space and female production.[5] In market towns such as York, Norwich, and Exeter married women also predominated as brewers through the middle of the fifteenth century. Even after losing their dominance over production, they still acted as retailers of ale and beer.[6]

In London, brewing was already a large-scale industry in the late thirteenth and early fourteenth centuries because its population (in excess of 60,000) was too large for extensive domestic brewing, and the housing did not permit home brewing for many people. The sheer problem of supplying the malt and water for the operation required more than household production. In-home brewing continued in larger establishments, with the wife or servants brewing for a household. A servant woman, for instance, was hired in a large household to do the brewing for the family, servants, and apprentices.[7] London women also engaged in brewing as wholesale traders. Indeed, the *Liber Albus*, refers to brewers as "she" throughout the ordinance on brewing.[8] About 10 percent of the members enrolled in the London Brewer's company were women paying their dues alone. Most of these were widows, but a few were single women. The number of women engaged in brewing, however, was much higher since couples paid dues together. In all, perhaps a third of the members of the Brewers guild in London were women.[9]

Taverns and inns not only sold drink, but also served meals and offered sleeping accommodations.[10] While these establishments might have brewed their own ale, many did not and most sold wine as well. The domestic nature of the business meant that the presence of women was desired and needed. Married couples ran most inns and taverns because the division of labor that typified an ordinary household translated well into serving strangers. The wife oversaw the running of the house and management of household servants, while the husband supervised the guests and provisioned the establishment.

The innkeeping business was rarely run by single females. In 1384 only ten women were listed as innkeepers compared to 183 men.[11] Women acquired inns either by taking over their former husbands' businesses or through inheritance, and they managed the premises themselves. The official tallies of inn and tavern keepers, however, underrepresent women's actual participation in the lodging and victualing business.[12] Taking in lodgers and boarders has been a time-honored by-occupation for women. In medieval London the frequency of such arrangements might well have been greater than it is today. Two factors contributed to both the supply and the demand for lodging. London women, when they married, contracted to contribute a dowry and were awarded a dower in rents and real estate should they outlive their husbands. At the very least, a widow would receive the principle dwelling as her home for life use. Many London widows, therefore, had rooms to rent and had a need for the extra income.[13] On the demand side, London, like other medieval European cities, did not replace its own population. It relied on immigrants from the countryside and, as a major trading and administrative center, it also had to house a number of foreign merchants, fortune seekers, suitors at court, and delegations to the Crown. Widows had a ready market for their rooms and meals, but they were not registered as innkeepers.

Despite the fact that some women owned breweries, taverns, and inns, most of the women who worked in those spaces served in other capacities such as wife of the proprietor, tapster, or domestic servant. A London hostelry could be a large establishment, including buildings for horses, draught animals, and fodder; a large courtyard with a well and latrines; and a house with a large hall for dining, drinking, and games, a kitchen, and chambers for sleeping. Such establishments employed a number of servants who were part of the innkeeper's *familia*. Taverns and breweries were simpler establishments that might consist of a place to drink and assemble, and a shop window for selling ale, beer, and wine as "take out." Both male and female help was employed in this important service industry.

Every female role associated with taverns and inns turned the domestic nature of the association on end and implied tainted womanhood. The disparaging term "ale-wife" was not the only insult directed at women associated with brewing and drink. For a *materfamilias* of a tavern, the titles of "procurer" or "bawd" were ready to the tongue and, for the tapster, the association with prostitution was all too much of a stereotype. In a mid-fourteenth-century London ordinance, brewsters were lumped with nurses, other servants, and "women of disreputable character" in a prohibition against adorning themselves with hoods furred with finer furs "after the manner of reputable women."[14]

Women who worked in the service occupations in taverns were at risk of being pimped by their masters and mistresses for the sexual satisfaction of male customers. Thus Thomesina Newton was said, in the London Consistory Court, to have worked for William Basseloy, the *paterfamilias* of a tavern who acted as her pimp. The owner of The Busche tavern was accused of pimping for his two servants, Mandeleyn and Alice. Others were accused of adultery with members of their establishment, as was the proprietor of The Lodyn Proche with his tapster, Mariota, and William le Hostler of Le Crown was said to have gotten his servant, Matrosa, pregnant and that her daughter was his.[15] The *materfamilias* was no better than her male counterpart. The one who kept "le tavern near the church" was accused of adultery with her servant and the one running Le Schippe procured her tapster as a prostitute.[16] The tapsters themselves acquired a neighborhood reputation. Elizabeth Machyn, tapster of the Red Lyon, was accused of adultery and of doing the same at "Le Cok" in Woodstreet, while Mariona, who was the sometime tapster at The Vine in the parish of St. Helen and at The Choker in the high street, was accused of being "a common scandalizer especially with Thomas, one of the deacons of St. Paul."[17]

A 1516 case demonstrates the role of the taverner or innkeeper as a go-between. Elizabeth Tomlins was in an alehouse next to The Bell Inn and sent for the hostler inquiring if Gregory Kyton, a priest, was there. The innkeeper told Kyton that there was a woman waiting for him. It was arranged that the priest would have her in his chamber, and the innkeeper then suggested that the priest go to The George in Lombard street and that Elizabeth would come to him there. The hostler took her into a chamber at The George and the priest came and joined them. The hostler's pay was a meal shared with them at the priest's expense.[18]

Taverns provided opportunities for pimps and prostitutes that apparently went unregulated by the proprietors. John Mande and his wife pimped his sister at a tavern, and others made contacts with prostitutes at taverns.[19]

The Pye in Queenhithe had a reputation as a place "which is a good shadowing for thieves and many evil bargains have been made there, and many strumpets and pimps have their covert there, and leisure to make their false covenants." The neighbors wanted it closed at night.[20]

Suspicion fell on ordinary female patrons of taverns as well as on servants and known prostitutes. The popular poetry suggested that female patrons of taverns were of easy virtue; thus the presence of the Prioress along with the Wife of Bath at The Tabard casts some doubt on their good sense. One of the few advice poems directed toward women specifically has been edited as "How the Good Wife Taught Her Daughter." Although probably not written by a woman, it reflects popular concepts of appropriate behavior for them. The "Good Wife" cautions her daughter that she should not spend all the money she makes selling her cloth in the city on taverns because "they that taverns haunt/From thrift soon come to want." The first warning then is that taverns are places to throw away money. The second warning is about the effects of drunkenness on reputation:

> And if thou be in any place where good ale is aloft,
> Whether that thou serve thereof or that thou sit soft,
> Measurably thou take thereof, that thou fall in no blame
> For if thou be often drunk, it falleth to thy shame.
> For those that be often drunk—
> Thrift is from them sunk,
> My lief child.

The poem presumes that the young woman might either be a tapster or a patron. The other warnings about the temptations of the city urge her to avoid going to wrestling matches or cock shooting for fear of being mistaken for a strumpet.[21]

The second type of literature to speak about women frequenting taverns was the drinking song. In one such song, the gossips—Elinore, Joan, Margery, Margaret, Alice, and Cecily—come together at a place where they can get the best wine and strong ale. Bringing cold dishes to enjoy with their drink, they come in twos so as to conceal their drinking from their husbands. At the taverns they drink, eat, and complain about men, particularly husbands who beat their wives:

> Whatsoever any man thynk,
> We com for nawght but for good drynk;
> Now let us go home and wynke,
> For it may be seen
> Where we have been
> Good Gossips myn, a!

The poem concludes that some women come once a week for wine, but others "be at the tavern thrise in the weke" or even every day until they are sick:

"For thyngis used/Will not be refused."[22] The latter indictment of women was also applied to their sexual appetites once they had lost their virginity.

The space of inns and taverns, being domestic, facilitated not only sexual contacts but also violence between men and women. For instance, five men with accomplices were indicted for being present with arms at the inn of John Fodard, a hostler, in Cornhill. The charge was that they broke into Katherine de Brewes' chamber and dragged her along the floor by her arms and clothing so that she was naked upwards to the waist and her hair was hanging over her bosom. She was only saved when the servants and neighbors came and rescued her.[23] In 1325 Walter de Benygtone with seventeen companions came to the brewhouse of Gilbert de Mordone with stones in their hoods, swords, knives, and other weapons. They sat in the tavern drinking four gallons of ale. Their objective was to seize Emma, daughter of the late Robert Pourte and a ward of Gilbert. Mabel, Gilbert's wife, and Geoffrey, his brewer, asked them to leave. They refused to do so, saying that it was a public tavern and that they had the right to stay and drink. Mabel took Emma to an upper chamber while the men dealt with the ruffians. A fight ensued and spilled into the streets, where the neighbors came to the rescue and one of the thugs was killed. In another brawl, two men were quietly playing checkers in a tavern when some rowdies came in and laid a woman across the checkerboard.[24]

The ambiguous space of the tavern and the battles between the sexes for control over it appears without a previous hint in Harry Bailly's reaction to the *Tale of Melibee*. *Paterfamilias* and *materfamilias* Bailly are in contention over the inn, its employees, and the sexual symbols of office. He explains that when he undertakes to beat the knaves who serve in the tavern, she complains that he is inadequate in his discipline—he has yet to break their backs or bones.[25] When she is in church and the neighbors fail to show respect for her social station by taking precedence at the pews, she returns home in a rage crying, "False coward, wrek thy wyf!/ By corpus bones, I wol have thy knyf, /And thou shalt have my distaf and go spynne!" (VII.1905–7). The symbolism of their disputed roles and control of the inn could not be more explicit. She proposes to give him the universal symbol of womanhood, the distaff, and take the phallic symbol of the knife for her own. His impotence, to her takes on a symbol of childishness when she describes him as a "milksop or a coward ape"(VII.1910). He goes on to lament that he can carry the knife only outside the disputed space of the inn, where he is a dangerous man: not a cowardly ape but a foolhardy "wilde leoun," apt to kill "som neighbor" (VII.1913–23). She has demonstrated that she can take over the inn's ambiguous domestic space very effectively and even drive him out of it. He is willing to leave it in her hands while he goes to Canterbury. Becoming a guide to pilgrims en route, a role not open to a *materfamilias*, is his way out of his embattled space. If his busman's holiday has some foolhardy bravado mixed with better sense and appropriate discourse, the reader can appreciate his sense of release as well as his professionalism as a host.[26]

DISORDERLY SPACES

London was famous for its many places to drink. One of the few complaints that FitzStephen made about thirteenth-century London was "the immoderate quaffing among the foolish sort."[27] By 1309 there were 354 taverns and 1,334 brew-houses in the city. The smallest measure in which ale was sold was a quart.[28] The disorder of taverns and inns centered not only on the gender mix within its space, but also on the other types of business and recreation that took place there. The vices available in inns and taverns were stock targets for sermons and homilies,[29] and also appear in *Piers Plowman* and *The Canterbury Tales*.[30] Official opinion about the potential for disorder in these places of resort was clearly stated in the Statutes for the City of London promulgated by Edward I in 1285. Complaining about those who wandered the streets at night with arms, the statute went on to say,

> Whereas such offenders as aforesaid going about by night, do commonly resort and have their meetings and hold their evil talk in taverns more than elsewhere, and there do seek for shelter, lying in wait, and watching their time to do mischief; it is enjoined that none do keep a tavern open for wine or ale, after the tolling of the aforesaid curfew; but they shall keep their tavern shut after that hour and none therein drinking or resorting.[31]

The *Liber Albus* copied the statute in the early fifteenth century, but it had been invoked and enforced from the time it was issued and long after.[32]

Court cases leave little doubt about taverns and inns encouraging concentrations of disorderly behavior, which took the form of noisy pranks, brawling, homicide, prostitution, rape, and insurrection. The king, the London magistrates, the taverners themselves, and the neighbors all had a stake in keeping such behavior under control if not entirely eliminated.

The disorderly nature of inn and tavern appears in a 1276 coroner's inquest from a ward near the Tower and close to Fenchurch. The case was brought ten years before Edward I's statute and indicates the type of problem the statute addressed. Agnes de Essex ran a lodging house and rented to knights of the household of Robert de Munceny and his son. After curfew had rung, one Richard Moys came to the house next door and banged on the door and shouted to be let in. Robert's men told him to "cease making noise," but he persisted. This roused Robert de Munceny, his son, and others of the household, who pursued the noisemaker into the nearby drinking establishment of Alice le Official. A number of people were drinking there and the door was open. One can sympathize with Alice: the location attracted the soldiers who assembled near or in the Tower and business was brisk on the Saturday on which the Eve of All Hallows fell that year. The noisemaker, Richard Moys, was able to hide among the barrels, but Richard de Parys challenged the hotheads and cried out "Who are these people?" He was stabbed through the body by Robert de Munceny's hot-headed young son and died. Robert de Munceny watched from the doorstep of his lodging, but did not move to stop the action. The youth fled, but his possessions and those of his father were confiscated. Agnes de Essex, Alice her maid servant, and all those connected to the house of Alice le Official were attached in connection with the homicide.[33]

Violence has often been perpetrated by young males, and fourteenth-century London had its share of problems from this group. As Thomas Hoccleve observed: "willful youthe" is tempted by taverns; Venus always can catch him in her snares; and he likes a good fight.[34] One such group of young servants had filled an empty cask with stones on a Monday at midnight and "set it rolling through graschirchestrate to London Bridge to the terror of the neighborhood."[35] Other rowdy behavior starting in taverns ended in homicide. The apprentices of the Bench who lived in and around the Inns of Court were responsible for some of the major riots in medieval London's west end. On one occasion it was the taverner who was the object of an old argument. When the taverner was attacked, he raised the hue and cry, which was joined by apprentices of the Bench and other taverners. An apprentice was killed in the resulting riot.[36]

The noise and disturbance from the less-established drinking places were also disruptive. Agnes de Louthe, who was described as a common and notorious prostitute, kept a house in Paternoster row beside the gate of the Lord Bishop of London:

> On account of her remaining there quarrels and contentions frequently arise between the neighbors, so that the neighbors dwelling near her can have no peace or rest in their houses at night-time, nor dare they oft times leave their homes for fear of death by the attack of diverse men unknown coming by night to the said Agnes with drawn swords and stones to throw through the windows of the neighbors.

Some of the neighbor women were cited for spending their "filthy lucre" in her house on drink.[37]

Taverns were also places for games, and, although those we know about often ended in homicide or accusations of cheating, we must assume that most games went on in an orderly fashion. Michael le Gaugenour and John Faukes had been playing a game called "hasard" in a brewhouse after curfew. John was apparently a sore loser and, when he left the brewhouse, he lay in wait for Michael, killing him with a sword. Stephen de Lenn, a taverner himself, was killed after winning a game at tables in another tavern where he was playing after curfew. The loser ran him through with a sword in the streets.[38]

The connection between dramatic homicide cases and taverns suggests the conclusion that drinking houses were very dangerous places, but drink was mentioned in only 6.2 percent of the 130 London homicides involving men. Taverns and brewhouses were the location of just 7.6 percent of all 144 homicides. In rural Northamptonshire only 4.3 percent of the 347 homicides mentioned drinking as a cause, and taverns figured as the place of homicide in 7 percent of the cases.[39]

All sorts of deals, both shady and legitimate, took place in taverns. They were places to draw up contracts, to arrange service and apprentice agreements, to share drink to seal a deal or a successful arbitration, to discuss business, and to plot. But, again, the deals that led to disorder were more likely to be reported than the thousands of peaceful transactions. Richard and William met at The Horn in Milk Street and were having a drink of wine together. Apparently William wanted to settle his debts to Richard and wanted Richard to turn over his bonds. Being illiterate, he asked Richard to read the bonds that he had in a box. Richard took them to read, but refused to give them back saying that William had diverse writings and muniments pertaining to his property. William became furious and said that "Richard should deliver them to him in his clenched teeth" and took up a pewter pot standing between them, intending to strike Richard. Richard disarmed him and went off carrying the bonds.[40] Other cases were much more sinister than that taking advantage of a poor illiterate. Nicholas le Barbour, Agnes de Houdan, his mistress, and John Joye, a webber, met in a tavern to lure a client to Agnes's house, where they killed and robbed him instead of entertaining him.[41]

Fear of disorder in taverns permeated all official ranks. The king's chief concern, however, was that taverns were places where people could meet to form "congregations, unions (*alligaciones*), and covins." Thus, in 1368 a group of skinners was attached to stand trial because they had met in a tavern and other places and formed a coven.[42] The Church was concerned about taverns as places to talk heresy and to slander the church.[43] The mayor and aldermen were concerned about keeping order in their city and continually prodded the taverners and inn keepers to take legal responsibility for their clients and for enforcing curfew and other city ordinances.

MANDATE FOR SOCIAL CONTROL

Expectations for the peacekeeping role of taverners and innkeepers were high and, as such, turned them into officers of the peace. In medieval England many people played such semi-official roles with no payment for executing them. In the case of London's purveyors of drink and lodging, their official stature came from statute law and London ordinances. In the absence of licensing, the presumption that an innkeeper or taverner would carry out the mandates rested on the force of the king's law, the necessary city, neighborhood, and client approval, and the honesty of the proprietors. Edward I's 1285 statute sought a solution to the problem of night walkers and plotters in closing down taverns after curfew:

> It is enjoined that none do keep a tavern open for wine or ale, after the tolling of the aforesaid curfew; but they shall keep their tavern shut after that hour, and none neither shall any man admit others in his house except in common taverns, for therein drinking nor resorting; whom he will not be answerable unto the king's peace. And if any taverner be found doing the contrary, the first time he shall be put in pledge by his tavern drinking

cup, or by other good pledge there found, and be amerced 40d; and if he be found a second time offending, he shall be amerced half a mark; and the third time ten shillings; and the fourth time he shall pay the whole penalty double, that is to say, twenty shillings; and the fifth time he shall be forsworn of his trade for ever.[44]

Penalties were gradual but severe, and presumed that the proprietors were both well-informed and answerable to the king for their tavern hours and their clientele.[45]

Control over foreigners, always a worry of governments that witness large influxes of aliens, was a second concern in the statute. The language has a modern ring in complaining that

some from parts beyond the sea, and others of this land, . . . do there [in London] seek shelter and refuge, by reason of banishment out of their own country, or who for great offense or other misdeed have fled from their own country; and of these some do become brokers, hostelers, and innkeepers within the City, for denizens and strangers, as freely as though they were good and lawful men of the franchise of the City; and some nothing do but run up and down through the streets, more by night than by day and are well attired in clothing and array, and have their food of delicate meats and costly.

The solution the statute offered was to allow only citizens or those who had become citizens and sworn their oaths to the mayor and aldermen to become inkeepers. Aspiring foreign innkeepers had to provide testimony from their home residence as to their good character, as well as to arrange for Londoners to stand surety for their willingness to enforce the law.[46]

The *Liber Albus*, in repeating the 1285 statute, added that no foreigner could have an inn or lodging-house on the waterside of the Thames because of the fear that foreigners lodging with foreign hosts were likely to form covens.[47] Zenobius Martyn, for instance, was indicted in Langbourne Ward as a common bawd and associate of prostitutes. He admitted to this charge and also confessed that he ran a "lodging-house for aliens and had acted as a broker against the ordinances of the City." He suffered the prescribed penalty of being put into prison.[48]

The distinction between denizen or local person and stranger or foreigner was very important to the medieval concept of order and peace. The *Liber Albus* begins its section on taverns, breweries, and inns with an injunction: "In the first place, that the peace of God and the peace of our Lord the King shall be well kept and maintained among denizens and strangers."[49] Local people's reputations were well known in their communities, as has been pointed out in chapter 1. But what did one do to ensure the good behavior of numerous people who wandered into London: migrant workers, minstrels, knights errant, foreign merchants, craftsmen, and pilgrims? The terms "stranger" and "foreigner" were applied to English men and women from another village or town as well as to those who came from Italy, Germany, or Flanders.[50]

The 1285 statute and the *Liber Albus* echoed the Anglo-Saxon customs, but put the innkeeper in charge:

> And that no one in the City shall harbor any man beyond a day and a night, if he be not willing to produce such person to stand trial. In case such person shall commit an offense and absent himself, the host shall make answer for him. And no one shall be resident in the Ward of an Alderman beyond a day and a night, if he be not in view of frankpledge, or if his host be not willing to produce him to stand trial.[51]

Essentially, the law held hosts responsible for the good behavior of their clients and forced them to stand surety for them if they committed an offense and did not appear for trial. The repeated appeals to innkeepers indicate ongoing scandals. In 1384, Mayor Nicholas Brembre again appealed for order, complaining that "larcenies and diverse evil deeds" were committed openly because innkeepers were not careful about those they harbored or how long they allowed them to stay. Inkeepers were to abide by the statute and not allow *"travaillyngmen"* and other strangers at their tables on pain of paying a £100 fine. At that time, Brembre had 197 innkeepers swear to obey the law and to report innkeepers who did not do so.[52]

Further ordinances made taverners and innkeepers responsible for informing guests about the laws regarding bearing arms, keeping curfew, holding guests' goods in safekeeping, and so on. Aldermen and wardmoots were to keep a close watch on the hosts to see that they complied with the laws.[53] The officials and citizens duly carried out their responsibilities; in 1372, for instance, Adam Grymmesby was committed to prison for not warning his lodger to leave his knife indoors after curfew. The watch confiscated the knife and Adam was instructed to redeem it for his guest.[54]

Innkeepers were also responsible for protecting the property of their guests. William Beaubek of Kent claimed remedy against John de Waltham, innkeeper, on those grounds in 1345, and John Sappy, knight, did so against Thomas Hostiller of Le Swerd in 1380. William Beaubek stated that he rented a room for 1 1/2 d. a week and that the innkeeper gave him a key to the room claiming that his goods would be secure. William relied on the help of the innkeeper to collect a debt and deposited the money in a box in his room. Later, not only was the money missing, but so too were gold and silver ornaments and plate that were in the box. The innkeeper claimed that his brewer had entered the chamber by a garden door, but William held the innkeeper responsible for recovery of the value of the goods stolen. The court upheld him and the law. Sir John Sappy was also successful in his suit.[55]

On the whole, innkeepers and taverners appear more often as breakers of the law than as enforcers. By far the most common complaint was that they did not use the correct measures for their beer and ale, or that they were mixing bad wine with good, or that they did not let customers see their wine drawn.[56] In addition to charges of prostitution, which have already been mentioned, charges of assault against taverners and innkeepers were also brought.[57]

It is the nature of court records and ordinances, our chief sources for information on taverns and inns, to record the negative rather than the positive side of the picture. Reissuing of regulations for taverners, suits against them for non-compliance with laws, complaints from the neighbors about noise, loose women, prostitution, and undesirable characters all appear with great regularity. Only occasionally does one find a case such as that of Margaret Rumbold, who was arrested for theft by John Grove, a taverner.[58]

HARRY BAILLY, HOST OF THE TABARD

Harry Bailly's character has a clear job description, as laid down in law, custom, and practice. Any traveler, such as Chaucer, could remind a host of his legal responsibilities, and any denizen of London knew them well because he had to enforce them. That the Tabard was located in Southwark rather than in London did not exempt it from most of the laws and customs that would have been typical of "gentil hostelrye" (I. 718), nor did it significantly alter Harry Bailly's responsibilities as an innkeeper.[59] Many of the statutes applied to England as a whole, such as the assize of ale and the ordinances regarding wine, while others, such as the responsibility of innkeepers for their guests and their goods, applied to all who made or sold alcoholic beverages or ran inns for respectable travelers. Sir John Sappy, mentioned above, made his claim against Thomas Hostiller "in accordance with the common custom of the realm that the keeper of a hostelry was responsible for the goods and chattels brought by lodgers to his hostelry." Richard Waldegrave, a knight, complained on the basis of the custom in 1384, and John Prene also appealed to the encumbrance of "every common innkeeper . . . bound by law and custom to guard his inn."[60] Chaucer's knowledge of inns and taverns would have been informed by his experience with a variety of London establishments rather than any specific innkeeper in one tavern. Too much can also be made of the location of the tavern in Southwark, the sexual suburb of London and location of stews, brothels, breweries, gambling, and animal shows. The juxtaposition of respectable housing and brothels was a problem about which many proper London citizens complained, as wardmoot court records demonstrate. Aldermen lived side by side with strumpets, bawds, and regraters.[61]

Although the ordinances and statutes do not specify the appearance or manners of innkeepers and taverners, certain physical and psychological types made for a successful trade:

> A semely man Oure Hooste was withalle
> For to been a marchal in an halle.
> A large man he was with eyen stepe—
> A fairer burgeys was ther noon in Chepe—
> Boold of his speche, and wys, and wel ytaught,
> And of manhod hym lakkede right naught.
>
> (I. 751–56)

Success as an innkeeper, lay in a ready wit heightened by some education, sharp eyes, a physical appearance and strength adequate to overcome resistance, and a certain presence and seeming gentility of manner. But Harry Bailley only *resembled* an exalted marshal serving in a lord's hall or one of the extravagantly wealthy merchants living and trading on Cheapside. He was neither a gentleman servant nor a goldsmith; innkeepers did not hold such high status. Chaucer's Host has the pilgrims pay their bills before proposing to accompany them (I. 760).

A smooth businessman knew how to address his diverse clientele while maintaining the appropriate social distance. Thus on the day they depart, the Host immediately singles out the two highest status pilgrims, "Sire Knyght, . . . my mayster and my lord" and "my lady Prioresse" (I. 837, 839). Polite address, however, has not always been successful in managing customers. Peacekeepers often have found that assuming a jocular manner or even the role of buffoon is an effective way of dealing with potentially violent people. If a medieval innkeeper jollied along the drunken miller or cook, allowing them to stew in their own juices, that too was acceptable within the medieval social hierarchy as long as it was effective in minimizing conflict. Direct physical contact with a burly drunk was dangerous. But the general form of address, "Lordynges," was an all-inclusive compliment.

The quasi-legal side of a host's job also appears in Chaucer's description of Harry Bailly, often in the same language used in statute and ordinance. In a sense, Harry Bailly has a doubly ascribed legal role because his name implies that he is a bailiff and that his occupation is that of enforcer of laws over his guests. The *Liber Albus*, in its section on "rebellious persons," enjoins that the bailiff is to have control over them, just as the hostelers or herbergeour shall not "harbour any man beyond a day and a night, if he be not willing to produce such person to stand trial." Furthermore, "the host has to make answer" for the person who commits an offense and absents himself.[62] These legal roles and those discussed in the section above appear again in the role the Host undertakes in the fellowship, offering to "be youre gyde " with a proviso: "And whoso wole my juggement withseye/Shal paye al that we spenden by the weye" (I.804–6). The party agrees to the extension of his role: "he wolde been oure governour," "oure tales juge and reportour" (I.813–14).[63] They seal the agreement with another drink of his good wine. This symbolic drink also had its judicial place, as we saw in chapter 3, "The Power of Word and Symbols." (The shared drink is similar to the kiss of peace exchanged by the Pardoner and the Host after the Pardoner's challenge to Harry's authority [VI.962–67].) Host Bailly reminds the pilgrims of his powers the next morning by outlining the punishment of "Whoso be rebel to my juggement" (I.833). By the "Parson's Tale," the Host announces that his "ordinaunce" has been fulfilled, an echoing of the municipal rules for taverns and inns (X.19).

The arrogant exercise of his powers seems, at times, to overtake the Host's judgment. For example, he addresses the Reeve "as lordly as a kyng" (I.3900), but the Cook (the natural enemy of the innkeeper as a rival for the victualing trade or as an employee) soon draws him back to reality. Running an "herbergage," the cook points out, means that the hostler is responsible for the behavior of those he harbors at night who may be very dangerous sorts (I.4329–34). Bailly responds that the cook has endangered the lives of many pilgrims by reheating meat pies and by overlooking the flies that abound in his shop (I.4346–52). It is, perhaps, because of his professional worries about having to produce his clientele before the law that the Host is so concerned about people straying from the party. Still, when a real scoundrel joins the party, the alchemist-Canon, Harry advises the yeoman to let his master leave—a prudent move for a responsible host (VII.697–98).

Whether he takes the role of a clown or a mock courtier, the Host does have the signal triumph of keeping the party together, keeping them from coming to blows, maintaining the social hierarchy, and earning their respect for *his* rules of the game. Most of the storytellers refer to the peacekeeping role that he occupies and accept his authority.[64] Only Harry Bailly's wife successfully challenges his abilities as a peacekeeper within the ambiguous space of the tavern.

NOTES

1. For a discussion of the historic Tabard Inn and the historical Harry Bailly see George R. Corner, "On Some of the Ancient Inns of Southwark," *Surrey Archaeological Collections*, 2 (1864): 50–81; W. H. Hart, "Further Remarks on Some of the Ancient Inns of Southwark," *Surrey Archaeological Collections*, 3 (1865): 193–207; Philip Norman, "The Tabard Inn, Southwark, The Queen's Head, William Rutter, and St. Margaret's Church," *Surrey Archaeological Collections*, 13 (1897): 28–38.

2. John M. Manly, *Some New Light on Chaucer: Lectures Delivered at the Lowell Institute* (New York: Henry Holt and Co., 1926), pp. 78–82. It is not the purpose of this study to add further to the discussion of the real Harry Bailly. Nonetheless, a discussion of London inns and taverns has considerable bearing on the language Chaucer used to describe Harry Bailly and his character development as framer of the tales.

3. A brief and unsystematic literature survey of the character of Harry Bailly has turned up many explanations for his behavior except the obvious one of his training and occupation in the demanding role of innkeeper. Kemp Malone, in *Chapters on Chaucer* (Baltimore: Johns Hopkins University Press, 1951), p. 193, found a comic inversion, with the innkeeper telling his customers what to do, and yet, he is performing exactly the role expected by statutes. Harry Bailly has been portrayed as a Christ figure and the prize banquet as the Eucharist, by Rodney Delasanta, in "The Theme of Judgment in The Canterbury Tales," *Modern Language Quarterly*, 31 (1970): 298–307; and as embodying Chaucer's concept of the monarchy by David R. Pichaski and Laura Sweetland, in "Chaucer on the Medieval Monarch: Harry Bailly in the Canterbury Tales," *Chaucer Review*, 11 (1977): 179–200. In "The Function of the Host in the Canterbury Tales," *Texas Studies in Literature and Language*, 12 (1970): 327, Cynthia C. Richardson por-

trayed him as "the middlest of the middle class," perhaps because she took literally that he was the fairest burgess in Cheapside (p. 325). But she also asked the shrewd question (p. 326) of "why an innkeeper" and answered it equally well by saying that only in an inn would one find the combination of social classes that one finds on the pilgrimage.

4. See Judith M. Bennett, "The Village Ale-Wife: Women and Brewing in Fourteenth-Century England," in *Women and Work in Preindustrial Europe*, ed. Barbara A. Hanawalt (Bloomington, Ind., 1986), pp. 20–22 for the production of beer in medieval villages. See also Judith M. Bennett, *Ale, Beer and Brewsters in England: Women's Work in a Changing World* (New York: Oxford University Press, 1996).

5. Bennett, "The Village Ale-Wife," pp. 23–30. Bennett found that about a fourth of the adult women in Brigstock (Northamptonshire) brewed beer, but most engaged in only minor commercial ventures. Only 11.5 percent of the brewers could be called real "ale-wives" who routinely produced beer for sale. These ale-wives usually came from families who had long been resident in their communities and who often came from the wealthier families or had married into them. Their brewing was intermittent, undertaken as time and opportunity permitted. All were married women (not widows), who seemed to have used family labor or to have hired village girls and women to help with brewing.

6. P. J. P. Goldberg, "Women in Fifteenth-Century Town Life," in *Towns and Townspeople in the Fifteenth Century*, ed. John A.F. Thompson (Gloucester: Alan Sutton Publishing, 1988), pp. 116–17.

7. Public Record Office, Chancery Petitions C1/142/18.

8. *Liber Albus: The White Book of the City of London*, ed. and trans. Henry Thomas Riley (London: Richard Griffin and Company, 1861), p. 238.

9. Judith M. Bennett, "Working Together: Women and Men in the Brewer's Gild of London, c. 1420," in *The Salt of Common Life: Individuality and Choice in the Medieval Town, Countryside, and Church*, ed. Edwin DeWindt (Kalamazoo: Medieval Institute Publications, 1996), pp. 181–232. In contrast to the brewers, women in the wine trade were rare. Widows could inherit the vintner trade, but carrying it on by themselves was difficult. Widows do appear collecting the debts of their vintner husbands. For instance, one wife sued to collect a debt of £40 because her husband was abroad (P.R.O. C1/46/341.) The trade required either travel or the use of agents and apprentices to do the traveling for them. A female vintner would not travel to Bordeaux and could have difficulty managing business factors and apprentices. It was not a trade that was easy to practice as an extension of other domestic occupations. See Margery Kirkbridge James, *Studies in the Medieval Wine Trade* (Oxford: Oxford University Press, 1971), pp. 160–71, for a description of the trade requirements.

10. Peter Clark, *The English Alehouse: A Social History 1200–1830* (London: Longman, 1983), p. 5. The distinctions between alehouses, taverns, and inns was not made until a statute in the sixteenth century which described alehouses as the lower end of the social scale (existing primarily for drink and perhaps some lodging), taverns as selling wine, and inns as being at the upper end of the scale providing respectable wine, ale, beer, food, and chambers. In the Middle Ages, taverns sold both ale and wine, while alehouses sold only ale.

11. Bennett, "Working Together"; Henry Thomas Riley, *Memorials of London and London Life in the XIIIth, XIVth, and XVth Centuries* (London: Longmans, Green, and Co., 1868), p. 182. Only two women were among the twenty-nine taverners who

shut their shops and would not sell wine in defiance of a city ordinance (1331) that all wine be sold from taverns with doors and windows open to the day-light.

12. Gervase Rosser, "London and Westminster: The Suburb in the Urban Economy in the Later Middle Ages," in *Towns and Townspeople in the Fifteenth Century*, ed. John A.F. Thomson (Gloucester: Alan Sutton, 1988), p. 53, observes that women in Westminster ran rooming houses.

13. Barbara A. Hanawalt, "The Widow's Mite: Provisions for Medieval London Wid-ows," in *Upon My Husband's Death: Widows in the Literature and Histories of Me-dieval Europe*, ed. Louise Mirrer (Ann Arbor: University of Michigan Press, 1992), pp. 21–45.

14. *Calendar of Letter Books of the City of London, A* (1275–1497), ed. Reginald R. Sharpe (London: John Edward Francis, 1899), p. 220.

15. Guildhall, Consistory Court 9064/1 ms. 5, 5v, 6, 26v, 30, 31, 64v, 65, 66, 81v, 114, 116, 116v, 119, 119v, 122v, 155v. P.R.O. C1/136/79. John Godwynn and his wife Agnes were accused in the wardmote of Billingsgate of keeping misrule in an inn called "the Mermaid" held on lease from the Chamberlain of London.

16. Guildhall, Consistory Court, 9064/1, ms. 68, 83, 84, 91v.

17. Ibid., ms. 110v, 114v.

18. Corporation of London Record Office, Repertory 5, fol. 52–52v. Hereafter re-ferred to as CLRO.

19. Guildhall, Consistory Court 9064/1 32, 43, 143.

20. Arthur H. Thomas, *Calendar of Plea and Memoranda Rolls of the City of London 1323–1482*, 4 (Cambridge: Cambridge University Press, 1943), p. 138.

21. Edith Rickert, ed., *The Babees' Book: Medieval Manners for the Young* (New York: Cooper Square Publishers, 1966), pp. 34–35.

22. Henry S. Bennett, *England from Chaucer to Caxton* (New York: Harcourt, Brace and Co., 1928), pp. 134–38.

23. Thomas, *Calendar of Plea and Memoranda Rolls 1323–1482*, 2 (Cambridge: Cam-bridge University Press, 1929), p. 184 (1374).

24. Reginald R. Sharpe, *Calendar of Coroners' Rolls of the City of London* (London: Richard Clay and Sons, 1913), pp. 17–18, 114–16.

25. *The Riverside Chaucer*, 3rd ed., ed. Larry D. Benson, (Boston: Houghton Mifflin Company, 1987), VII.1897–1900. All subsequent references to Chaucer's poetry will be from this edition, and hereafter fragment and line numbers will appear in text. The Host's treatment of the women on the pilgrimage, the Prioress, and even the Wife of Bath, is courteous. His general reactions to women and wives fall within the misogynistic tradition of the period. In the epilogue to the "Mer-chant's Tale" (IV.2419–2440), he returns to his complaints about his wife, but they are in more generalized terms than those pertaining to their struggle for control of the inn.

26. The ambiguity of who controls public taverns came out in a case in 1395 in which a brewer complained against William Rothewell, chaplain, that he had entered his house at night, against his will, and carried off his goods worth £66 13s. 4d., and that he also "suspected relations with his wife." He had, therefore, denied him entrance to his house. The defendant claimed that the house was a "com-mon inn" and that he had entered as a lodger and the plaintiff was an innkeeper. *Calendar of Plea and Memoranda Rolls*, 3 pp. 218–19 (1359).

27. Quoted by John Stow, in *The Survey of London* (Oxford: Oxford University Press, 1908), p. 74. Taken from the 1603 edition of Stow's *Survey*.

28. Gwyn Williams, *Medieval London from Commune to Capital* (London: Athlone, 1963), pp. 21–22.
29. Gerald R. Owst, *Literature and the Pulpit in Medieval England*, 2nd ed. (Oxford: Blackwell, 1961), pp. 435–41.
30. See William Langland's, *Piers Plowman: An Edition of the C-Text*, ed. Derek Pearsall (Berkeley: University of California Press, 1987), (VI.350–441), in which Glutton stops at a tavern on the way to mass. In *The Canterbury Tales* the "Pardoner's Tale" has an excellent description of the games, drink, and vices one finds in a medieval tavern and the appropriate condemnation of them (VI.463–73).
31. *Statutes of the Realm: Printed by the Command of George III* (1810), 13 Edward I, 102.
32. *Liber Albus: The White Book of the City of London*, ed. and trans. Henry Thomas Riley (London: Richard Griffin and Company, 1861), pp. 240–41.
33. Riley, *Memorials of London and London Life*, pp. 9–11.
34. "La Male Regle," in Bennett, *England from Chaucer to Caxton*, pp. 138–41.
35. *Calendar of Early Mayor's Court Rolls Preserved among the Archives of the Corporation of the City of London, 1298–1307*, ed. Arthur H. Thomas (London, 1924), p. 124 (1302).
36. *Calendar of Coroners' Rolls*, pp. 134–35.
37. Corporation of London Record Office, MC1/1/153.
38. *Calendar of Coroners' Rolls*, pp. 38–39, 77–78.
39. Barbara A. Hanawalt, "Violent Death in Fourteenth and Fifteenth Century England," *Journal of Comparative Studies in Society and History*, 18 (1976): 297–320.
40. *Select Cases of Trespass from the King's Courts, 1307–1399*, ed. Morris S. Arnold (London: Selden Society, 1985), p. 28.
41. *Calendar of Coroners' inquests*, pp. 143–44. See also Just. 2/94a ms. 1, 1d. for other plots ending in homicide.
42. *Calendar of Plea and Memoranda Rolls*, 2, p. 88. For a larger suspected rebellion see *Calendar of Plea and Memoranda Rolls*, 3, p. 278 (1406).
43. Guildhall, Consistory Court 9064/1 m. 133 (1470–73).
44. *Statutes of the Realm*, 1, p. 102.
45. *Calendar of Plea and Memoranda Rolls*, 2, pp. 218–19. The churches that rang curfew were St. Mary le Bow, Kerkyngcherche, St. Bride, and St. Giles without Cripplegate. The hours of curfew were nine or ten o'clock to prime.
46. *Statutes of the Realm*, 1, p. 104.
47. Ibid., pp. 234–35.
48. *Calendar of Plea and Memoranda Rolls*, 2, p. 151.
49. *Liber Albus*, p. 228.
50. Felicity Heal, in *Hospitality in Early Modern England* (Oxford: Clarendon Press, 1990), pp. 1–22, discusses the shifting attitude toward foreigners and extending them hospitality. As early as the London Eyre of 1244 the Anglo-Saxon law was reiterated:

> Be it known also, that the mayor and citizens say that no one may be in the City as a citizen, and stay there and enjoy the law of the City for more than three nights, unless he finds two pledges and thus is in frankpledge; and if he stays longer in the City in the manner aforesaid, and does not stand his trial, the alderman in whose ward he was, ought to be in mercy for harboring him in his ward when he is not in frankpledge. (*The London Eyre of 1244*, ed. Helena M. Chew and Martin Weinbaum, London Record Society, 6 [London: Chatham, W. & J. MacKay, 1970], p. 25)

51. *Liber Albus*, p. 234.
52. *Calendar of Plea and Memoranda Rolls*, 3, pp. 78–79. Because this ordinance is contemporary to both Chaucer and the Revolt of 1381, a quote is in order:
Whereas larcenies and divers evil deeds are commonly perpetrated more openly, notoriously and frequently in this present than in past times in the city of London, its suburbs and neighbourhood, which would not have been possible, if the thieves and evildoers had not been maintained and harboured by persons dwelling in the city and suburbs and residing with innkeepers, who cared little what kind of men they received, to the great damage of the citizens of the city and those repairing there to the great disgrace and scandal of the same, and in order to prevent such damage and scandal of the same, it was agreed that Sir Nicholas Brembre, Mayor, and the Aldermen that the innkeepers within the liberty should be sworn to harbour no one longer than a day and a night unless he were willing to answer for them and their acts, nor to receive to their tables any strangers called "travaillyngmen" or others, unless they had good and sufficient surety from them for their good and loyal behavior, under penalty.
53. *Letter Book A*, p. 127; *Calendar of Plea and Memoranda Rolls*, 1, pp. 18, 45, 154, 156, 163; *Letter Book G*, p. 294.
54. *Calendar of Plea and Memoranda Rolls*, 3, p. 146. The proclamation was repeated in 1376 (pp. 218–19) "No one shall carry arms within the city except the 'valet' of great lords of the land carrying their masters' swords in their presence, the serjeants-at-arms of the King and the Prince and the King's children, and the officers of the City and their companies."
55. *Calendar of Plea and Memoranda Rolls*, 1, pp. 220–21; 2, pp. 260–61. Sappy claimed loss of £18 6s. 8d. from two chests when the door of his room was broken open. The innkeeper tried to blame Sappy's servants, but the mayor and aldermen viewed the evidence of the broken door and sided with Sappy, making Hostiller responsible under "the common custom of the realm that the keeper of a hostelry was responsible for the goods and chattels brought by lodgers to his hostelry."
56. *Calendar of Plea and Memoranda Rolls*, 1, pp. 45, 235; 4, pp. 119, 121, 125, 131, 135–36, 139–40, 145, 159. See also *Letter Book F*, pp. 19, 77.
57. See *Calendar of Plea and Memoranda Rolls*, 2, p. 30, in which Isabel de Chepsted complained that William Dyne, taverner, had beaten and wounded her in 1365 to her damage of 40s. He confessed to the assault and was mainprised by John Chaucer (probably the poet's father).
58. CLRO, Journals I, m.6.
59. Frederick B. Johassen, in "The Inn, the Cathedral, and the Pilgrimage of The Canterbury Tales," in *Rebels and Rivals: The Contestive Spirit in The Canterbury Tales*, ed. Susanna Greer Fein, David Raybin, and Peter C. Braeger (Medieval Institute Publications: Kalamazoo, Mich., 1991), pp. 12–13, has made a great deal of the exemptions of Edward III to Southwark from London laws and the general reputation of the borough, but this interpretation is forced by his argument of going from sin to salvation or inn to cathedral.
60. *Calendar of Plea and Memoranda Rolls*, 3, p. 11 (1382) and pp. 172–74 (1390).
61. *Calendar of Plea and Memoranda Rolls*, 4, pp. 1551–54.
62. *Liber Albus*, pp. 231, 234.
63. For a discussion of the terms applied to the Host see David Wallace, *Chaucerian Polity: Absolutist Lineages and Associational Forms in England and Italy* (Palo Alto: Stanford University Press, 1997), ch. 2.

64. The Clerk defers by saying "Hooste, . . . I am under your yerde; / Ye han of us as now the governance, / Ane therefore wol I do yow obeisance" (IV.22–24). The Squire also defers to the host and will not be a rebel; and the Nun's Priest promises the host to be merry (V.3–4; VII.2816–17). The Franklin also agrees to obey when receiving a reprimand that he must tell a tale of pay up (V.700–706).

8

Whose Story Was This? Rape Narratives in Medieval English Courts

A crime might have many narrators: the victim, the alleged perpetrator, the witnesses, the law enforcement agents, the jurors, and the judges. But in medieval English criminal records, the victim's voice is often lost, particularly if she was a woman. The predominant voice is the laconic one of the sheriffs' or justices' clerks who recorded the bare necessities of the case and entered the verdict. In only two criminal actions did the law accord a woman a strong legal voice: an appeal involving the murderer of a woman's husband and an appeal involving her own rapist. In both cases she narrated a story of the event and named the culprit. It is tempting to conclude that at last we can read a legal record and hear the woman's voice, after these many centuries, recounting the calamity and horror that has entered her life as a victim of crime. The voice, however, is not a clear, unambiguous woman's narrative. Even if she is the one bringing the charges, she must do so within a set formula for making an appeal. She may, instead, have told of the crime to a group of neighborhood men who brought the indictment against the suspect in the king's name, or her father's voice may be that reporting his despoiled property in the loss of his daughter's virginity. Finally, the trial jurors might retell the story in their own words and the justices might also add their versions before reaching a decision. Through all of these filters, one can still hear the woman's own agonized tale. But what distortions do the filters add to the narrative?

Using three accounts of the alleged rape in 1320 of an eleven-year-old London girl, Joan daughter of Eustace le Seler (Saddler), I will look at the variations in the narratives that surround this rape case. While multiple versions of property disputes are common,[1] three versions of a rape are very rare. The first version, of course, is that of the girl herself in the form of an appeal. She alleged that Reymund of Limoges, a merchant of Bordeaux, seized her, at twilight, outside her father's house in the Vintry and carried her off to his lodgings where he raped her. The second version is a rebuttal by the accused man, and the third is the discussion by the justices of eyre before whom the case was eventually tried. Each teller presents different details and embellishments to the basic story, which subtly changed the motivations of the participants and the outcome of the case. Analysis of the case is presented from these three different perspectives so that a full understanding of the voices in the case can be assessed in their own contexts.

Rape narratives unfold in competing and complementary frameworks that do much to mold the structure of the story. An understanding of the girl's appeal and its narrative form is enhanced by a brief history of the legal status of rape and its prosecution in the thirteenth and fourteenth centuries. Statute law, legal treatises, and practice put constraints on a woman's narrative. Formulaic requirements play a large role in the narrative structure, emphasizing a violent intrusion on normal routines, resistance, and injury. Eleanor Wachs, in *Crime-Victim Stories*, has pointed out that "crime-victim narratives are stylized and structured formulaic stories that recapitulate incidents between a victim and offender."[2] In this respect, they are similar to the medieval appeals of rape. A second element in rape narratives is the difference in the ways that the victim and the accused tell their versions of the crime. When the alleged offender is the storyteller, the narrative may contain the same elements, but he or she may twist the facts around, thereby exculpating him or herself. Yet a third version is that of third parties—the neighbors, the community, and the judicial system. Those who retell the story from the viewpoint of a nonparticipant, according to Wachs, have a variety of motivations in mind, including didactic tales that warn how to avoid rape situations, triumphant stories that create heroes out of rescuers or courageous women who resist, moral parables of foolish women who "ask for" rape, and exculpating stories that allowed the accused to be acquitted or to get off with a lesser punishment. The recitation of the cases reinforces a sense of community belonging, values, and survival tactics in a generally threatening environment.[3]

Third parties can, of course, tell a salacious story about rape as well, and this type, as we shall see, appears to be what the court officials and judges favored. The pornographic elements of the version the judges hear of Joan's rape may have titillated the auditors, but did not influence their narrow legal conclusions. This third version, however, had a lasting appeal in legal circles and appeared again years later in *Novae Narrationes*, a book of examples for lawyers on how to present a case.[4] Did this early-fourteenth-century child pornography add levity to a law text, or did it teach a number of coded messages to legal apprentices about gender roles, legal narratives, and privilege in courts?

THE LEGAL FRAMEWORK OF A RAPE NARRATIVE

As Natalie Zemon Davis has shown in *Fiction in the Archives*, court narratives were told within a legal framework, but also within one that reflected the societal mores of the time.[5] In the case of rape, medieval law had explicit rules that framed the tales, but an additional body of unofficial male folklore also shaped how the stories were told and tried.[6] Rape carried with it the idea of violence—*violentus concubitus*—and was treated as a bootless crime from the Conquest onwards, as long as the woman pressed her suit successfully. The prescribed punishment for the convicted offender, castration and blinding, seems not to have been practiced frequently. If the woman did not pursue her appeal or failed to get a conviction, then the man was tried at the king's suit. The first Statute of Westminster in 1275 tried to regularize the appeal of rape, giving a woman forty days to make her appeal and prescribing two years' imprisonment and ransom at the king's pleasure in cases of conviction. Essentially, the punishment made rape a trespass rather than a felony. By the second Statute of Westminster (1285), ten years later, the felonious status of rape was clarified, requiring punishment in life and member, as was the case for other felonies, and permitting indictment by jury as well as appeal by the victim for prosecuting offense.[7]

Until Westminster II, the burden of proof rested on women, and even after 1285, a woman could bring an appeal of rape. The law left little room for spontaneity or emotion in the appeal. Glanville, a legal theorist writing in the late twelfth century, described the constraints surrounding a rape appeal:

> In the crime of rape [*raptus crimen*] a woman charges a man with violating her by force in the peace of the lord king. A woman who suffers in this way must go, soon after the deed is done, to the nearest vill and there show to trustworthy men the injury done to her, and any effusion of blood there may be and any tearing of her clothes. She should then do the same to the reeve of the hundred. Afterwards she should proclaim it publicly in the next county court.[8]

The victim must bear witness herself not only in her own voice and words, but also with her body both clothed and unclothed. Torn clothing and wounds were evidence of struggle, and "effusion of blood" indicated the breaking of the hymen. Her testimony was not to be made to a jury of matrons, but to an audience of males in a public setting. Her narrative was repeated to the hundred reeve, to a coroner at a later date, to the country court, and to the royal justices.

The story could not be a simple recitation of wrongs done to her. Appeals were, in many respects, ritualized recitals that had to be reproduced not once, but multiple times and in exactly the same words, covering all the necessary legal points. The legal magic required to render an appeal efficacious included exact repetitions. Even approvers, those confessed felons who turned king's evidence and appealed their confederates in crime, had to follow the prescribed formula during their trial and name the same names with the same crimes, stolen goods, and places as in their first confession to the coroner.[9] A women who had undergone the trauma of rape, therefore, needed to rehearse her story and receive advice on its telling before making the appeal. By the Statute of Westminster I (1275) a woman had forty days to make the appeal.

In *De Legibus et Consuetudinibus Angliae*, attributed to Henry de Bracton, the formula was laid out. Bracton used not only legal treatises but also plea rolls, and his formula relates practice as well as theory.

> A., such a woman, appeals B., for that whereas she was at such a place on such a day in such a year etc. (or when she was going from such a place to such, or at such a place, doing such a thing) the said B. came with his force and wickedly and against the king's peace lay with her and took from her maidenhood (or virginity) and kept her with him for so many nights (and let thus set out all the facts and the truth). And that he did this wickedly and feloniously she offers to prove against him as the king's court may award.[10]

Apparently, it was difficult for the women to get the appeal in the correct words. They might use "rape" instead of the formula or leave out "against the king's peace," or add or leave out some part of the circumstances in one of the versions. In the Wiltshire eyre of 1249 eight of the twenty appeals of rape contained some mistake in the formula.[11] The stakes were high in the legal storytelling, because the woman would be imprisoned and fined for making a false appeal.

In the eyes of the men writing legal theory in the thirteenth and early fourteenth centuries, not all raped women stood equally before the law. Bracton felt that payment in life and member (true felony) was only applicable in conviction for rape of a virgin, whereas a man convicted of raping a married woman or widow would suffer corporal punishment only.[12] In practice monetary fines and imprisonment were common. In other words, some rapes were felonies and some were trespasses depending on the woman's virginity before rape. But a later theorist, Britton, added even further complications in arguing that a defendant in an appeal of rape could confess his deed, but the rape would not be considered a felony if the woman conceived as a result of rape. Medical opinion was that a woman could not conceive if she did not consent to intercourse.[13] In the eyre of Kent in 1312–13 a man was acquitted because the woman who appealed him had a child that resulted from the rape.[14] Male ideas about medicine, as well as about differential suffering as a result of rape, played into the interpretation of the law, disadvantaging mature, married women. Loss of virginity, perhaps viewed as a property value, influenced legal discourse. Or perhaps it was the usual medieval misogynistic view that once women had sex they desired it always, and this insatiability exculpated their rapists.[15]

At age eleven, Joan fit into all the legal stereotypes for making a successful appeal: she was a virgin of a young and tender age and had not conceived a child. Her appeal followed the formula as Bracton had laid it out. The first record of Joan's appeal [13 April 1320] was made before the sheriffs of London and recorded in the Coram Rege Roll no. 240 for Easter 1320.

> And the said Joan appeals the said Reymund of rape and breach of the
> King's peace, saying that the said Reymund on the night of the Sunday next
> before the feast of Gregory the Pope in the thirteenth year of the reign of
> the King who now is [9 March 1320], at the hour of curfew, in the City of
> London, in Walbrook Ward by force and arms and against the will of the
> said Joan took her by her left hand and led her away to the room of the
> same Reymund in the parish of St. Martin in the Vintry, and there flung
> her to the ground and lay with her against her will, feloniously as the lord
> King's felon, and utterly robbed her of her maidenhead, against the peace
> of the lord King and his Crown and dignity.

All was correct with this appeal, and the record went on to say that "Joan
followed him up, raising the hue and cry, from ward to ward, to the next
four wards, and beyond the court of the lord King, so that the said Reymund is attached at the suit of the said Joan."[16]

One does not imagine that Joan could have known all the legal niceties
to make this appeal without some coaching. Nor does one assume that, after this violent trauma, she herself pursued the rapist from ward to ward.
Her two pledges to prosecute were her father, Eustace the saddler of London, and John le Boys. Her father and other neighbors would have taken up
the hue and cry and probably helped her formulate and memorize her appeal.

THE STORIES OF THE VICTIM AND THE ACCUSED

Joan's appeal and Reymund's rebuttal in his defense are not the loosely told
stories that Wachs has recorded for urban folklore, but one can see similar
patterns in crime-victim stories from modern New York and those of court
records from the fourteenth century. Beyond simply getting all the right
words into the appeal, Joan's narrative voice does appear, and Reymund
tells an exculpating tale that has a familiar modern ring. Reading the stories
through the lens of time and formula, however, raises complexities of interpretation over such basic issues as dates.

Although filtered through the set legal formula, Joan's story has elements that are common to Wach's crime-victim tales. Crime victims describe
their behavior before the crime as ordinary and routine. They may even por-
tray themselves as too trusting. What happens to them is "bad luck" or being "in the wrong place at the wrong time."[17] Joan's story is of an ordinary
evening that she might have passed any night of her young life. She was
outside her father's house at the hour of curfew. She describes herself as
"hard by" her father's house when Reymund came up and took her by the
left hand. Perhaps she knew him and was too trusting. But this is only the
first version of the story.

In her second version, which purports to be a verbatim appeal in French,
more details were added. This version was entered in a jail delivery session
held in 1321 and records an appeal she made to the coroner on 6 February

1321, almost a year after the event. The basic narrative is the same, but more details are recorded. They may have been part of her initial story, but the King's Bench scribes did not put in all the details. In this version of the appeal she says that she was "two feet" from her father's house, or well within a safe radius for a child, but the hour was after curfew—a dangerous and illegal time to be out. Rather than taking her by the hand, Reymund "took the body of the said Joan . . . and carried her off and took her into the house of the said Reymund, that is to say, to the house rented by Ellis Pers in the parish of St. Martin in the Vintry." He took her to his chamber, which was in a solar or the upper story of the house. He kept her there all night and "there deflowered her . . . against her will" and "so vilely and cruelly handled her limbs that her life was despaired of, and still is, and she has lost all hope of recovering her health."[18]

This more complete version speaks of other characteristics of crime-victim stories. We are given details that, while not strictly necessary for the formula, communicate her horror during the attack. She was bodily carried off, not led away, for the distance of about a quarter of a mile from her parish and ward to his. She was kept in a confined space where escape was impossible. The attack lasted all night, rather than being a single event, and the brutality was life-threatening. The extensive wounds that are hinted at are those that are often encountered when an adult male has forced intercourse with a young girl. The voice of a terrified victim comes through, even though it is told in the sparse style of a crime-victim tale.[19]

Faced with the appeal of rape, which meant hanging if sustained, Reymund tried a number of evasion tactics. His first ploy at the King's Bench hearing was to claim that he was a clerk and that he would not answer to the felony charge until his ordinary had come from the bishop. He was, in other words, claiming benefit of clergy, which would permit him to be tried in the lenient ecclesiastical court where he would have a penance rather than capital punishment.[20] The justices charged jurors to inquire into his clerical status and delayed the hearing until 4 June. Reymund changed his story, probably knowing that the jury did not or could not substantiate his claim to be a clerk, and put himself "on the country,"—that is, he agreed to have a jury trial. Perhaps he knew that Joan would not come, because he had either paid her off or intimidated her. In any case, he was acquitted because she did not appear to prosecute her appeal. She was to be arrested and put in prison for false appeal (forgiven because of her age), and her sureties (her father and the other man) were amerced or fined. By law, Reymund was then tried at the king's suit and was acquitted on 25 June.[21]

Reymund's next tactic, in a civil suit, was to claim to be more sinned against than sinning. He told his own crime-victim story. The jurors had said, in response to questioning by the justices of King's Bench, that Reymund had suffered damages from the false appeal to the value of £40 and that Joan could not pay these damages. They suggested that Joan had been abetted in her false appeal by her father, Eustace, and four other men. At the autumn court sessions in 1320 Reymund presented a full narrative of his losses. He complained that "the said Eustace and others" on 7 February 1320 (over a month before the alleged rape) "falsely and maliciously abetted Joan the daughter of Eustace the saddler in appealing the said Reymund before the King in his court of the rape of the said Joan." Reymund was arrested and spent the time between 23 March and 25 June in prison, whereby he suffered loss and damage of £100. He sued Eustace and the others for financial loss, and both he and they put themselves on the country in the Michaelmas term of 1320, but the case was not resolved.[22] It is perhaps because of the pending civil suit that Joan made the second appeal in 1321.

Joan, probably with the advice, coaching, and maybe even prodding of her father, told her story again to the coroner in 1321, as related above, and the case came into jail delivery. This time Reymund pointed out that she had not gotten her story right. She claimed in the appeal before the coroner that the rape had occurred on 9 March 1320, but when she repeated the appeal to the justices of jail delivery she said it was 19 March 1320. Having been acquitted already in King's Bench, he could afford to be jocular, claiming "she could not twice be deprived of one and the same maidenhead." The case ends with the comment, "Joan cannot deny this." Reymund was obviously well-connected, and when he was tried at the king's suit after the failure of Joan's second appeal, he produced a sealed copy of the King's Bench decision and a writ from the King commanding the justices to admit the copy. Again he was acquitted.[23]

Joan's mistake was not a simple, understandable slip of days and numbers from nine to nineteen. The dates were given by church holiday and by regnal year so that 9 March was the "Sunday in Mid Lent in the thirteenth year of the reign of our lord the King who now is" (*le demeyne en le my quarem Lan de Regne nostre siegnur le Roy qe ore est qu dieu gard, treszime*). This is the date that appears in the jail delivery records, but Reymund is able to show that her appeal to the coroner was different: "the Wednesday next before Palm Sunday in the said year" (*die Mercurii proxima ante diem dominicam in Ramis palmarum anno supradicto*), or the 19th of March. In her first appeal to the sheriff and that which is recorded in the King's Bench she apparently used, or at least the scribes wrote the date as, "Sunday next before the feast of Gregory the Pope" (*diei dominice proxima ante festum Gregorii Pape*), which would also work out to 9 March 1320.[24] Even if the appeals had all been rendered in French, they would not have resembled each other closely enough for a slip to occur.

Did Joan know French, or did she have to memorize her appeal in a language that was foreign to her? Three languages were current in legal proceedings at the time. Latin was the formal language of the judicial records, but French was the language of the courts for ordinary judicial discussion. The justices in eyre heard Joan's case and discussed it in French. Joan, however, may have told her case to the coroner in English.[25] Coroners' clerks customarily did immediate translations from English into Latin when they entered the cases into the coroners' rolls. If Joan's words were translated, as they certainly were in her first version and might have been in her second "verbatim" version, then the deviations may not have been her own, but those of an inattentive (or bribed?) clerk. By the early fourteenth century, it is unlikely that Joan would have known French even if her father was called "le Seler." English had become the common language; Edward III (who came to the throne in 1327) was the first monarch to speak English at court. Was she forced to repeat her appeal in a foreign language at the jail delivery session, or did she know French and was part of a foreign French community? Alternatively, if she was a Francophone, that might have made her more susceptible to the blandishments of Reymund, who was from Limoges. We cannot know the answer to this question from the evidence we have.

The surrounding records have little to tell about the main characters in the case. Other court records for London and the royal government do not hint of a previous relationship between Eustace and Reymund. Eustace and Joan do not appear in these records, nor do the men who stand surety for her or are accused with him. No obvious trade connection would have existed between a saddler and a vintner, and yet Reymund was able to make an argument that Joan's father and his friends were pursuing a vendetta against him that predated the rape. The records that we do have imply that Reymund was wealthy, considering the amount he claimed to have lost while in prison, and that he was well-connected at the royal court.[26] He used his wealth and power to manipulate his narrative effectively. When he was tried in jail delivery, he not only could argue that he had already been acquitted, he "puts forward the (copy) of the record of the acquittal of the said Reymund under the seal of the same Henry [le Scrope, justice of the King's Bench], together with the King's writ directed to the same Henry about sending that copy to the Justices here, and also a writ of the lord King to the Justices here (commanding them) to admit that copy and to do further what they rightly should."[27]

The presence of both the victim and the accused in the courtroom situations implies a dialogue, if not with each other, then through the intermediary of justices and jurors. Wachs found that the victims told the more complete and detailed story in the courtroom situation.[28] It is, however, in the accused's interest to add as few details as possible in order to avoid emotional and factual entanglements. Reymund keeps his story to technical details and responds with a counter suit in civil court to silence charges and accusations. Perhaps Reymund had a further advantage in the courtroom dialogue that Joan could not access, not only because she was a girl whose father was not well connected with power: If Joan knew only English, then Reymund could have talked with the justices in French and further excluded Joan's voice from the proceedings.[29]

Before looking further into Joan's experience in the courts, we need a context in which to assess whether her story was typical of women's appeals. Was there any point to reporting a rape to authorities? Women who made the appeal of rape had very little chance of success. Rape was a rare form of criminal action. Between 1202 and 1276, in other words, before the Statute of Westminster I, only 142 rape cases appeared in 20 eyre records compared to 3,492 homicides. Of these, 56 percent of the women did not continue to prosecute after their initial appeal. The women who failed to pursue their appeal were imprisoned and fined unless, like Joan, they were young or poor. The king did prosecute when the appealor failed to do so, but only five (16 percent) of the 142 alleged rapists were found guilty. Of the 44 percent of women who did pursue their cases, most found that the alleged rapist had fled and had to be outlawed. Twenty-three men did stand trial on appeal, and of these twenty were acquitted. Of the three convicted, two were clergy and so avoided punishment when they were turned over to the ecclesiastical authorities; the layman was fined £1 6s. 8d. The overall conviction was 8 percent of those tried for homicides and 6 percent for rape. But while 7 percent of the convicted murderers were hanged, none of the rapists paid with life or member.[30]

In the ten-year period between Westminster I and Westminster II thirty-seven rape cases appeared in the plea rolls, of which sixteen originated through indictment and twenty-one by appeal. Again, the pattern was for eleven of the twenty-one appeals either to be quashed in court or abandoned by the woman. Only two of the cases originating from indictments ended in conviction, but only one of the men appealed of rape was convicted.[31] The courts, therefore, showed a reluctance to accept the evidence of appeals. Again, punishment in life and member was not practiced.

Following Westminster II, when the penalty was hanging as it was for other felonies, indictment increasingly replaced appeals for rape. In an eight-county survey from 1300 to 1348 only 79 rape indictments were made out of 15,952 felony indictments, or only .2 percent of the cases. Only 10 percent of those indictments ended in conviction, close to homicide, which was 12 percent. The successful convictions were usually in cases of the rape of young virgins. For instance, a man was convicted for raping Agnes daughter of William Neilesone and Isabel daughter of Simon Gregesone, who were both only fourteen years old.[32]

With the odds so stacked against a rape victim's success in making an appeal and with the punishment for small blunders in recitation and non-appearance being punished with imprisonment and fines, why did women bother to make the appeals? Since appeals of rape were so rare in the courts— 2 cases per year in 74 years between 1202 and 1276 and scattered throughout England—it is possible that the women who made appeals did not know about the futility of their effort. Statistics were not kept at the time, so that word of mouth would be the only indication of potential defeat in the courts. Still, those women did have legal knowledge or advice about making an appeal in the correct form, and so women obviously had access to the common parlance of legal matters. Legal theorists attributed the motivation of marriage to women making an appeal. Because the theorists thought that an appeal of rape could be used to force a marriage that might disparage either the victim's or the attacker's family, rape participants had to have a license from the king in order to marry. Historians, also, perhaps to shield themselves from acknowledging the brutality of rape, have assumed that the rape appeal was useful to a young couple when there was an impediment to marriage such as class differences or parental opposition.[33] If this romantic explanation for rape appeals was true, historical records are not forthcoming in substantiating it. Only two of the thirteenth-century cases mention that the couple married.[34]

Having made an appeal, why did so many women fail to appear and pursue the case? The least savory explanation, of course, is that the accused or his friends intimidated the victim from appearing in court or paid her off in advance. It is also possible that if marriage was not the objective, women did manage to force some other compromise such as a monetary payment that would compensate them for their loss of virginity and any complications that this might cause in the marriage market. A few cases mention that an out-of-court settlement was reached, but these were as rare as marriages. Only in the Chancery petitions of the fifteenth century does one get a sense of how such bargains worked. For instance, Robert Trenender, a brazier, and his wife complained the Philip Rychard had deflowered their daughter. They took the matter to arbitration, and Philip bound himself by £100 to abide by the arbitration. He agreed that he would give their daughter, Agnes, a pipe and a half of woad or £20 as compensation and agreed not to "vex" the family again. Another man who had criminally assaulted a girl younger than fourteen years old was to pay £40 to the chamberlain, who would keep it until the victim either arrived at full age or married. In other words, the compensation was a dowry that would make the girl attractive for marriage.[35]

I suggest, however, that for the victim the telling of the tale itself was some compensation. Part of the reason that crime-victim narratives are such a popular folklore genre in New York is that so few crimes are punished. Reciting the incident is a way of coming to grips with the violence itself. The telling of the tale among friends and acquaintances in New York is a compensatory exercise even when the name of the perpetrator is unknown.[36] It was, perhaps, an even greater satisfaction to tell the tale and name the culprit in medieval times. In a society in which one's "good fame" was what got loans, pledges for land transactions, and even acquittal in courts, a man blackened by an accusation of rape might find himself isolated in his community. While a woman risked her reputation by admitting to her violation, she might have been able to discredit her attacker sufficiently to ruin him in the local community and the county at large. The number of accused who fled and were outlawed gives some indication of the subtle and complete punishment the victim's story could bring, even if it did not terminate in castration or hanging.

COMMUNITY VALUES AND THE RAPE TALES

We must turn to the role that third parties played either as reciters of rape stories or as audiences. Joan's rape story was told a third time in the official records. London experienced one of the rare eyres of the fourteenth century in 1321. Since the case was still very current, the justices of eyre heard and discussed it. In this third version, the formulaic parts are again the same, but the narrative is not directly attributed to Joan, although the narrator makes clear that both she and Reymund were present. The additional narrative elements may have been supplied by Joan, but there are hints that they were added by the third-party narrator, probably the coroner.[37] In this version, Joan was "hard by" her father's house at a distance of only three feet. The time is sunset. Reymund took her by the hand against her will to his chamber.

The addition of another voice becomes obvious here because this version gives the exact location of Reymund's chamber and its orientation south to north with "one end of it abutting on the high street of our lord the King which is called the Vintry and the other end (being) three perches from the river Thames, which chamber in length adjoins the house of Sir Hugh Gissors towards the north and the house of James Beauflour towards the west." The third-party narrator goes on to detail Reymund's attack:

> Reymund . . . took this same Joan the daughter (of Eustace) who is here, between his two arms and against her consent and will laid her on the ground with her belly upwards and her back on the ground, and with his right hand raised the clothes of the same Joan the daughter of Eustace up to her navel, she being clothed in a blue coat and a shift of light cloth, and feloniously as the felon of our lord the King who now is, with both his hands separated the legs and thighs of this same Joan, and with his right hand took his male organ of such and such a length and size and put it in the secret parts of this same Joan, and bruised her watershed and laid her open so that she was bleeding, and ravished her maidenhead.

Nothing is said about how long the rape lasted, but, rather, the story reverts to the first version in which he fled and Joan raised the hue and cry.[38]

The added details are not those that Joan was likely to have knowledge of or to remember. She would certainly have known what she was wearing at the time since she would have had few changes of clothing, but the length and size of Reymund's penis would not be part of her observation, the orientation of the chamber and the nearest neighbors would not be part of her description. Another legal formula has entered—the correct pleading of a case in eyre with details of place, size, and injuries that add a verisimilitude.

The disjuncture between this dramatic rendering of the tale and the eyre justices' legalistic discussion that follows is striking. It is apparent that another story is embedded in their deliberations. Having heard this more lurid version, the justices discussed the legal points of case. They do not address the question of whether or not the rape occurred or if her father forced her into making the appeal. Their sole concerns were about the discrepancies of dates, the late appeal to the coroner (long after the 40 days that the statute required), and the fact that she did not pursue her appeal in King's Bench.

They concluded that, since Reymund had been acquitted already in King's Bench, he could not now be tried in eyre. Joan was again to be remanded to prison for false appeal, but was excused because of her young age.[39]

The seeming indifference of eyre justices in hearing the sad tale of Joan's rape needs an explanation, as does the vivid detail that is added to her story of the rape. The male voice looms very large in court records: it speaks through the laws, the legal treatises, the formulas for making appeals, the officials, justices, juries, scribes recording testimony, and even the audience at legal proceedings. That male concerns and male bonding might override women's voices is not surprising. The distortions of a woman's story in the court deliberation, however, are instructive.

Reconstructing the eyre deliberations on Joan's case gives a sense of the very maleness of the encounter. The Eyre of 1321 was held on the third floor of the White Tower (Tower of London), with the Pleas of the Crown held in the Lesser Hall. Janitors and ushers guarded entry into the hall and clerks with sacks of documents scurried about. The London coroners, sheriffs, and ward bailiffs were there as were jurors waiting for trials. All of these officials were, of course, men. Even among litigants there were few women.[40] Perhaps Joan was accompanied by her father and her other pledge, but she was essentially in a room of strange men, standing not very far from her alleged attacker—the narrator apparently pointed to Reymund "who is there" and Joan "who is here." The most likely third-party reciter of Joan's tale, the coroner, answered the justices' questions. There are voyeuristic elements in this description of Joan's rape, and one is reminded of Chaucer's description of Pandarus loitering at the foot of the bed for the rape of Criseyde. The dramatic recounting of the rape had nothing to do with the deliberation, which considered only narrow legal points.

The primary legal issue was that Joan "ought to prove [rape] against a man as a woman ravished of her maidenhead." One obvious male perception that influenced legal deliberations was the varying status accorded to rape victims. Bracton, as we observed, felt that the degree of punishment of an offender should depend on the victim's status: "Virgins and widows as well as nuns are dedicated to God, and their defilement is committed not only to the hurt of mankind, but indeed, in scorn of Almighty God Himself." Men who violated these women were to be punished to the fullness of the law, including castration, so that "the offender should lose his eyes which gave him sight of the maiden's beauty for which he coveted her . . . and the testicles which excited his hot lust." He suggests, however, that the violators of wives, concubines, and prostitutes might receive a lesser punishment, although he does not spell this out.[41] Male jurors and justices seem to have shared his preoccupation that virginity was a valuable object and its violent loss by a young girl was particularly grievous.

One thing that the dismal record of rape convictions shows, including Joan's loss of her appeal, is that the males involved in all aspects of the judicial system found the punishments of mutilation or hanging too severe for their perceptions of the degree of damages a woman suffered from rape, even when it entailed loss of virginity. An examination of several thirteenth-century cases indicates the lengths to which the jurors and justices would go to avoid the full letter of the law. For instance, the jurors found that Emma, daughter of Christine, had been raped by Hugh fitz Henry de Alkyndoun, but they stated that Emma was not a virgin so Hugh should not be mutilated. Westminster I made no distinction about virginity, but the justices upheld the jury's conclusion and he was imprisoned. When Alice, daughter of William le Brewere appealed Adam le Taverner of rape, the jury upheld his version that she consented to intercourse. Another man claimed that the woman who appealed him was married so that she could not have lost her virginity in the rape. He was acquitted, although the law said nothing about married, non-virgins being ineligible of making an appeal of rape.[42]

In their eager desire to let men accused of rape off lightly, the jurors in Hertfordshire in 1287 became very literal in their definition of virginity. Agnes, daughter of John de Enovere, appealed Hugh fitz Thomas le Renur of rape. Agnes was seven years old at the time and was minding sheep in the fields. Hugh came upon her and violently threw her onto the ground in order to rape her. He squeezed her so hard that blood issued from her mouth and nose. But the jurors said that because of her young age, he was able to penetrate her, but was not able to break her maidenhead. The jurors concluded, therefore, that Agnes had not been raped and that Hugh had only committed trespass because he had beaten her. Because it was a trespass, he had to pay her a compensation.[43]

Men's stories about rape victims, therefore, were about their balance of a woman's loss of virginity as opposed to a man's loss of his penis or his life. Men's scales definitely tipped toward the accused's intact organ rather than the victim's lost hymen.[44] If the law had to be twisted slightly to define virginity, so be it. If the appeal contained small inconsistencies, then the accused was free. If the accused compensated the victim or married her, then the jurors no doubt went home happier; they would find it easier to confront the father and brothers of the victim if some arrangement could be made. The victim herself was of little consequence. The invisibility of the victim is particularly striking when one considers that a woman pursuing her appeal was present before the eyes of the jurors and justices and, at an eyre, she would have to be present even if the case had already been decided against her. In Joan's case, not only was she in the room, but it was claimed that she was still suffering the physical effects of the brutal rape.

The immediate audience of official rape stories was primarily male, as we have observed. But Joan's story lived on for a male audience for generation after generation of aspiring lawyers. It was included in the popular *Novae Narrationes*, a manual for instruction in pleading. The *Novae Narrationes* is a collection of cases (*narratio* or *conte* in Anglo-Norman) giving detailed statements of the plaintiff's argument and the defendant's denial. Lawyers used them as models of how to plead in various actions involving land, dower, wardship, writs, and so on. Many of the cases simply used initials or stereotyped names, but Joan's case is preserved in exactly the form that it appeared in the eyre of 1321. It was not part of the usual formulary, but was a popular addition to this much-copied manuscript.[45]

The inclusion of this particular rape appeal as an afterthought in various editions of the book is curious. Rape virtually never appeared in the year books that were also meant to instruct practitioners of law. Indeed, felonies generally do not appear in either the year books or the *Novae Narrationes* because attorneys could not be used. A woman had to make the appeal herself and in her own words. The case, therefore, was not instructive for methods of pleading or presenting a case. It was useful for its emphasis on getting the details correct, but other cases served just as well. I suggest that it was popular because of its titillation value—a bit of fourteenth-century soft pornography for lawyers. Indeed, the translator of the *Novae Narrationes*, Elsie Shanks, found the rape scene so shocking, that she did not translate it from the Anglo-Norman. Kathryn Gravdal has noted that in one of the fourteenth-century French criminal registers the court recorder also moved from his usually laconic presentation of cases to more detail when he described at length the rape of young girls. The descriptions in the French court are not only similar to the rape of Joan, they also appear as a literary topos.[46]

Beyond the courts, however, when people in communities listened to crime-victim rape tales, what subtexts did they hear? I have argued that the telling of accidental death cases was a didactic exercise that instructed the public about the dangers of certain activities or, in "Narratives of a Nurturing Culture," taught parents and community about child care.[47] Wachs has pointed out that the crime-victim stories were part of an ongoing socialization process. They demonstrate that not all members of society will obey the laws or will be forced to obey them even if caught. They speak of spaces that are dangerous and those that the victim assumed would be safe. They emphasize how the victim might behave to escape victimization or at least to survive an attack. And they speak to social order and social values.[48]

If the lesson for male audiences of rape cases was that the courts were friendly to rapists, what would women glean from hearing these tales? First, there would be the question of places in which a woman was safe. It would seem that being in one's own home or close to it, as was Joan, would be a safe place for a young girl. Joan would not have been in the street alone on a March evening in London. London streets were crowded, and there must have been bystanders who did not intervene; perhaps because she was too trusting and did not protest. On the other hand, Agnes was out in the field minding sheep. In another attempted rape case in Bedfordshire at about the same time, a girl of thirteen was minding sheep near a wood while her father worked near by. A man came up and threw her to the ground to rape her. Her father rushed to her rescue, but the assailant shot an arrow and killed him.[49] Minding sheep was dangerous for girls, and it is perhaps for that reason that Joan of Arc's interrogators asked her whether she had minded the sheep.[50]

Finally, what lesson would the crime-victim narrator take away from her day or days in court? Humiliation would be the chief lesson to bring away from confronting the attacker in a court of law. Appeals did not end in conviction and, as a consequence of having either not appeared or of losing the case, the woman herself could suffer imprisonment and fines. The view of the social order that these women would find once again driven home was that the courts and society were a man's world and that they defined the behavior of women. As Catharine MacKinnon has observed of modern American law: "The rule of law—neutral, abstract, elevated, pervasive—both institutionalizes the power of men over women and institutionalizes power in its male form."[51] For a woman to take her crime-victim story into a court was to submit herself and her story to a series of intrusions and distortions that would alter both the teller and the tale. The accused would be acquitted or outlawed—in either case he went physically free. At best the victim might get some compensation or a marriage, at worst she will have further humiliated herself by publicly proclaiming her rape and be fined and imprisoned.

We cannot know what happened to Joan daughter of Eustace le Seler. Although the court never established that she was raped, she would have had to show her wounds to the sheriff and coroner, and the extent of her wounds are probably correctly reported in the eyre version. But we do not know who bore the greater responsibility for her suffering—Reymund never denied the rape, having argued from technicalities, but he does suggest that her father may have forced her into the rape situation for goals of his own. Historical records do not reveal the psychological traumas of rape, possible parental betrayal, and public humiliation that Joan suffered. Indeed, the historical records do not even tell us if she lived beyond the year of her rape.

NOTES

1. Robert C. Palmer, *The Wilton Dispute, 1264–1380: A Social-Legal Study of Dispute Settlement in Medieval England* (Princeton: Princeton University Press, 1984).
2. Eleanor Wachs, *Crime-Victim Stories: New York City's Urban Folklore* (Bloomington: Indiana University Press, 1988), p. xv.
3. Ibid., pp. xix, 7, 12.
4. *Novae Narrationes*, ed. Elsie Shanks, with a legal introduction by S. F. C. Milsom, Selden Society, 80 (London: Bernard Quarith, 1963), pp. 341–44.
5. Natalie Zemon Davis, *Fiction in the Archives: Pardon Tales and Their Tellers in Sixteenth-Century France* (Stanford: Stanford University Press, 1987).
6. Kathryn Gravdal, in *Ravishing Maidens: Writing Rape in Medieval French Literature and Law* (Philadelphia: University of Pennsylvania Press, 1991), has the best description of the literary topos of rape and its relationship to the law and legal cases in medieval France.
7. Frederick Pollock and Frederic William Maitland, *The History of English Law before the Time of Edward I*, 2nd ed. (Cambridge: Cambridge University Press, 1968), pp. 490–91. The best analysis of the Statutes of Westminster, their provisions,

and their enforcement is Harold N. Schneebach, "The Law of Felony in Medieval England from the Accession of Edward I until the Mid-Fourteenth Century" (University of Iowa, Ph.D. thesis, 1973), pp. 433–506. See also John B. Post, "Ravishment of Women and the Statutes of Westminster," in John H. Baker, *Legal Records and the Historian: Papers Presented to the Cambridge Legal History Conference 1975* (London: Royal Historical Society, 1978), pp. 150–64; Ruth Kittel, "Rape in Thirteenth-Century England: A Study of the Common-Law Courts," in *Women and the Law: The Social Historical Perspective*, ed. D. Kelly Weisberg, 2 (Cambridge, Mass.: Schenkman Publishing Company, 1982), pp. 101–15; Barbara A. Hanawalt, *Crime and Conflict in English Communities* (Cambridge, Mass.: Harvard University Press, 1979). The crime of rape became distinct from that of ravishment, which was directed at securing the property of a woman through carrying her off. The expert on this subject is Sue Sheridan Walker, in "Common Law Juries and Feudal Marriage Customs in Medieval England: The Pleas of Ravishment," *University of Illinois Law Review*, 3 (1984): 705–18; "Punishing Convicted Ravishers: Statutory Strictures and Actual Practice in Thirteenth- and Fourteenth-Century England," *Journal of Medieval History*, 13 (1987): 237–50; and "Wrongdoing and Compensation: The Pleas of Wardship in Thirteenth- and Fourteenth-Century England," *Journal of Legal History* 32 (1988): 267–309.

8. *Tractatus de Legibus et Consuetudinibus Regni Anglie qui Glanvilla Vocatur [The Treatise on the Laws and Customs of the Realm of England Commonly Called Glanville]*, ed. and trans. George D. G. Hall (London: Nelson, 1965), pp. 175–76. Glanville goes on to say that the convicted rapist cannot get out of punishment by offering to marry the woman because this might lead to marriages between the servile and the well-born and "thus the fair repute of their [victim and convicted] would be unworthily blackened." Only the king or his justices could license such marriages with the consent of the families.

9. F.C. Hamil, "The King's Approvers," *Speculum*, 11 (1936): 238–58.

10. *Bracton on the Laws and Customs of England*, 2, ed. George H. Woodbine and Samuel E. Thorne (Cambridge, Mass.: Harvard University Press, 1968–77), pp. 416–17.

11. John M. Carter, *Rape in Medieval England: An Historical and Sociological Study* (Lanham, Md.: University Press of America, 1985), p. 43. Post, in "Ravishment of Women," pp. 155–56 says that the judges were becoming ever more technical about the details in the appeals.

12. Bracton, 2, pp. 414–15, 417.

13. *Britton*, ed. Francis M. Nichols (Washington, D.C., J. Poyrne, 1901), Bk. I, chapt. xxiv, pp. 17, 55; *Fleta*, ed. Henry G. Richardson and George O. Sayles, Seldon Society, 72 (London: 1953), Bk. I, chapt. xxxiii, p. 89; and *The Mirror of Justices*, ed. William J. Whittaker. Selden Society, 7 (London; 1895), p. 103; and Kittel, "Rape in Thirteenth-Century England," pp. 104–5.

14. *The Eyre of Kent Six and Seven Edward II, 1331–1314*, 1, ed. Frederick William Maitland, L.W.V. Harcourt, and W. C. Bolland, Seldon Society, 24 (London, 1910), p. 111.

15. In *Toward a Feminist Theory of the State* (Cambridge, Mass.: Harvard University Press, 1989), p. 173, Catharine A. MacKinnon gives the modern version of this piece of male folklore: the male incomprehension that, once a woman has had sex, she loses anything when subsequently raped.

16. *The Eyre of London, 14 Edward II, A.D. 1321*, 2, ed. Helen M. Cam, 2, Selden Society, 26 (London: 1968), pp. cxxiii–cxxiv, 91.

17. Wachs, *Crime-Victim Stories*, pp. 16–17.
18. *London Eyre*, 1, p. 90.
19. Wachs, *Crime-Victim Stories*, p. 16, and ch. 3, "The Traditional Style of the Crime-Victim Narrative."
20. Leona C. Gabel, *Benefit of Clergy in England in the Later Middle Ages*, (Northampton, Mass.: Smith College Studies in History 14, nos. 1–4, (Northampton, Mass.: 1928–1929).
21. *London Eyre*, 1, pp. 90–91.
22. Ibid., pp. 91–93. The other men were John Botoner le Clop', John Longchamp, Thomas Sherman of Walbrook, and John de Goys, locksmith. Nothing about them appears in the surviving records, and their occupations and surnames do not indicate a connection with a vintner or with French merchants. They appear in court in the Michaelmas term of 1320 through their attorney John Bernard, denying Reymund's accusation. A jury was summoned but did not appear in sufficient numbers in successive court sessions through 22 June 1321. The case reappeared in P.R.O. KB 27/246 m. 37d, 27/247 m.1, 27/248 m.80d. Either the jurors or the sheriff did not come. The case then disappeared from the record.
23. Ibid., pp. 90–91.
24. Ibid.
25. See Roy F. Hunnisett, *The Medieval Coroner* (Cambridge: Cambridge University Press 1961), pp. 55–74 for appeals before the coroners.
26. *London Eyre*, 1, p. 90. Cam found a mention of him in the *Calendar of Close Rolls 1318–1323*, p. 490, indicating that a Reymund de Lymoges, merchant of Bordeaux, was named on 16 August 1322 as an attorney for Reymund de la Brunye to prosecute a writ of arrest in the Chancery. He is mentioned as attorney for Reymund du Mas, 9 June 1321, in the *Calendar of Patent Rolls, 1315–1321*, but his name does not appear subsequently nor does it appear in the London records. He apparently was able to function as usual after the alleged rape.
27. *London Eyre*, 1, p. 90.
28. Wachs, *Crime-Victim Stories*, p. 16.
29. Post, in "Ravishment of Women," pp. 155, 159–60, notes that women were in any case being excluded from a role in appeals of rape.
30. Kittel, "Rape in Thirteenth-Century England," pp. 107–10.
31. Schneebach, "Law of Felony in Medieval England," 2, pp. 445–55.
32. Hanawalt, *Crime and Conflict*, pp. 59–66, 153.
33. Pollock and Maitland, in *History of English Law*, 2, p. 491, cites both Bracton and Glanville. Maitland says that "an appeal of rape was not infrequently a prelude to marriage." Post, in "Ravishment of Women," pp. 152–53, also argues this position with selected cases but not with statistics.
34. Kittel, "Rape in Thirteenth-Century England," pp. 105–6.
35. P.R.O. C1/45/24. Corporation of London Record Office, *Letter Book L*, p. 103.
36. Wachs, *Crime-Victim Stories*, p. 15.
37. Hunnisett, *Medieval Coroner*, pp. 106–7.
38. *London Eyre*, 1, pp. 87–88. Gravdal, in *Ravishing Maidens*, pp. 137–38, quotes French sources that express rape of young girls in much the same terms: "there in the cellar he forced her to go, against her will and by force, the said Perrete la Souplice. He threw her to the ground, and pulled down her underwear, and got on top of her, and forced himself against her private parts as hard as he could. And because she cried out, he beat her, struck her, and left her there."
39. *London Eyre*, 1, pp. 87–90.

40. Cam, *Eyre of London*, pp. xxiii–xxiv.
41. Bracton, 1, p. 147.
42. Schneebeck, "Law of Felony in Medieval England," pp. 445–60.
43. Ibid., pp. 464–67.
44. Gravdal, in *Ravishing Maidens*, pp. 125–28, also found that any excuse was a good one in terms of exculpating the alleged rapist in French court.
45. *Novae Narrationes*, Elsie Shanks introduction, pp. ix–xiii. See the case in pp. 341–44.
46. Gravdal, in *Ravishing Maidens*, pp. 131–40, notes that the descriptions in some respects parallel the pastourelle poems of rape: "I did not want to quarrel with her anymore, so I threw her on the grass. But when I tried to pull her legs apart, oh what a cry she let out. At the top of her lungs she cried aloud."
47. Barbara A. Hanawalt, "The Voices and Audiences of Social History Records," *Social Science History*, 15: 159–75.
48. Wachs, *Crime-Victim Stories*, p. 12. Gravdal, in *Ravishing Maidens*, p. 18, discusses the psychoanalytical literary theories that rape scenes in literature taught female audiences to enjoy the idea of male aggressiveness. Historical evidence for such a view is, of course, lacking.
49. *Bedfordshire Coroners' Rolls*, trans. Roy F. Hunnisett (Bedfordshire Historical Society, 41) pp. 27–28.
50. Gravdal, in *Ravishing Maidens*, chap. 4, discusses the sexual violence that was characteristic of the pastourelle, in which the knight deflowers the shepherdess. The undefended shepherdess was a standard of literature throughout medieval Europe, and therefore this is an instance where literature and history of rape must have intersected in forming the opinions of both men and women about rape situations.
51. MacKinnon, *Toward a Feminist Theory of State*, p. 238.

9

Men's Games, King's Deer: Poaching in Medieval England

Poaching is a game—a dangerous, thrilling game of hide-and-seek that has changed little over time. Poachers' boasting stories and newspaper accounts casually refer to poaching as play. In *The News and Observer* of Raleigh, North Carolina, for instance, an article on poaching comments that "in a way, it's a game the officers and hunters play: Both know their territory intimately, and often they know each other." A nineteenth-century poacher, a country man, filled a small book with stories of how he outsmarted both animals and gamekeepers. When an exasperated landowner finally allowed him to hunt, the poacher commented, "Now you've given me permission it won't be half as much fun."[1] Historians have traditionally looked at poaching as a legal problem or, more recently, as a continuing battle in class warfare pitting hungry country men against the landholding class.[2] While the spoils of poaching, particularly in eighteenth- and nineteenth-century England, did supplement poor men's diets and the act of poaching did encourage explicit inter-class tensions, their significance is far more basic to men's nature than a matter of simple economics. A poor man can put meat on the table by other means and can express class hostility through other avenues. The appeal of illegal hunting is that it is a manly game.

Using literary sources in combination with the thirteenth-century forest eyre cases,[3] this chapter investigates poaching as a game that reinforces male gender identity. Detailed descriptions, including dialogues of participants, make forest eyre cases a particularly rich source. The class element does not have a predominant place in this study because most of the cases involve members of the gentry, clergy, and nobility who illegally hunted the king's

This essay was first published in *The Journal of Medieval and Renaissance History*, 15 (1988): 137–48.

deer. Although these same groups engaged in political battles against the forest laws and their infractions can be seen as part of the thirteenth-century baronial revolts, this study focuses on the direct, local interactions between poachers and foresters. Furthermore, the offenses discussed here involve the taking of deer only, and not the lesser game or other trespasses against the vert (vegetation in the forests). While the main theme of this study is male gender identity, the evidence also indicates the reaction of Englishmen to their encounters with a first regular policing force. Arrests for other offenses such as felonies were made by the sheriff or bailiff acting on indictments or through citizen arrest. These officers and citizens did not go out looking for crimes; they reacted when crimes happened. The forest laws created the first officers who had a regular patrolling function and a territory that was their beat.

The poaching game is a complex one that is perennially played on a number of different levels and involves a multiplicity of symbolic meanings for the participants. Poaching has all of the elements of play that Johan Huizenga outlined in *Homo Ludens: A Study of the Play Element in Culture*: fun, sport, playing fields, players, and rules.[4] The players are the illegal hunters, the quarry, and the state or lord and their foresters. The playing ground is not simply the forest, but also the courts, the capital, and the battlefield. At their most basic, the elements of the poaching game are the same as those of hunting: knowledge of nature and woodcraft, the cunning of man against that of animal, reinforcement of gender identification, and the possession of a meat that society values highly, both for ritual and for status. To pursue these valued rewards in stealth and with bravado, man against cunning man, under risk of personal danger or death, and asserting freedom from authority, lends titillation to the hunt. The rules of the game are the same as those of hunting, but the poacher must outwit the forester as well as the quarry. He can shoot at both the deer and the forester.

The game centers on elements that define male identity. Women may participate in the legitimate hunts and they may receive stolen venison, but they can be neither poachers nor foresters. Few scholars have studied the cultural role of animal theft and poaching and yet, for pastoral and woodland economies, these illegal activities played a major role in men's lives. The anthropologist Michael Herzfeld calls his exploration of the male identity of sheep and goat stealers in the Cretan mountains *The Poetics of Manhood*.[5] To understand the elements of what he calls a "male discourse," this chapter analyzes separately the components of poaching: the origins and administration of game laws, the symbolic significance of venison and hunting in medieval culture, the delight in combining knowledge of nature with its violation, and the importance of poaching to male gender identity and social bonding. The study then brings these elements together by analyzing specific cases that show the nature of play between foresters and poachers.

THE FOREST LAW

Our game began when William the Conqueror established the royal forests in England. Of the many hardships and atrocities that he visited upon England, none seems to have impressed the general populace more than his forest laws. The *Anglo-Saxon Chronicle* quotes several stanzas of a rhyme that expressed the popular opinion:

> He made great protection for the game
> And imposed laws for the same,
> So that who so slew hart or hind
> Should be made blind.

> He preserved the harts and boars
> And loved stags as much
> As if he were their father.
> Moreover, for the hares did he decree that they should go free.
> Powerful men complained of it and poor men lamented it,
> But so fierce was he that he cared not for the rancour of them all.[6]

William's subjects perceived the new forest laws as brutal, arbitrary, and an infringement on their long-established custom of using the forest's various spoils to supplement their economy or to provide sport requiring special skills.

As Charles R. Young has pointed out, resentment increased under the Norman and Angevin kings.[7] By the thirteenth century roughly one-fourth of the land in England was turned over to royal forest, and in the process of creating homes for the king's deer, human dwellings were destroyed and people driven from the land. The economic complaints went beyond control of access to supplemental meat for the Englishman's diet, because the forest law also protected trees and other forest byproducts. Furthermore, forest administration required a set of laws and a judicial machinery that developed alongside common law but apart from it. Because the king mandated it rather than letting it evolve as did common law, it always contained an arbitrary element. Abuses of the forest law were common among kings and their officials. The *Dialogue of the Exchequer* commented explicitly: "The forest has its own laws, based, it is said, not on the Common Law of the realm, but on the arbitrary legislation of the King; so that what is done in accordance with forest law is not called 'just' without qualification, but 'just, according to the forest law.' "[8]

The population resented the harsh punishment for poaching, finding an imbalance in a law that punished the killer of a deer and the killer of a man in the same way. Although castration and blinding were replaced by fines in the thirteenth century, the change only provided kings with an opportunity to use forest laws to exact money from powerful subjects. King John, who abused many laws and customs, also abused the forest law. Thus, along with Magna Carta, the Forest Charter gradually became embodied in thirteenth-century statements of baronial rights and became part of the baronial complaints that fueled Simon de Montfort's rebellions. Part of the game against the forest laws, therefore, was a political one played at the council and on the battlefield.[9]

The Forest Charter of 1217 established the administrators of forest laws, and, therefore, the targets of hostility. The royal forests were put under the direction of two justices of the forest. Below these officials was a warden for each forest who administered forest law at the local level, hearing and determining less serious offenses (trespasses of grazing animals, cutting brush, killing lesser game) than the taking of venison or oak trees. The latter were reserved for the forest eyres. Foresters, both riding and walking, did most of the daily patrolling, along with their assistants, called "garçons." Their job was to arrest culprits caught in the act of poaching or find evidence for an attachment (arrest) when a poaching had obviously occurred. Foresters were normally appointees of the warden, but some inherited their positions and were called "foresters-in-fee." In addition, foresters usually had four verderers elected to office in the county court. These men were selected from among the men of standing who had lands within the forest. The verderers participated in the process of attaching suspects in the local forest court and also presented a roll of attachments to the justices in eyre. The forest eyre justices made infrequent visits, but the population hated them no less for it, probably because the continued surveillance by the various forest officials kept the enforcement very visible.[10]

Complaints of injustice can exaggerate a law's oppressiveness, and one wonders if this was not true of the forest laws. Charles Young has demonstrated that their administration was both corrupt and inefficient. Foresters often exploited their office, and one of the reasons for having verderers and inquiries about official conduct in the forest eyres was to uncover their misconduct. Their abuses included exploiting forest products for personal economic gain, keeping too many officials at public expense, and harassing the inhabitants on forest edges with extra charges for forest use or threatening to imprison them for poaching. A numerical assessment of cases in the forest eyres suggests that enforcement of the venison laws was lax. Offenses against the vert, including cutting wood and illegal pasturing, were much more common than poaching cases. With the yearly average of cases for venison in various forests ranging from two to eight, with four being the mean, it is apparent that more poachers were successful than those who were caught. By the thirteenth century, Young has concluded, the fines were levied according to the ability to pay. The wealthy paid heavily and the very poor were excused. Since the eyres were so infrequent—every seven years at best—it was common for the suspect to die or procure a pardon before the justices arrived. Still, one is haunted by the cases of poor men put into prison on suspicion of poaching and dying there, only to have their innocence proved later, or of innocent men hiding in the bushes at the approach of the foresters. People who could afford bail were released, and the poor could only be detained for a year and a day.[11] Although innocent men were routinely retained in prison before trial in criminal cases as well, forest laws were still regarded as more onerous.

The hatred of forest law came not because it was relentless in its efficiency and punishment, but because it encroached on one of the perceived rights of medieval men of all classes and status groups: freedom to exploit the natural environment. The presence of arbitrary and patrolling officials seems to have lent a particular fear and hatred to forest detentions. The enforcement of forest laws aroused a defiant game between law breakers and law enforcers, poachers and foresters, not present in other areas of the administration of justice, because it represented an invasion of male gender identity.

THE SYMBOLIC VALUE OF VENISON

The appeal of hunting forest animals, particularly the hart and the hind, derived in part from the festive significance of eating venison. No holiday celebration seemed complete without venison, and the incidence of forest violation increased before Christmas, Easter, and Whitsuntide. A wedding feast was all the more impressive when venison was served. Two young brothers, Walter and Nicholas, sons of Sweyn and Simon the woodward, were part of a friend's wedding party. They went into the forest on the wedding day and brought a deer to the bridegroom's house, where everyone feasted on it. Walter Paston wrote home saying that his baccalaureate feast went well even though the people who had promised to supply him with venison failed to produce it. Some of the suppliers of venison for special occasions were poachers who made considerable profit from their illicit kills.[12]

Although most people did not have the good fortune to celebrate special occasions with venison, everyone in society shared the ideal that it was the appropriate luxury for major festivals. Although not normally admitted to the dominant culture, Jews engaged in poaching as well. A party of some twenty Jewish men, mostly from Northampton, but including two from London, were on their way to a wedding in Stamford. On the way they poached a deer for the festivities. As with many poachers, however, the celebratory occasion was not the only motive for hunting, because on their way back from the wedding they took another deer. Their hunting methods differed from other poachers in that they observed Kosher laws. As was common for a wealthy fellowship traveling through the woods, they ran the deer down with their greyhounds. But, as the record observes, they killed it according to their own custom. While a boy held its feet, Mosse of Oxford cut its throat.[13]

For the prototypical medieval poacher, Robin Hood, the luxury of venison picnics in Sherwood forest is underscored by the addition of the fine white bread and good red wine—elite fare to accompany an equally prestigious meat. Indeed, new episodes in the "Gest of Robin Hood" always begin with Robin declaring that he plans to dine but will not eat alone. Accordingly, Little John goes off to Wattling Street to find a knight, abbot, sheriff, or even the king to dine with his master in the greenwood:

They [i.e., Robin and the knight] washed together before they ate,
And sat them down to dine,
And their meat it was of good red deer,
And plenty of bread and wine.

The king was invited to dine *al fresco* on his own deer.

And many a noble deer was slain,
Upon the king's own land.

Anon before our royal king,
Fat venison was set down.
The good white bread, the good red wine,
And the good fine ale and brown.[14]

The irony of the king being invited to a feast of poached venison and pilfered wine must have delighted an audience who hated the forest laws.

Because of venison's special status, when an animal died of murrain or some other disease or when it was found dead of wounds, the foresters were directed to give the food to the local poor or hospital.[15] Alms delivered in the form of such prized meat have been regarded as particularly efficacious for the health of the king's soul, but diseased or spoiled venison must have been only barely palatable to the beggars and lepers who received it.

The status symbols extended beyond the meat to the skills and instruments of poaching. While peasant poachers worked quietly with snares and traps, the majority of the poachers were gentry or of higher status, who possessed not only the accoutrements of hunting, but delighted in displaying their skill in using them.[16] Foremost among the prized equipment were highly trained hunting dogs—limers, bracelets, greyhounds, and mastiffs—whose expertise ranged from tracking to killing. The dogs were expensive because of their breeding and training. Owning one indicated not only wealth, but also the prestige of possessing a superior domestic animal that could outwit a wild one. Hunting dogs either tracked the deer or ran them down; the coup de grace came from the hunter's bow or spear. These hunting instruments varied in quality and luxury, but the chief status symbol was the ability to shoot well, because such virtuosity could only come from having the leisure to practice.

THE PLEASURE OF THE HUNT

To poachers, the meat itself, even considering the high regard in which it was held, was often secondary to the sport of procuring it. The meaning of the hunt went far beyond taking a deer, for a wide range of social and emotional experiences came together in the hunt, and poaching only intensified them. The match of woodcraft and cunning against the animals, the skill of the hunter and his dogs, the initiation of taking a first deer, the bonds of *camaraderie* in joint poaching expeditions, and the outsmarting of the foresters combined to intensify pleasure. Even when an economic motive such as hunger on the part of peasants or profit for men who sold venison entered into the hunt, the other pleasures of the hunt still obtained.

The pure enjoyment of woodcraft and match of cunning against both the buck and the foresters unfolds in the prologue to the *Parlement of the Thre Ages*. The narrator, a late fourteenth-century man of the North Midlands, must have had first-hand knowledge of hunting and describes the beauty of the wood in May, where he has gone to "werdesto dreghe" (try his luck) in taking a hart or a hind. He details the early morning woods with the mists rising, the jewel-like colors of the primroses, periwinkles, and daisies, the song of the cuckoo, and the movement of small, predatory animals; but amidst this woodland scene he is preoccupied with thoughts of stalking. Displaying his knowledge of woodcraft, he camouflages himself and his bow with leaves and hides behind a tree. Shortly he beholds a fine hart, full grown with five and six tines on his antlers, accompanied by a younger buck that attends to him. The hart, he observes, is "a coloppe (tasty treat) for a kynge."

The opportunity arrives for the poacher to test his cunning against the buck and his attendant soar (the younger buck). He ties the leash of his dog to a birch tree, and, taking note of the wind so that his scent does not betray his presence to the deer, he stealthily stalks the two bucks. Creeping to a sheltering crab apple tree he winds up his crossbow. But the soar becomes wary and the buck looks up from his eating. Despairing that he might lose his prey, the poacher stands without moving while gnats bite at his eyes; if he makes any motion, he says, "All my layke (sport) hade bene lost that I hade longe wayttede." His cunning prevails and the hart returns to eating. Loosing his bolt, he sends a dart through the left shoulder, a shot displaying the hunter's skill. The big beast brays and crashes through the forest. The hunter returns to his dog, unties his leash, and the dog tracks the noble animal to a cave where he lies, "ded als a dore-nayle."[17] The poacher has successfully matched his cunning of woodcraft against that of the hart.

Abruptly the mood of the poem changes. The noble beast becomes meat, the poacher becomes a butcher, and the game of skill becomes outwitting the forester. It would be brazen and foolhardy to carry a full deer carcass out of the forest in broad daylight, so the poacher must dismember it on the spot. The butchering is described in the same rich detail as was the lively throbbing of a misty May morning. He takes the hart by the head and drags him out of the cave. Turning the tines, he fixes them into the earth and "Kest up that keudart (raskel) and kutt of his tonge"—the prize of the hunt and usually given to the most prestigious male present. The skilled hunting dog receives the next reward: "Brayde (pulled) [owte] his bewells my breselet to fede." We are then treated to a complete description of the stages of butchering. I will not spare the reader the guts and shanks of the scene, or as one of my neighbors in the Indiana countryside might have put it, "the flaying of Bambi," since the literary example aptly sets the scene for the judicial cases that follow.

After master and dog receive the first rewards of the hunt, the poacher follows the standard procedures recommended in hunting manuals:

And I s[lit]te hym at the assaye to see how me semyde,
And hew was floresched (lined with fat) full faire of two fyngere brede.

Starting at the jowels, he slits down to the tail in one sweep. Then he rapidly skins the legs, moving on with his fist to separate the hide from the body working towards the backbone. Taking out his knife he cuts out the "corbyns bone and kest it a-waye." This piece of cartilage at the end of the breast bone is thrown to the crows as an offering of good luck and peace. Then,

I slitte hym full sleghely (deftly) and slyppede in my fyngere,
Less the poynte shoulde perche the pawnche or the guttys:
I soughte owte my sewet and semblete it to-gedire,
And pulled oute the paw[n]che and putte it in a hole.

After he removes and buries the innards, he decapitates the carcass and puts the head in a hollow oak tree so foresters cannot find it. He then slits the carcass up the back, quartering it, so that he can hide it in a hole covered with fragrant fern, heath, and hoarmoss to disguise the smell so that "no fostere of the fee schoulde fynde it ther-aftir." He leaves the scene because he fears discovery and waits to see what will happen.[18]

The juxtaposition of a wood's beauties teeming with life and the sudden death of one of nature's finest creatures would not have disturbed medieval audiences. The poem captures the joys of being in nature and the manly domination over it. The butchering is as sensuously satisfying, or perhaps even more so, than the earlier sensations in his description of a perfect spring dawn. To the listeners as to the author-cum-poacher, the kill is the denouement of a perfect day. The rich descriptions of the hunt are reminiscent of episodes in *Sir Gawain and the Green Knight*, while the joyous parallel of a spring day with manly slaughter recalls Bertrand de Born's "Joys of War" in which the blood and cries are those of the battlefield.

Occasionally, one has the sense that blood sport has overwhelmed the poachers. The Earl of Derby, for instance, was accused of killing more than two thousand deer in the forest of High Peak in the course of six years.[19] Legitimate royal hunts could kill hundreds of deer in a day, so the earl was indulging in familiar excesses. A particularly chilling account of a royal hunt juxtaposes Henry VIII's slaughter of deer with his simultaneous executions.[20]

Another part of the primordial male experience associated with hunting was the triumphal rite of passage in taking a first deer. Unfortunately, neither literary nor court cases refer to this aspect of hunting. The cases suggestive of the practice are those in which boys are taken with hunting equipment when they are out alone in the forest. For instance, foresters come across a boy, Roger the son of Lawrence of Wadenhoe, in the forest carrying a bow and barbed arrows, and a Welsh arrow. They arrest him on suspicion of poaching. John, son of Simon Cut, is taken with a dead fawn in his arms and put into prison for his trespass. After being in prison for a year, it is decided that he is too young to have killed the deer and that he must have found it dead.[21] Since most poachers hunted with dogs and with several companions or set snares if hunting alone, this type of case is our only hint of a very traditional ritual of manhood.

The pleasures of the hunt extended beyond taking deer to include male bonding among poaching party members. For adult males, particularly the nobility and higher clergy, poaching was both an entertainment and a way of solidifying connections with local clergy, knights, and even royal officials. Although all members of the nobility from earls to barons had the right to take a certain number of deer from the forests yearly,[22] they easily exceeded their limit. Since they routinely traveled armed for hunting and with their huntsmen and dogs, a trip through the royal forest could hardly be accomplished without some sport. Poaching added entertainment to the weary work of travel and provided a house gift of valued meat that was sure to please the host of the evening. Among the offenders who appeared in the Cannock Eyre of 1262 were Archbishop Boniface of Savoy of Canterbury and Archbishop Fulk of Sanford of Dublin who took four deer on their way through the forest. Hamo L'Estrange, who, as a Marcher baron, regularly traveled through the royal forests, was convicted for a number of offenses.[23]

In addition to the casual hunt, nobles relied upon poaching for entertaining themselves and their guests. Thus, "after dinner he [Richard of Clare, earl of Gloucester] went to his wood of Micklewood to take a walk, and there he caused to be uncoupled two braches, which found a hart in the same wood. And they chased it as far as the field of Desborough above Rothwell; and it was taken there." Among the hunting party were Robert de Mares (another nobleman) with his three greyhounds, Robert Basset (sheriff) with his three greyhounds, the forest verderer, and another man. Robert Basset got a side of the deer, perhaps to silence him. This distinguished company had all been to dinner with the Earl, and the presence of their hunting dogs at the dinner was not an accident but part of the planned festivities. One imagines that they stayed for supper as well and had venison.[24]

As in commission of felonies, men often paired off with fathers or brothers in poaching expeditions. Walter Capel hunted with his two sons, and Earl Beauchamp poached on several occasions with his two brothers and an uncle along with other members of his household. The familial bonding of poaching together leads me to repeat my observation about criminous families: "The family that slays together stays together."[25]

Among the local knights and lesser noblemen patterns of regular poaching parties emerge, indicating that poaching was more than a sport. In addition to family, the parties included the local clergyman, squires, pages, members of the *meinie*, local royal officials, and even forest administrators. Local nobles poached relatively frequently, with shifting members of the party. In all cases they repaired with their booty to the castle of the most powerful man among them, where they held a feast.[26] For the nobility, therefore, poaching was not simply a pastime but a way of strengthening local alliances and loyalties. Sharing in the hunt and the theft created strong bonds among the participants. They were bound by the need to cooperate in the hunt, to observe rules of prestige in conducting it (such as allowing the most powerful noble to take the first deer), and to protect the identity of the local notables.

Frequently included in these poaching parties were men so skilled in poaching that they were a valuable asset to the local nobles. The foresters knew these men well, and when a deer head, entrails, or legs were found they often gave orders to round up the usual suspects. To avoid easy recognition, some of these men wore masks. We have a very good description of one of these habitual offenders from a forester who explained to the court that he saw two evildoers in the forest who shot at him and a fellow forester with bows and arrows. They recognized one as Dawe, son of Mabel Sudborough, but "the other had a mask over his head, wherefore they suspected that he was William of Drayton, and more especially because he was accused before of an evil deed in the forest. The said William of Drayton is with no one constantly, and is sometimes in one place and sometimes in another."

Drayton appears to have hired himself out for his forestry skills. He dressed for his part, for, in addition to the mask, he wore a tunic of green hue. Four herdsman testified that while they were sitting at their dinner under a hedge he passed by with a party including eight greyhounds, two pages, two other men on foot, and a man on horseback carrying a fawn before him on his saddle.[27]

THE POACHERS VERSUS THE FORESTERS

It is time to pull together the elements of the sport of poaching and analyze the game between poachers and foresters. The scene has been set: armed foresters patrol on both foot and horseback; verders and the warden listen to gossip about the known poachers; the poachers, also armed, either move stealthily so as not to alarm the deer and the foresters or travel brazenly with their hounds and horses. The potential for violent confrontation is great, and both foresters and poachers may die in a shoot-out.[28] But the interaction between the poachers and the foresters is a subtle one that includes defiance, cooperation, and cunning. The two sides knew each other and socialized together. Their encounters could be teasing and humorous as well as violent.

The complex relationship of foresters and poachers clearly emerges in some of the case narratives. In the following case, for instance, the foresters were actually present at the poaching and were bribed:

> Colin of Geddington, Roger Caperun, walking forester, William Bolle, walking forester, William of Warmington, the younger, Russell, the man of Benedict the forester, and Robert, the keeper of Langley, were present at the taking of two beasts in the wood of Geddington; and that Hugh Kydelomb of

Geddington and Thomas the son of Roger of the same town were privey to the acts of the aforesaid evil doers, and had their share of the said beasts; and the aforesaid Hugh Kydelomb took the shoulders and two necks of the aforesaid venison to the house of the vicar of Geddington; and that the spenser of the said vicar received the said shoulders and necks for the use of his lord.

The practice was common and the English had a word for it, the *waith*, or custom of placating people who might inform the authorities by giving them parts of the animals taken. The case is similar to one in which the earl shared his prey with the sheriff. An ironic twist is that one of the pledges for the guilty foresters was a notorious poacher himself, Henry Tuke. The price of not paying the bribe can be seen in a case in which a man was riding through the forest and saw a deer caught with a snare. He sent his page out to ask for a piece of the meat, but when the page was refused, he reported the poachers.[29]

Open contempt for the foresters and the forest laws is also evident, particularly among the nobility, who routinely upheld their household poachers against the law. When Sir Richard, Earl of Gloucester, was planning to move from Huntingdon to Stamford he sent his cook, marshall, and a clerk of the chamber ahead of him to prepare his house. On the way they took a doe with the earl's greyhounds. When the foresters made known the incident to the Earl, he "vouched it well." Even members of the king's household casually took deer. Some lords used elaborate subterfuge to free household members. Gervais of Dene, cook to Sir John of Crakehall, was caught poaching and put into prison. Sir John, with the help of the bishop of Lincoln, organized some chaplains from Huntingdon and the bishop's bailiff to appear before the foresters with bell, book, and candle. They threatened to excommunicate the foresters if they did not release Gervais. The foresters responded that they were powerless to release Gervais, but the chaplains insisted that he was a clerk and should be released to his lord bishop. Adjourning to the prison, they took off Gervais's hat and found the crown of his head freshly shaven in the manner of a monk. The foresters suspected that it had been done that day in prison, but they released Gervais to the chaplains.[30]

The actual conversation between a poacher and a verderer is recorded in one case and indicates the contempt that the poacher had for this royal official. Richard Aldwinkle, a verder, had testified at an inquest that William, the spenser for Sir Nicholas of Bassingbourn, might have been involved in an incident in which poachers shot arrows at the foresters and escaped. Some time later Richard entered the forest looking for his pigs and came across William the spenser and greeted him:

William replied: "I do not greet you."
"Why not?"
"Because you stole our buck."
"Certainly not," he said.
"Richard! I would rather go to my plough than serve in such an office as yours."

William insulted the verderer by saying that it was worse than being a peasant to have an office that interfered with poaching. He set up an inversion
of guilt by accusing the verderer of "stealing" the buck.[31]

A few cases contain explicit political protest against forest laws. Master
Robert le Baud of the Hospital of Huntingdon came and complained that
the king ought not to have the right to attachments for vert and venison.
The record says that his chatter, *propter garulacionem suum*, interfered with
the functioning of the court and he was imprisoned until he paid 13s. 4d.[32]
When news of Henry III's death reached the West Midlands, some of the local gentlemen celebrated by taking their greyhounds and bows and arrows
into the forest for the day "with clamour and tumult."[33] Here the political
protest in poaching combined with the pleasures of the hunt.

Symbols of manhood and sexuality played a dominant part in the interaction between foresters and poachers. When the poachers managed to
tie up the foresters, they took from them their symbol of office, their horns.[34]
Horns, of course, had sexual connotations and appear in the cuckold's horns.
Thus taking the horns of office (hunting horns) was a way of emasculating
the foresters by literally removing their potency. Poaching thus set up a
struggle for male domination of the forest.

The nobleman, Simon Tuluse, devised even more elaborate and insulting symbols. He and a group of his household and neighbors were on a
poaching spree that lasted three days and earned them a kill of eight deer.
On the last day, when they had already killed three deer, Tuluse cut off the
head of a buck. He "put it on a stake in the middle of a certain clearing, which
is called Harleruding, placing in the mouth of the aforesaid head a certain
spindle; and they made the mouth gape towards the sun, in a great contempt
of the lord king and of his foresters." At the inquisition it was stated that it
was the head of a doe, and he put a billet (club or stick) in its throat.

Whether it was a spindle or a stick, the gross sexual insult is apparent
and it took the form of a sexual inversion. The male animal had a woman's
symbol—a spindle—in its throat, and the female had a male symbol—a club.
If the first version is correct, the action was premeditated, for no man would
have been carrying a spindle—the preeminent symbol of the female role in
medieval society—on a poaching party. The symbolic overtones suggest sexual inversion, with the buck's throat representing the vagina and a female
implement the penis. As we know from the *Parlement of Thre Ages*, the tongue
would have been removed. Turning the head toward the sun was also an
insult, perhaps their defiance in acting in open daylight rather than under
cover of night. The foresters saw the insulting message, but when they tried
to attach them, Tuluse and his gang shot arrows at them and boldly carried
off the venison in a cart.[35]

The combination of hunting and male sexuality was a common literary
theme. Even the very terms have parallels: the hunter takes a deer as a man
takes a woman. Among the most obvious literary examples are Henry VIII's
hunting poems. Designed for entertainment, the poems dwell on the double entendre of the hunter as a man stalking the doe qua woman:

> Sore this dere strykyn ys,
> And yet she bledes no whytt;
> She lay so fayre, I cowde nott mys;
> Lord, I was glad of it!

Others play upon the theme of the jolly hunter and his potent horn:

> Wherefor shuld I han up my horne
> Upon the grenwod tre?
> I can blow the deth of a dere
> As well as any that ever I see;
> I am a jolly foster.

Lady Venus, he tells us, sent him out hunting.[36]

We may now draw some conclusions about the significance of poaching for medieval English males. The act was a complex one involving the assertion of rights, political protest, reaction to policing, and pursuit of pleasure and meat. At its most fundamental, it powerfully reinforced male gender identity.

The men of England, whatever their class, perceived the poaching laws as an encroachment on their ancient rights to serve venison on special occasions and to hunt for the pleasures of the chase. For the upper classes the hunting rights were also entwined with political rights and privileges. Even given the risks of being caught, imprisoned, and fined, nobles and clergy traveling through the forests and peasants and knights living on their edges made free with the king's deer. In this regard, poaching was an assertion of independence and an act of private rebellion.

An important difference exists, however, between merely breaking an unpopular law and defying the king and his officials. In large measure the enforcement of the forest laws set up the conflict. The royal foresters were England's first policing force that had a regular beat and made routine rounds. Sheriffs, coroners, and bailiffs arrived after a crime was committed or not until an indictment directed arrest, but foresters went out patrolling and looking for potential offenders. With their horns, they were a highly visible symbol of the hated laws, and they had authority over noble and commoner alike. Furthermore, the procedure upon finding a dead animal or evidence of poachers was the same as that used in the case of homicide or some other bootless crime: to hold an inquest and clap the suspect in prison. This practice tended to equate deer and humans under the legal system. The unusual arrangement of having officials on the spot to enforce unwanted legislation set up that remarkable game between forester and poacher. It was a hide-and-seek in the woods with poacher stalking animal and forester stalking poacher.

The most fundamental element in poaching, however, was and still is the expression of male gender identity. Poaching permits all of the same challenges and skills of hunting, but adds elements of stealth, danger, violence, sexuality, and assertion of independence. Not only does the act of poaching offer opportunities for the assertion of manliness, but so too does the recounting of the exploits.

One can well imagine that the poacher who successfully eluded the forester enjoyed telling the story to his cronies at the local tavern or crowed over his hunting prowess and cunning at the lord's or bishop's banquet table. His status might turn heroic if he were detected and had to use violence, or his craftiness might be immortalized in explaining how he negotiated a compromise by bribes. Tuluse must have relished recounting his clever sexual inversion and how that was the ultimate insult to the impotent foresters. It is easy to appreciate the sense of ironic enjoyment that the audience of the *Gest of Robin Hood* must have felt when the king was served his own venison. Even without the white bread and red wine the illicit meat served to the licit king would have been a delicious inversion.

It may appear strange that the poachers' clever ruses are preserved among the documents generated by those called upon to enforce the game laws, and one may wonder if the foresters did not have equivalent tales of outwitting poachers. One must remember, however, that the cases in the forest eyres record the triumph of officialdom over poachers. It is always more satisfying to arrest a wily adversary than a docile or stupid one. The very recounting of a poacher's daring makes his capture more valued. Thus for the enforcers as for the culprits, the game was an opportunity to display male virtuosity.

NOTES

1. *The News and Observer*, Raleigh, N.C., 3 Jan. 1988, pp. 1A, 8A; *A Victorian Poacher: James Hawker's Journal*, ed. Garth Christian (London: Oxford University Press, 1961), p. xxi.
2. See Edward P. Thompson, *Whigs and Hunters: The Origins of the Black Act* (New York: Pantheon Books, 1975); and Douglas Hay, "Poaching and the Game Laws on Cannock Chase," in *Albion's Fatal Tree: Crime and Society in Eighteenth-Century England*, ed. Douglas Hay, Peter Linebaugh, Edward P. Thompson (New York: Pantheon Books, 1975), pp. 189–253. Roger B. Manning, in *Hunters and Poachers: A Cultural and Social History of Unlawful Hunting in England, 1485–1640* (Oxford: Clarendon Press, 1993), has by far the most sophisticated analysis. His book was published after this article, and is therefore not included.
3. In *The Royal Forests of Medieval England* (Philadelphia: University of Pennsylvania Press, 1979), (pp. 99, 118–21), Charles R. Young presents tables and graphs that indicate the uneven preservation of the forest eyres. The material is too sporadic for reliable trend analysis or even ascertaining the number of cases in a typical year. The cases are, therefore, more appropriate for a content analysis.
4. Boston, 1955.
5. Michael Herzfeld, *The Poetics of Manhood: Contest and Identity in a Cretan Mountain Village* (Princeton: Princeton University Press, 1985). I am indebted to Michael Herzfeld for his several readings of this chapter and for his many helpful suggestions in interpretation.

6. *The Anglo-Saxon Chronicle*, ed. Dorothy Whitelock (London: Eyre and Spottiswoode, 1961), pp. 164–65.
7. Young, *The Royal Forests*, pp. 3–32.
8. Ibid., p. 22.
9. Ibid., pp. 60–73.
10. Ibid., pp. 74–113. See also Nellie Neilson, "The Forests," in *The English Government at Work, 1327–1336*, I, ed. James Willard and William A. Morris (Cambridge, Mass.: Medieval Academy of America, 1940), pp. 394–467; and the introduction to *Selected Pleas of the Forest*, ed. G. J. Turner, (London: Selden Society, 13, 1901).
11. Young, *The Royal Forests*, pp. 103–7.
12. Jean Birrell, "Who Poached the King's Deer? A Study in Thirteenth Century Crime," *Midland History*, 7 (1982): 19; Turner, *Selected Pleas of the Forest*, p. 36; Henry S. Bennett, *The Pastons and Their England* (Cambridge: The University Press, 1922), p. 107.
13. Birrell, "Who Poached the King's Deer?", p. 19.
14. *A Lytell Geste of Robin Hode*, ed. J.M. Gutch (London, 1847), Fytte, p. 228 and Fytte VII, pp. 286–87.
15. See *Select Pleas of the Forest*, pp. 82, 83, for examples.
16. Young, in *The Royal Forests*, pp. 107–8, cites a study that indicates that one half of the poachers engaged in poaching for sport and the other half for meat.
17. *The Parlement of the Thre Ages*, ed. M.Y. Offord, (London: The Early English Text Society, 246, Oxford University Press, 1959), pp. 1–2. See also the informative notes that draw from contemporary hunting manuals.
18. Ibid., p. 3. At this point the poem becomes a dream sequence on the moral ills of England. The poaching prologue is an odd introduction to the rest of the poem and may be a protest against the forest laws.
19. Young, *The Royal Forests*, p. 106.
20. *The Lisle Letters*, ed. Muriel St. Clare Byrne (Chicago: University of Chicago Press, 1981), 6, p. 177. These letters describe a vast hunt staged by Henry VIII in which 240 stags and does were taken in one day and that the feat was repeated the next. The editor draws an unforgettable parallel between this hunt and the reign of terror following the Pilgrimage of Grace that was going on at the same time in the north.
21. *Select Pleas of the Forest*, pp. 29, 82, 90. Young noblemen appeared with servants rather than alone. Thus Thomas Basset, the son of Sir Ralph Basset of Weldon, and two attendants were arrested on suspicion because four deer limbs had been found in a ditch. See also p. 89.
22. Ibid., p. xli.
23. Birrell, "Who Poached the King's Deer?", p. 11.
24. Turner, *Selected Pleas of the Forest*, pp. 34, 98–99.
25. Barbara A. Hanawalt [Westman], "The Peasant Family and Crime in Fourteenth-Century England," *Journal of British Studies*, 8 (1974): 16. Unfortunately, Lawrence Stone, in *The Family, Sex and Marriage in England, 1500–1800* (New York: Harper & Row, 1977), used this phrase without quotation marks, and thus many authors have attributed the line to him.
26. Turner, *Selected Pleas of the Forest*, p. 36; Birrell, "Who Poached the King's Deer?", pp. 12–13.
27. Turner, *Selected Pleas of the Forest*, pp. 97, 102. Dawe's brother was already in trouble with the law for poaching (pp. 29, 83). See also Birrell, "Who Poached the King's Deer?", pp. 13–14.

28. Young, *The Royal Forests*, p. 81.
29. Turner, *Selected Pleas of the Forest*, pp. 37–38. For other examples see p. 8, on which there is an account of two poachers giving a thigh to the servant of the sheriff who came across them; and p. 112.
30. Ibid., pp. 12–13, 34, 77–78. The Abbot of Pipewell also harbored poachers (see pp. 78–81). In a shoot-out between the foresters and the poachers, one of the foresters was hit by an arrow and died of his wounds. None of the poachers were caught because it was getting dark and they headed for the underbrush. But the foresters had a good opportunity to observe the dogs who were with the malefactors. Some time later they were guests at Pipewell Abbey, and while they were eating, they saw the greyhounds in the courtyard. The abbot had sheltered the poachers who killed the forester and then entertained his companions.
31. Ibid., pp. 100–102.
32. Ibid., p. 25. In "Between the Battles of Lewes and Evesham," Robert, Count of Ferrieres and his servants took four deer in a park that was in the custody of Peter de Montfort (see p. 40).
33. Birrell, "Who Poached the King's Deer?", p. 15.
34. Ibid.
35. Turner, *Selected Pleas of the Forest*, pp. 38–39. Stith Thompson, in *Motif Index of Folk Literature* (Bloomington, Ind.: Indiana University Press, 1955), does not list any comparable folk theme under deer, sun, spindle, throat, or poaching.
36. John Stevens, *Music and Poetry in the Early Tudor Court* (New York: Cambridge University Press, 1979), pp. 249–50, 400–401, 408–9, 410–11.

10

Narratives of a Nurturing Culture: Parents and Neighbors in Medieval England

A current trend in thinking about the problems of neglected children and unruly youth is to look more seriously at the community we have lost rather than the family we have lost. Recent newspaper articles speak of community members' inhibitions about taking any role in intervening with someone else's children for fear of lawsuits. Governments have increasingly stepped in where a more informal community of neighbors fear to tread. In studying the medieval world, scholars have assumed that it had a strong sense of community and corporate organization, generating not only cooperative action but also emotional loyalties. We who study medieval childhood have been as remiss in ignoring this simple truth about the past as have modern social commentators.

Medieval historians and others have focused too much attention on a one-cause battle—proving that a concept of childhood existed in the Middle Ages and thereby proving that Ariès, Stone, and the other early modern historians were wrong as usual.[1] By concentrating our attack on one front only, definitions of childhood, we have neglected the two-way relationship between parents and children, and we have overlooked entirely the importance of community in raising and protecting children. It is time to turn our attention toward the dynamics of the relationships among the three. We have followed Ariès too closely in trying to point to a clearly defined concept of childhood, to a parental attitude toward children that can only be loving if it is cast in the mold of twentieth-century sentimentality about childhood. Our interest in community responses to children and childhood has been limited to cultural expressions of love of children rather than to the disci-

This article was first published in *Essays in Medieval Studies: Proceedings of the Illinois Medieval Association*, 12 (in electronic issue, 1996): 1–21.

pline, training, and oversight the community might be willing to assume in rearing children.

The culture of nurturing was continually articulated in medieval sources ranging from coroners' inquests to Chaucer's "The Prioress's Tale" about the martyred little schoolboy. It is easy to ignore this simple value because it was repeated so frequently that it seems formulaic. In the "The Prioress's Tale," for instance, when her son fails to return home,

> This poure wydwe swaiteth al that nyght
> After hir litel child, but he cam noght;
> For which, as soone as it was dayes lyght,
> with face pale of drede and bisy thoght,
> She hath at scole and elleswhere hym soght.

When she finally finds him in a pit, "The Christene folk that thrugh the strete wente" gather around and quickly send for the provost.[2] The parents and the neighbors are the ones to seek out the missing children when they fail to appear, and it is they who undertake to protect the orphans and the vulnerable young people sent off as servants and apprentices. The presence of these important adults in children's lives as at their deaths escapes our attention because of their mundane frequency.

In this chapter I look at both record and folkloric sources such as the *Miracles of Henry VI*,[3] to show how a consistent, didactic narrative, reinforced by law, continually emphasized the theme of adult responsibility for children. Lessons for such a parental role are surprisingly absent in liturgy, penitentials, advice to parish priests, and sermons.[4] Instead, I argue, they were better and more frequently taught by lay recitations of miracles involving children, coroners' inquests into childhood accidental deaths, and the public application of laws that protected children. Both the narratives and the practice coincided to form coherent moral values for the protection of vulnerable children. Indeed, in the case of the late-fifteenth-century miracles of Henry VI, fourteenth-century coroners' inquests into the death of children, and the hagiography of child saints such as William of Norwich and Hugh of Lincoln, the narrative style is so similar that one detects a common topos for childhood violent death and for parental and community response.

THE NARRATIVES OF CHILDREARING

The official and popular demand for public narratives about children were numerous. Passing time on pilgrimage was certainly an occasion for pious tales about the child-saints Hugh of Lincoln and William of Norwich and probably also the miracles of Henry VI. Such narrative occasions extended to every type of trip. One of the miracles of Henry speaks of three late adolescents walking beside a loaded wagon occupying "themselves in their customary stories and in trifles (for thus they relieved the labor of their journey, and in a way shortened the distance of it)."[5]

More formal storytelling, however, revolved around various inquests. When the pious went to a tomb or a shrine, such as the tomb of Henry VI, to report a miraculous cure or when the clerical investigator came to inquire about the veracity of the miracle the whole story would be told again. But it would have been recounted and embellished many times in the twenty or so years before the cleric came to ask them to recollect the miracle. A retelling of the story, then, was not limited to the version that was preserved in a miracle book.

Likewise, when a child was found dead in a medieval village or town the coroner was called to investigate the death. Since there were four coroners in the county, it could take a day or so for one to arrive. Starting with the discovery of the body, the condition of the corpse, and the scene of the accident, the inquiries and hypotheses of the child's actions, the scene and hour of the death, the whereabouts of parents or other responsible adults must all have been thoroughly discussed and a story pieced together before the coroner appeared. The coroner arrived on horseback, as did his clerk, who would record the local people's testimony about the homicide, suicide, or misadventure (accidental death). The locals spoke in English and the clerk rendered this into Latin. The coroner's charge was clear: he must inspect the body by stripping it and turning it over to explore the extent, nature, and depth of the wounds and other evidence to establish the probable cause of death. If he suspected homicide, he had to find out who should be indicted. If death was accidental, he had to find out what caused it, assess the *deodand*, and collect that money for the king. The *deodand* was a gift to God collected from the value of the instrument that caused the death and, in the Anglo-Saxon period, used for prayers for the soul of the dead person. The Norman kings collected the money for their own uses. Solely examining the body would not yield the coroner all of this information, and so by law the adult males of the four surrounding vills in the countryside or the four neighboring wards in London were called upon to testify or offer verification of the story.[6]

All the elements of dramatic narrative were present at the inquest: A sudden death provided a conclusion to a tale that needed a beginning (an explanation); a big audience of interested speakers and listeners assembled; a recognized leader asked questions to structure the narrative; and someone recorded the story.[7] An investigation into a miracle was similar in many ways: a death and, in this case, a miraculous restoration to life; an audience of interested listeners and interlocutors; a clerk to structure the questions; and a record of the narrative.

In both the coroners' inquests and the miracles attributed to Henry VI, children were the central element in many of the narratives. Henry was associated particularly with children because he was born on St. Nicholas day, the patron saint of children.[8] Children are accident-prone, then as now, and the cases in both sources bear this out with details surrounding children's accidents, including the activity, cause, first finder, witnesses, hour, date, location, and so on. Thus both sources are rich for the study of childhood and the adults who assumed responsibility for them.

In law, twelve was the age at which children moved into adult ac-
countability for their criminal offenses, and at which male children became
members of a frankpledge (tithing group). The coroners had reason to record
this age, but they carefully recorded the ages of children even when they
were much younger and when they were victims of accidents rather than
suspects in homicide. People generally knew the names and ages of their
neighbors' children, and officials were concerned enough about young innocent victims of crimes to record details of their identities and manners of
death. This eager concern for recording children's ages down to the month
reveals a community fascination with childhood. The king did not require
information about how a child died or at what age because his sole interest
in accidental deaths was to collect the value of the *deodand*. The details
recorded in the coroners' inquests, therefore, reveal community values that
accorded special status to childhood. It was only in the second half of the
fourteenth century that the ages of adults gradually became part of the
record, but, again, not because the king required such information.

To understand the parallels between the coroners' inquests and the miracles, it will be helpful to juxtapose two examples, chosen for their similarities rather than their dramatic events. While the basic narrative is the same
in both, the miracle stories have colorful and emotional embellishments that
would not be appropriate to an official coroners' inquest. The resonances
between the two texts, however, is striking:

> Saturday before the Feast of St. Margaret [20 July 1322] information was
> given to the aforesaid Coroner and Sheriffs that a certain Robert, son of John
> de St. Botulph, a boy seven years old, lay dead of a death other than his
> rightful death in a certain shop which the said Robert held of Richard de
> Wirhale in the parish of St. Michael de Paternostercherch in the Ward of
> Vintry. Thereupon the said Coroner and Sheriffs proceeded thither and hav-
> ing summoned good men of that Ward and of the three nearest Wards, viz.:
> Douegate, Queenhithe, and Cordewanerstrete, they diligently enquired
> how it happened. The jurors say that when on Sunday next before the Feast
> of St. Dunstan [19 May] the said John (Robert?), Richard, son of John de
> Cheshunt, and two other boys, names unknown, were playing upon cer-
> tain pieces of timber in the lane called "Kyrouneland" in the Ward of Vin-
> try, a certain piece fell on the said John (Robert?) and broke his right leg.
> In the course of time Johanna, his mother, arrived, and rolled the timber off
> him, and carried him to the shop aforesaid where he lingered until the Fri-
> day before the Feast of St. Margaret when he died at the hour of Prime of
> a broken leg and of no other felony, nor do they suspect anyone of the death
> but only the accident and the fracture.[9]

The coroner recorded the age of the young victim, his activities, the close
presence of his mother, and the place of death as the shop of his father. Family, playmates, and community were near at hand.

The record of a miracle, on the other hand, invites much editorial comment but tells essentially the same story:

> I must not pass over without mention of an important miracle which, I am
> told, took place through the merits of the renowned King Henry some time

ago in Wiston, a Sussex town. For though I have known some of the dead
coming back to life, in spite of all reluctance of nature, at the Saints' interces-
sion, I can scarce restrain my pen: the greater the wonder which the mind
feels, the richer is the matter for discourse, although in my case the emotion
of my full heart is far greater than my capacity for writing the record. A girl
of three years old was sitting under a large stack of firewood, in the company
of other children of that age who were playing by themselves, when by a sudden and calamitous accident a huge trunk fell from the stack and threw her
on her back in the mud, pinning her down so heavily as to deprive her in-
stantly of the breath of life. It was not possible that the breath should remain
in her when her whole frame was so shattered; for the trunk was of such a
size that it could scarcely be moved by two grown men. You may be assured
that the horror of the sight soon scattered the company of the child's friends,
who forthwith ran to and fro in all directions, shewing that something unto-
ward had occurred by their screams or their flight, not by words. Perhaps it
was this warning which made the child's father come up to see what had happened: and he, looking from some distance off, could see that it was his little
Beatrice who lay stretched out there. Not a little alarmed, he hastened forward and, on drawing near and finding her already carried off by so cruel a
death, found his face grow pale, and his heart wrung with an agony of grief:
yet, lifting the log with some difficulty, he raised her in his hands. Then the
fountains of his eyes were loosed, and calling his wife, he put the poor corpse
in her arms. She took her unhappy burden and laid it on her bosom; and so,
almost fainting in her grief, and giving expression to it with heavy groans and
loud wailing, made for the church that stood hard by.

The account, which was later verified, went on to say that the mother invoked King Henry and vowed a pilgrimage to his tomb. Continued prayers
brought a breath of life to the child, and "she spoke to her mother, albeit
with difficult utterance, complaining of the pain she felt" and "when she
had drunk once of her mother's milk" she needed no other medicine.[10]

Both the coroners' inquests and the miracles are at pains to show the innocent nature of children in general. The coroner's reports speak of children
trying to pluck feathers or flowers from streams, playing with balls, or un-
dertaking tasks beyond their motor skills such as dipping bowls in streams
to get water.[11] The miracles make off-hand comments about childhood such
as: "The boy, given his liberty, was playing about somewhere, as boys will,
while his grandfather was all intent upon his work," or "The boy climbed
up a tree about ten o'clock in the morning, bent on some childish prank—
or perhaps birds'-nesting," or "The girl, careless and mischievous as children will be . . ."[12] None tries to paint a picture of holy innocence such as
that of the boy in "The Prioress's Tale" who merrily sings "O Alma Re-
demptoris" on the way home from school,[13] but then again the children in
these tales were not candidates for sainthood either.

The miracle narratives also make a central theme of devotion of parents
and neighbors when confronted with the loss of a child. The grandfather
who had gone to the mill with his curious grandson called for him and
searched all around until he found the boy in the mill race. Being too old to

remove him, "he made all haste to find the neighboring farmers, and collect all those whom he could get within a circuit of three furlongs." The efforts were unsuccessful until one of the onlookers, "bolder than the rest," accomplished the rescue. The parents arrived and the whole crowd fell into prayer to Henry. When a little girl accidentally hanged herself while her parents were away, the mother "called her fellow townspeople and neighbors from their houses, and, to be brief, in a short time a large crowd of both sexes had hurried into the house and were all bewailing the unfortunate mother's lot."[14]

The coroners' inquests indicate that neither the parents nor the community took children's accidental deaths lightly. Both the urban and the rural coroners' inquests show community censure of parents who left children with inadequate care. The rural inquests also suggest that child accidents were seasonal. For example, accidents involving infants and toddlers in the countryside occurred predominantly in the harvest months, when all able-bodied people were in the fields.[15] The times of day (21 percent in the morning and 43 percent at noon) for the accidental deaths of babies under one year of age coincide with times when mothers were particularly busy about the house. When they were not working with such intensity, however, parents tried their best to supervise their children, because villagers did not approve of the practice of leaving them alone. For example, jurors entered into the record that a child wandered outside its father's house and "was without anyone looking after him" when he drowned, and a two-year-old died when she was "left without a caretaker." Often, however, a caretaker was ill-equipped to mind a child. Maude, daughter of William Bigge, was left in the care of a blind woman while her mother was visiting a neighbor. When her mother returned, she found her daughter drowned in a ditch. Parents often entrusted their babies to the care of other children. Thus a thirty-week-old child was left in the care of a neighbor's three-and-a-half-year-old son. The attention span of other children in tending to their young brothers and sisters was obviously limited. William Senenok and his wife went to church on Christmas Day 1345, leaving their infant daughter, Lucy, in a cradle and in the care of their daughter Agnes, who was three. Agnes went out into the courtyard to play and the younger child burned. In another case villagers commented that a five-year-old boy who had failed to take adequate care of his brother was a "bad custodian."[16]

Those who are familiar with fairy tales will already have perceived that the typologies and the sorts of anxieties portrayed in them are close to the narratives related here. A Proppian analysis would see in this commonality of narrative a thread of similar functions. The reader must allow for the absence of some attributes of the fairy tale formula in the records because of their official nature, but, although the familiar villain (a witch or wicked stepparent) is usually not present, many other elements are. One finds members of the family absent on business, injunctions for good behavior ignored, guilt over innocent children endangered, and in some of the miracles the victim is deceived by the devil. One tale that Propp analyzes in depth relates specifically to the type of narrative with which we are dealing. A girl is charged by her parents to look after her younger brother, but after amusing him for awhile, she goes into the street to play and abandons her charge. The swan-geese abduct him. The horrified little babysitter goes on an adventure and recovers the child from a witch.[17]

Even the cadence of the fairy tale or ballad is caught in the miracle tales. Alice Newnett, a young girl, is dying of the plague and the curate is called to give extreme unction. He concludes that she is dead already and instructs her mother and other women to prepare her for burial and sew up a shroud. But the daughter suddenly sits up in her shroud and says, "Mother, have me measured with a tape longways and broadways, whence a candle may be made to King Henry's honor." The measurement made, the child is restored to health with all plague blotches gone. This folk custom of taking the measurements for a candle appears in other miracles and won the snide remarks of the cleric who investigated the miracles as being in the "fashion ignorant folk have."[18]

All elements of the tradition—fairy tales, true-life misadventures, miracles, and child saints' lives—were woven together to form part of a general culture of stories that articulated the dangers that children should be aware of, and cautioned adults on childrearing. Other narratives about childhood appear in other types of court cases such as proof of age of inheritance, London's orphan court, and ecclesiastical courts, but it is best to deal with this sort of evidence within the reality of the adult community and its commitment to childrearing. It is important to realize from the beginning, however, that we are telling both true stories and plausible ones.

NURTURING OF CHILDREN

The primary nurturer in a medieval English family was female rather than male, mother rather than father. The birth of a child occurred exclusively in the female domain. The mother, the midwife and her assistants, female friends and kin brought the child into the world, bathed it, swaddled it, and fed it.

The religious images of the time also reflect that society valued Mary as nurturer. The prevalent visual image of Mary was with the baby or child Jesus. Devotional literature and sermons refer to the comfort of this maternal scene, and even the popular carols express delight in the maternal role for Mary, comparing her with other mothers. Joseph's paternal role was weak by comparison. Beyond the spiritual models, nurturing in the early years of a child's life rested chiefly with women. It is they who would nurse or feed the baby, wash and dress it, and soothe its crying. Early socialization in terms of talking, training, and walking fell mostly to women, either mothers or other females around the house.

To say that women were the primary nurturers does not mean that children did not enjoy the affection of both parents, as the coroners' rolls indicate. In accidental deaths, the first finder of the body was often recorded. Practice varied from county to county, and some seem to have preferred to designate someone in the village as the "official" first finder. But in 268 cases of rural accidental deaths of children twelve and under during the four-teenth century, kin were the first finders. Of these first finders, 51 percent were mothers and 39 percent were fathers. Brothers and sisters constituted 3 percent each, and male and female kin made up 2 percent each. When the first finders are divided by the sex of the child, fathers are more likely to appear as first finders of their male children. Thus, in 43 percent of accidents among boys, the father found the body compared to 33 percent of the acci-dents among girls. The mother was first finder in 45 percent of the cases in-volving boys and 59 percent of the cases involving girls.[19] In the London ac-cidents, the mother was the first finder in all cases (but there are only a dozen cases).

One must avoid the temptation, however, to rush to the conclusion that fathers cared more for their male children than their female children or that there was a special bond between mothers and daughters, because the pat-tern of place and activity of accidental deaths dispels such conclusions. In traditional societies the division of labor between the sexes was determined not only by the work that they did, but also by the space in which they worked. In peasant society men did the construction, road work, digging in marl pits, and, above all, the field work. For most of the day, particularly during planting and harvest seasons, they were outside the village and away from their children. Women, on the other hand, not only took care of the children but also swept out the houses, cooked, brewed, looked after the do-mestic animals, tended the garden and fruit trees. Those activities kept them around the house and the village and, therefore, with their children.[20]

The activities of the children who died from misadventure also indicate the spatial division of labor. Of the fifty-eight children under one year of age appearing in the coroners' inquests, 33 percent died in fires in their cra-dles. The percentage drops to 14 percent for one-year-olds and to only 1 per-cent for two-year-old children. Unattended babies who were not in cradles also died in house fires; 21 percent of their deaths occurred in this circum-stance. By one year old, however, babies were actively adventuring and even walking. Forty-six percent of the victims were described as playing with wa-ter, pots, fire, and with other children, and 13 percent were described as walking when the accident occurred. As in modern accidental-death statis-tics for children this age, the baby boys tended to be more active and ag-gressive at play (63 percent of the boys' accidents compared to 54 percent of the girls' accidents).[21] Given the sexual division of labor, the space in which women worked, and assumptions about nurturing, mothers were most likely to be the parent nearby when these infants suffered their acci-dents.

By the age of two and three one can see that the children were re-sponding to the role models around them and identifying with parental work and space. Little girls were already prone to accidents that paralleled their mother's routine, working with pots, gathering food, and drawing water (17.2 percent of their fatal accidents), even though these accidents only involved playing at these tasks. For instance, a two-year-old girl tried to stir a pot of hot water but tipped it over on herself.[22] The boys were more actively involved in play and observation of men working. One three-year-old boy was following his father to the mill and drowned; another was watching his father cut wood when the ax blade came off the handle and struck him.[23] Identification with the work roles of the parents became stronger as the boys and girls matured. Boys herded, imitated their fathers' games, and rode the plow horses to water them, while girls gathered herbs and fruit, helped with cooking and brewing, fetched water from the well, and did other tasks performed by their mothers.[24]

Thus it seems inappropriate to assign value judgments to the motivations of the first finder. A more prosaic assessment is that the children's bodies were found by the parent who was physically closest. Since boys were following their fathers about from the ages of two and three, the likelihood that a father would be first finder of his son's body after an accident increased. The evidence suggests strong gender-linked bonds, but not necessarily value-laden preferences. Nothing suggests that fathers did not love and value their daughters equally or even more. They were, however, engaged in training their sons to assume their work and roles.

As the children became more mobile, the community began to play a larger role in their care and socialization. Again, the coroners' inquests indicate a pattern not only of mobility, but also perhaps of visits and even of childcare arrangements. The majority of fatal accidents suffered by toddlers (49 percent) still occurred at home, but 18 percent occurred in another person's home, 20 percent in public places, and 12 percent in bodies of water. As one looks at the places of death for children, the number that happened outside the home increased as children's ages increased, but even adolescents were more likely to meet misadventures in their homes.[25]

While the coroners' inquests are mostly from the fourteenth century, the miracles are from the late fifteenth century. The spiritual genre elevates the role of parents in the nurturing of children and adds dramatic, emotional outpourings to enhance the narrative. The sample size is smaller for the miracles, but it shows that the father was the first finder of the body after a child's fatal accident in two cases, the mother in three, and the parents jointly in four cases. Kin and neighbors found the body in four cases. A second variable is added by the chief intercessor with King Henry: eight are mothers, two fathers, and eight the parents jointly. Neighbors initiated the prayers in eleven of the revivals. The numbers according to the sex of the restored victims are very evenly distributed: 21 males and 19 females.[26] Again, a sex bias is not apparent in parental or societal nurturing of children.

Fewer children died of accidental deaths in the city than in the countryside. In part, this was because European urban centers had fewer children. Marriages were delayed until a woman had accumulated a dowry from wages and a man had established a business or employment. There was also a high percentage of unmarried young people in the population. Furthermore, urban centers were unsanitary environments and less healthy than the countryside for children as well as for adults. Thus infant mortality was high. But the coroners' inquests indicate another reason for the lower number of accidental deaths. Paradoxically, London children were probably better supervised, even though their risks of dying from disease were greater than in the countryside. The child care may or may not have been organized, but the streets and houses were crowded with adults going about their business or pleasures. Parents worked in shops located in their homes, as we have already seen in one London case, and so they were able to supervise their children, rather than leave them for periods to go to the fields or attend to domestic animals. In London, in contrast to the countryside, many of the houses had servants or tenants who lived with the family or in rented rooms. It was easier to protect London children from their own disastrous adventures because there were more eyes watching and hands restraining.

Childrearing as a community venture on the London streets appeared both in court cases and in the miracles. Thomas Seint John, for instance, had to prove that he was of age in order to claim his inheritance. He called upon the usual round of people present from his early years: his godmother, the curate who had taken over the year after he was baptized, the husband of his nurse, his first schoolmaster, an apprentice of his father who knew Thomas was six when he arrived, and a neighbor who remembered that his younger brother was a playmate of Thomas.[27] Such touching scenes also appear in the miracles, as in the case of Miles, the son of William Freebridge living in Aldermanbury in London. Miles, nine months old, was being carried about by a somewhat older boy who had given him a circular pilgrimage badge of St. Thomas to play with: "anon, as is the way of such, he must put it into his mouth, and, since children love nothing better than swallowing things, he had no sooner got it in his mouth than he would have it in his belly."[28] Like the little boy in the "Prioress's Tale," who begged an older schoolboy to teach him a hymn as they walked home from school, Miles had an older boy accompanying him.[29] With the presence of traffic in streets and the absence of strollers, children in London must have been carried, lifted, and held in their early years more often than were children in the countryside.

London parishioners and neighbors often put their own lives on the line when they intervened where children were involved. For instance, John de Harwe, a porter, was going about his business in the street, when a young esquire came riding through at too fast a gallop and knocked down a mother and child. John took the bridle of the horse and warned the man to ride more carefully or he would kill a child. The esquire drew his sword and killed the well-intentioned neighbor.[30]

The move to reprimand carelessness also appears in one of the miracles. A small girl was wandering in the streets, "as children will," about eleven o'clock on the eve of Corpus Christi when a servant in the employ of nuns drove over her with a cart. "Because he drove with little prudence or care, the whole weight of the cart ran over the poor child . . . so that it left her young body shattered on the ground, well-nigh as flat as a pancake." The neighbors came to see the calamity and the distraught mother ran after the carter with "loud and reproachful cries." A neighbor woman had the presence of mind to called on Henry to revive the child.[31]

Because of the widespread assumption that infanticide was common in the Middle Ages, we cannot leave the issue of parental and communal attitudes toward nurturing without assessing the issue. Evidence of active infanticide is difficult to find in medieval English court records. Of the more than 4,000 cases of homicide that I have read in the coroners' inquests and criminal indictments, I have only found four cases of infanticide.[32] The Church took an interest in the newborn child and prescribed penances for mothers who killed them. But studies of church court records reveal that here, too, cases of infanticide were rare.[33] The accidental deaths of seventy-eight children under the age of one in the coroners' inquests do not indicate a pattern of willful destruction. The majority of them died in fires in their cradle or in the house, thus indicating that they were being cared for rather than exposed or drowned. If infanticides were being concealed by accidental deaths, then one would expect a higher proportion of female infants to appear among the cases, but the ratio between the sexes is quite close, with males suffering somewhat more accidents, as we have seen; the miracles reflect a similar pattern.[34]

A CULTURE OF OVERSIGHT

The sources that we have looked at so far speak of voluntary care and concern on the part of the family and community. No laws required parents to care for their children or for the community to come to the aid of children in distress. Orphanages were non-existent, foundling hospitals rare, and child assistance programs centuries away from being created. Church instructions dwelt more on honoring father and mother than on protecting children from their parents. The record sources and miracles speak of children becoming involved in accidents through no fault of the parents. If reports of infanticide are rare, those of child abuse are even rarer in the records.[35] Nonetheless, the popular culture of nurturing children did, in some instances, translate into legal protections. Furthermore, the concern of parents and friends did not end when children moved away from home. Intervention through various formal and informal means are observable, particularly in London, where so many young people came to further their fortunes at a far distance from their families.

In the absence of archival research, historians have allowed the opinions of a fifteenth-century Italian businessman to color their conclusions about both parental and community concern with children. With emotional language he argues that through "want of affection" the English put their male and female children out to "hard service" in other people's households when they are only seven to nine years of age, and that they bind them to seven to nine years of service in which they perform "the most menial offices." Even the wealthy put their children out and accept "strangers" into their own houses. The English respond that they send their children off to other families so that they can learn better and be disciplined. If they undertook such an important trust themselves, they would not be able to beat the poor youngsters sufficiently to see that they are well raised. True to his business background, the Italian opines that the English can get better service from strangers than from their own children.[36]

His report raises several problems about childrearing that need further elaboration. One is the extent of fostering; a second is his claim of the abandonment of English children to the tender mercies of surrogate parents; and a third is the late medieval English concept of looking after children's best interests or a love for children.

Actual fostering, that is, placing young children with another family, was common only among the nobility. Peasant children stayed with their natal families until they married or, perhaps, had a period of service or apprenticeship. Since the peasantry were the vast majority of the population (about 90 percent), fostering was not the most common experience in England. Urban children, few though they were, went into apprentice or service positions in their early to late teenage years. Some children, of course, also went to various schools. For his analysis, the Italian would have ignored the peasants and looked only at the urban elite and nobility. In any case, fostering arrangements did not mean abandonment of children by parents or by community.

An obvious place to look for an official culture of oversight is at the protection of orphans with property. In medieval society orphans might be defined as having lost both parents, but usually orphan status occurred with the loss of the father (the chief source of property and wealth for the family). Our modern inclination would be to argue that single-parent children are not really orphans and, furthermore, that orphans with inheritances are not the first who need oversight and official protection. But the medieval world saw the problem differently. It was not a matter of seeing a poor orphan as a person of no consequence, but rather one of legal issues that included the right to inheritance for all classes. A poor young orphan deserved the attention of charity, but a propertied orphan was more likely to be victimized.

Feudal custom, of course, gave the overlord protection (or perhaps more accurately, the use) of a vassal's orphaned children and their inheritance. The lord was obligated to see that the person and the property of the ward prospered and to punish those guardians who abused either. The abuses of wardship are well known and perhaps better chronicled than the interventions and rectifications. Selling the sheep or cutting down timber stands that belonged to his ward were often too tempting for a guardian of underaged children to resist. Lords found that they could make an immediate profit by selling off wardships. Abuses of all kinds were hard to control, although recourse to the law had a good measure of success. Still, as Sue Sheridan Walker's work has shown, young wards usually ended up in the care of their mothers even if their property went into other hands for the duration of the wardship.[37]

London law took care to protect children from unscrupulous relatives, stepparents, and guardians. The orphans of artisans and merchants, along with their inheritances, were put into the hands of the mayor, aldermen, and chamberlain of London. The law stated that the mayor was responsible for the goods and well-being of orphans, insuring that their persons, their wealth, and their marriages were arranged without detriment to them or their estates. With a skeptical regard for the morals of mankind, the London law stated that no one could become the guardian of orphans who could profit from their deaths. Because most of the wealth orphans inherited came from their fathers, and because an older brother or the father's uncle would be in direct line to inherit if the orphan died, the mother was usually recognized as guardian of the bodies of her children.[39]

An orphan's material wealth, however, was usually not awarded to the care of the mother because, again, London law stipulated that the inheritance along with a fair increase from its investment should be returned to the orphan upon his or her reaching the age of majority. Since women were seldom in the market place, this meant that the goods were given to the charge of a man. If the widow remarried, however, the children and their inheritance were given into her care and that of their stepfather. But here again, law protected the children. The person, usually the stepfather, assuming the investment of the orphans' inheritance had to produce sureties, and if the contract was not honored the sureties themselves would have to come up with the money for the payment to the children. Furthermore, to protect against a guardian marrying off the children and reaping a reward for the marriage, the mayor was given the right to arrange marriages that were not to the disparagement of the orphan's social and economic status. The laws were enforced, as we know from court cases that were brought against those who broke the contracts.[39]

Londoners placed their trust in the laws guarding their orphans, in the honesty of their officials, and, for men, in the devotion of their wives. Most citizens left the designation of guardians to custom and to the mayor. In the late medieval Husting Wills only 210 men (out of over 1,500) designated guardians for their children,[40] but their overwhelming preference (55 percent) was for the mother to assume this role. After her, the testator looked to friends (27 percent), kinsmen (8 percent),[41] executors (6 percent), and finally, apprentices, servants, and churchmen.[42]

The mayor followed the same pattern when he selected guardians for the citizen's orphans. The mother was the favored guardian: 30 to 57 percent of the children were in the care of their mothers, either alone or with a stepfather. This percentage obtained during the plague years of 1350–88, when a number of the mothers must have died of the plague. On the whole, the mayor and aldermen seem to have made an attempt to keep the children with kin. Until the onset of plague, 61 percent of children were placed with kin. The percentage fell to 36 in the worst of the plague years and only gradually recovered to 54 by the middle of the fifteenth century. For city officials, therefore, the nurturing of children by their kin was high in their priorities in granting wardship.

In rural areas as well men favored their wives as guardians of their children: 65 percent made their wives executors and left their children in their care. In manorial courts a husband could make such an arrangement at marriage by entering the land in the wife's name as well as his own, so that she would automatically come into control of the land and children should he predecease her while the children were still minors. As in the urban community, the juries of neighbors in manorial court oversaw the provisions for widows and orphans. Such a community actively participated in the welfare of its children.[43]

In the three classes we have looked at so far—the nobility, the peasantry, and the bourgeoisie—orphaned children had inherited property and generally had kin who could look after their interests. Did oversight only mean oversight of wealthy children? The London laws clearly limited their jurisdiction to children of London citizens, but they protected destitute orphans as well as wealthy ones. The city Chamberlain became responsible for the rearing of poor, young citizens. Thus when Walter, son of Richard the cook, appeared as a vagrant orphan the chamberlain provided for his upbringing. The mayor and other city officials showed their concern for abuses of noncitizens' orphans by hearing their cases and trying to determine if there was a way to claim the child as a citizen. If they could not so claim, they were powerless to do anything to rectify the matter.[44] In the countryside, the prevailing ethos dictated that the villagers take care of orphans if there were no immediate kin. The value of extra hands to work in the fields was of use to wealthier households and worth the investment in childrearing.[45] One cannot say that all orphans were taken care of, and, perhaps, one cannot be as optimistic as John Boswell's assessment in *Kindness of Strangers*,[46] but official culture reinforced the societal assumption that orphaned children should be cared for.

The other major "fostering" arrangements were apprenticeships and service. Such contracts meant that the children or adolescents left their natal homes and moved into those of their masters. Many of these young people were very far from home. Of the 536 apprentices listed in the chamberlain's register from 1309 to 1312, 185, or 35 percent, had names with a place reference that was certainly from outside London. Another 221, or 41 percent, had surnames that indicated an origin outside London. The rest of the names were occupational and so are hard to identify. By the middle of the sixteenth century, 83 percent of the apprentices were from outside London, with half coming form northern and western counties.[47] Did this imply the abandonment of children to a stern taskmaster with no hope of succor? Chapter 11, *"The Child of Bristowe* and the Making of Middle Class Adolescence,"* shows how close this relationship could be.

When the relationship soured, the mayor and aldermen, along with the guild wardens, intervened, punishing masters who broke the contract or abused the apprentice and disciplining recalcitrant apprentices. So that the contracts and their terms were publicly known, the city enrolled apprentices and maintained courts that would intervene if the contract was broken. Apprentices or their friends could appeal to either the specific guild or to the mayor for redress. A common complaint was that the master was not teaching the apprentice his trade. For instance, John Malmayn of Jerking complained that his master, John Coggeshale, a haberdasher, had agreed to a ten-year apprenticeship contract with him, but after four years he had learned only to make points and had been clothed only in a russet gown and an old "paltokes." He said the only work he did "was to carry a child in the streets." After four years of babysitting, he finally protested and was transferred to another master. Other apprentices complained that their masters did not keep a shop in London and so had not trained them; or that the master was dead and the widow did not keep up the trade; or that the master stole their money; or that the master had not enrolled them at the Guildhall and they could not establish the legal end of apprenticeship. Excessive physical punishment and failure to provide adequate food and clothing were also common complaints.[48] If no compromise could be reached that would satisfy the parents and friends of the apprentice, then the guild wardens or the mayor removed the apprentice and placed him with another master or returned the money he had paid to be trained.

THE EMOTIONAL UNDERPINNINGS OF NURTURING

Record sources are among the worst for assessing emotions because they so often deal with the negative side of any relationship. When all else has failed, the parties come to court. Even the very full coroners' inquests do not describe the emotions of a mother or father as first finder of a child's body. Lamentations are not part of the inquest record. When coupled with the miracles and other sources, however, the emotional underpinnings of the nurturing culture become more apparent.

We must go back to the Italian visitor's account and listen again to what the natives told him. They were so concerned about the future of their children that they sent them to other homes where they would receive the proper discipline. Parental love need not be measured by one yardstick, they argued, and they pursued their practices in the best interests of their children. We too must move away from the assumption that only one acceptable type of relationship between parents and children can exist—the affectionate, sentimental, unquestioning bond of "modern" families. Our modern sentimentality ignores the great importance that parents in former times placed on the training and placement of their children to insure their well-being and, therefore, their survival and, perhaps, even their happiness. Happiness was certainly the subordinate category to well-being and basic survival in the medieval era. Pre-modern parents did not assume that the state would take care of their children's education, clothes, or even food. They understood that their children's survival depended on their resources and training.

The fifteenth century saw an enormous explosion of books of advice for training children, as well as books for youth who wished to make their way up the social ladder or find profitable positions. Like the recording of ages in the coroners' inquests, the proliferation of such books and poems indicate a real societal concern about children and young people and a genuine desire to make as much out of youths as possible. If the lessons that the advice books offered were self-discipline, adherence to the ten commandments, acceptance of the social hierarchy, and subdued behavior in dress, discourse, and social interactions, it was because these were the very forms of behavior that society expected their children to adopt in order to survive in a harsh world. If the child were recalcitrant, then the books and poems urged that parents, teachers, or others in charge of their instruction be sure not to spare the rod in correction.

Discipline, corporal punishment, and fostering, however, did not imply public tolerance of abuse or a lack of love for children. The presumption of continued protection and support from parents and friends appears clearly in the mayor's court rolls relating to abuse of apprenticeship. When an apprenticeship or service arrangement went fearfully wrong, the first refuge the young person sought was his or her family. He or she might run away to family homes or the father, or another relative would come to London to investigate. One father complained to the mayor that his son had been apprenticed to one master, who had not trained him and then sold him to another master, who had beaten him and not fed him so that he permanently lost the use of an arm. When the father came to complain, the master's servants beat him as well.[49] Family and community vigilance did not end with the move of the child from its natal home.

The miracle stories reinforce not only parental and community concern for children, which we have already demonstrated, but also provide lessons on the behavior expected of employers of young people. John Wall, a seventeen-year-old servant of Robert Pokeapart, "a man of honorable birth and rank," was crushed to death as he returned from London with two other young men. They were following a wagon loaded with casks of salt fish and salt that upset on John, killing him. The other two young men panicked and hid the body by the road, but remembered to bend a penny double for King Henry. Arriving home they told their guardian, Robert Pokeapart, what had happened. In the morning, he gathered several neighbors and collected the body, carrying it to town. There he exposed the body for all to see so that there would be no suspicion of the other two young men in his guardianship. Lamentations to Henry and the bent penny paid off. John Wall rose from the dead and Robert, one of his wards, and John Wall's father went to the tomb of Henry together on a pilgrimage of thanksgiving. An abbess whose ten-year-old servant climbed a tree, "as boys are wont to do," and fell on his head, responded to the laments of the others by praying to St.

Henry for his recovery. When he was restored to life, she took the boy with her on a pilgrimage to Windsor. Dame Margery Hacket, likewise, was instrumental in restoring life to her servant girl. She had sent the seven-year-old to draw water from a well that had no winch. The girl slipped in and "went to the bottom like a lump of lead." When she did not return, her mistress went looking for her in dread and found the floating bucket. She despaired of what "one old woman" could do, but thought of an active young servant at home and went to get him. He rescued the little servant and prayed to King Henry with success.[50]

Wills also demonstrate the continued commitment of parents and masters to their children, servants, and apprentices in terms of bequests or intimate responsibilities placed on them.[51] But perhaps more interesting as evidence of the widespread emotional attitude toward succor of children are the general rather than individual bequests of dowries for poor maidens, lying-in hospitals for illegitimate births, foundling homes, and grammar schools.[52] The 1497 will of John Carpenter illustrates the specificity of mission that these testators felt for the children of the community. Carpenter charged the mayor, the chamberlain, and the commonality to take from his bequests to the city money to maintain

> four boys born within the City of London who shall be called in the vulgar tongue "Carpenters Children" to assist at divine service in the choir of the chapel aforesaid on festival days and to study at schools most convenient for them on ferial days, and that such boys shall be boarded and shall eat, drink and live within the college of the said chapel, or in another place nearby, or in the neighbourhood thereof. . . .

He goes on to specify the amount of board for the boys and the amount paid for gowns, tunics, hose, shoes, and shirts every year, as well as for bedding, laundry, and a barber. Not content with providing money for these services, he went on to require that the chamberlain hire a tutor to "supervise them in washing, shaving and other things convenient and necessary for the same boys" as well as teaching them their lessons.[53]

As we have seen, there is very persuasive evidence for a narrative tradition that both taught and enforced nurturing; a tradition that mirrored an official policy of nurturing, and that expressed the deeply embedded moral value that communities placed on that policy. We must, however, add a caution. Medieval parents and neighbors wished to preserve and nurture children into productive adult status. But this does not imply a lack of love and attention on the part of parents and guardians; indeed, childrearing required a great deal of oversight. Furthermore, the society was well aware that sentiment could be misleading and that self-sufficiency was ultimately more important. If children were to learn survival, they might themselves have more of a sense of survival than of love. A parable common to all of medieval Europe was the story of the divided horse blanket. The father instructs his son to take the horse blanket out to his grandfather, who was sleeping in the stable because it was a cold night. The son returns with half the blanket. When the father inquires why he cut the blanket in two, the son explains that he is saving the other half for his father when he is old.

NOTES

1. Philippe Ariès, *Centuries of Childhood: A Social History of the Family*, trans. Robert Baldrick (New York: Knopf, 1962); Lawrence Stone, *The Family, Sex, and Marriage in England, 1500–1800* (New York: Harper & Row, 1977).
2. Geoffrey Chaucer, *The Canterbury Tales*, trans. Nevill Coghill (Harmondsworth: Penguin Books, 1960), pp. 190–91.
3. *The Miracles of King Henry VI: Being an Account and Translation of Twenty-three Miracles Taken from the Manuscript in the British Museum (Royal 13 c.viii)*, ed. Ronald Know and Shane Leslie (Cambridge: The University Press, 1923). The collection of miracles was put together under the direction of Henry VII with the intention of moving toward the canonization of Henry VI. The collection of the miracle stories pertaining to children is very similar to the coroners' inquests over the death of children.
4. The *Medieval Handbooks of Penance: A Translation of the Principal Libri Penitentiales*, trans. John T. McNeill and Helena M. Gamer (New York: Columbia University Press, 1938) has very little on the parent-child relationship. Nicholas Orme, in "Children and the Church in Medieval England," *Journal of Ecclesiastical History*, 45 (1994): 563–87, speaks of the Handbooks' sparse reference to children other than baptism and the duties of the godparents to teach the basic prayers.
5. *Miracles of Henry VI*, p. 66.
6. The recording of accidental deaths had its roots in the Anglo-Saxon practice and the Norman Conquest. The Anglo-Saxons, having a tender concern for the souls of people who died suddenly without the opportunity of confessing their sins, had imposed the *deodand* on the community. When someone died suddenly and violently the price of the instrument that killed him or her was charged on the community and the proceeds were to go to prayers for the salvation of the soul of the deceased. The Normans continued the practice but kept the profits for the crown. For a fuller account of the source, see Roy F. Hunnisett, *The Medieval Coroner* (Cambridge: The University Press, 1961). The coroners' rolls are preserved in the Public Record Office in London under the classification of Just. 2. Hereafter referred to as P.R.O. Just. 2.
7. See Barbara A. Hanawalt, "The Voices and Audiences of Social History Records," *Social Science History*, 15 (1991): 159–75 for a more complete discussion of the narratives to be found in coroners' inquests.
8. See Barbara A. Hanawalt, *Growing Up in Medieval London* (New York: Oxford University Press, 1993), pp. 79–80 for a discussion of the customs surrounding St. Gregory and the boy bishops.
9. *Calendar of Coroners' Rolls of the City of London, A.D. 1300–1378*, ed. Reginald R. Sharpe (London: Richard Clay and Sons, 1913), pp. 63–64.
10 *Miracles of Henry VI*, pp. 50–54 (Latin transcript given in footnote).
11. Barbara A. Hanawalt, "Childrearing among the Lower Classes of Late Medieval England," *Journal of Interdisciplinary History*, 8 (1977): 1–21.
12. *Miracles of Henry VI*, pp. 35, 85, 115.
13. Chaucer, *Canterbury Tales*, "Prioress's Tale," p. 189. See Donald Weinstein and

Rudolph Bell, *Saints and Society: The Two Worlds of Western Christendom* (Chicago: University of Chicago Press, 1982), pp. 19–47, for the character of child saints.

14. *The Miracles of Henry VI*, pp. 35–37, 116–17. See also pp. 55, 56, 85. ("The news roused the whole household; the men servants came round shouting, or ran to and fro lamenting aloud.")

15. Barbara A. Hanawalt, *The Ties That Bound: Peasant Families in Medieval England* (New York: Oxford University Press, 1986), p. 176.

16. P.R.O. Just. 2/18 ms. 42d, 45; 2/104 m. 18d.; 2/200 m. 2; 2/199. *Bedfordshire Coroners' Rolls*, trans. R. F. Hunnisett, (Bedfordshire Historical Record Society, 41, 1961), pp. 25, 45.

17. Vladimir Propp, *Morphology of the Folktale*, trans. Laurence Scott (Austin: University of Texas Press, 1968), pp. 25–29, 96–98.

18. *Miracles of Henry VI*, pp. 88, 104, 171–76, 179–81, 195.

19. Hanawalt, *Ties That Bound*, pp. 87–89.

20. Hanawalt, *Ties That Bound*, pp. 141–55. See also Martine Segalen, *Mari et Femme dans la Société Paysanne* (Paris: Flammarion, 1980); and *Historical Anthropology of the Family*, trans. J. C. Whitehouse and Sarah Matthews (Cambridge: Cambridge University Press, 1986), pp. 205–19.

21. Albert P. Iskrant and Paul V. Joliet, *Accident and Homicide* (Cambridge, Mass.: Harvard University Press: 1968), pp. 23, 138.

22. P.R.O. Just. 2/113 m. 37. See also Just. 2/113 ms. 32, 33, 46.

23. P.R.O. Just. 2/109 m. 8. See also Just. 2/106 m. 1d., 2/77 m. 5d.

24. Hanawalt, *Ties That Bound*, pp. 158–59.

25. See Hanawalt, *Ties That Bound*, pp. 272–73 for tables on children's activities and place of death; p. 171 for tables on adults.

26. Figures from *Miracles of Henry VI*.

27. *Calendar of Plea and Memoranda Rolls*, 5, pp. 11–12, 1439.

28. *Miracles of Henry VI*, p. 164.

29. Chaucer, *Canterbury Tales*, p. 189; "His comrade was a boy of senior station"; "So every day his comrade secretly/As they went homewards taught it him by rote."

30. *Calendar of Coroners' Rolls of the City of London*, pp. 34–35.

31. *Miracles of Henry VI*, pp. 159–61.

32. See Barbara A. Hanawalt, *Crime and Conflict in English Communities, 1300–1348* (Cambridge, Mass.: Harvard University Press, 1979), pp. 154–57 for a discussion of evidence for infanticide. For a discussion of the legal basis for a pardon for infanticide in medieval society see Naomi D. Hurnard, *The King's Pardon for Homicide before A.D. 1307* (Oxford: Clarendon Press, 1969), p. 169. Until the sixteenth century the law did not clearly state that a mother was culpable of murder when she killed her infant. Jurors were thus unsure about whether indictments could be brought or not and, if indictments were brought, what was to be done with the woman who proved to be guilty of killing her newborn child.

33. Richard H. Helmholz, "Infanticide in the Province of Canterbury during the Fifteenth Century," *History of Childhood Quarterly*, 2 (1975): 384.

34. Hanawalt, *Growing Up in Medieval London*, p. 58. One curious figure comes from the London court of orphans. At the time that children entered wardship, 780, or 45 percent, were females and 951, or 55 percent, of the children were male. The shortfall of females should not have occurred because of inheritance, since male and female children inherited equally. The figure will need more investigation.

35. Hanawalt, *Ties That Bound*, p. 181.

36. C. A. Sneyd, ed., *The Italian Relation of England*, (London: Camden Society, 37, 1847), p. 24. One of the most naive uses of the quote is in Barbara Kaye Green-

leaf, *Children through the Ages: A History of Childhood* (New York: Barnes and Noble Books, 1978), who has distilled Philippe Ariès's writings into a book for education students.

37. Sue Sheridan Walker, "The Feudal Family and the Common Law Courts: The Pleas of Wardship in Thirteenth- and Fourteenth-Century England," *Journal of Medieval History*, 14 (1988): 13–31.

38. *Calendar of Letter Books of the City of London*, A-L, 11 vols., ed. Reginald R. Sharpe (London: John Edward Francis, 1899–1912). Hereafter referred to as *Letter Book* with an alphabetical number. See *Letter Book C*, p. 207; *Letter Book I*, pp. 220–21. See also *Liber Albus: The White Book of the City of London*, ed. Henry Thomas Riley (London: R. Griffin and Company, 1861), pp. 95–96; and Elaine Clark, "City Orphans and Custody Laws in Medieval England," *American Journal of Legal History*, 34 (1990): 168–87.

39. *Letter Book C*, pp. 81–82; *Letter Book E*, p. 121; *Letter Book G*, p. 91.

40. See *Calendar of Wills Proved and Enrolled in the Court of Husting, London, A.D. 1258–A.D. 1688*, ed. Reginald R. Sharpe (London: John E. Francis, 1890) for the years 1300 to 1500.

41. These included uncles or aunts of the child, grandparents, elder sons, and a nephew.

42. *Letter Book G*, p. 95 (1358) records the terms of a will in a wardship enrollment. Thomas Bedyk gave to Simon Fraunceys, mercer, the wardship, custody, and marriage of his son Henry during his minority.

43. Hanawalt, *Ties That Bound*, pp. 221–25. Cicely Howell, in "Peasant Inheritance Customs in the Midlands, 1280–1700," in *Family and Inheritance: Rural Society in Western Europe*, ed. Jack Goody, Joan Thirsk, and Edward P. Thompson (Cambridge: Cambridge University Press, 1976), pp. 112–55, has a good discussion on strategies of inheritance and responsibilities of the widow should she have young children.

44. Hanawalt, *Growing Up in Medieval London*, pp. 97, 103.

45. Hanawalt, *Ties That Bound*, pp. 250–53. Adoption as we know it was not one of those aspects of Roman law that passed into the medieval tradition. Foundling homes were also not common, although some hospitals for unwed mothers were established, thus recognizing the problem.

46. John Boswell, *Kindness of Strangers: The Abandonment of Children in Western Europe from Late Antiquity to the Renaissance* (New York: Pantheon, 1988).

47. *Calendar of Plea and Memoranda Rolls of the City of London*, 1–4, ed. Arthur H. Thomas (Cambridge: Cambridge University Press, 1926–61), Introduction, vol. 2, pp. xxxiii–xxxv. See also Steve Rappaport, *Worlds within Worlds: Structures of Life in Sixteenth-Century London* (Cambridge: Cambridge University Press, 1989), pp. 77–84.

48. Corporation of London Record Office, hereafter referred to as CLRO with manuscript reference. MC1/2/5, MC1/2/116. See Hanawalt, *Growing Up in Medieval London*, pp. 157–63 for a more complete discussion.

49. Hanawalt, *Growing Up in Medieval London* pp. 146–49, 157–63.

50. *Miracles of Henry VI*, pp. 65–72, 84–87, 206–10.

51. See Hanawalt, *Growing Up in Medieval London*, pp. 170–71 for the close relationship between masters and apprentices as seen largely in wills.

52. Ibid., pp. 33, 43. See also Charles Pendrill, *London Life in the Fourteenth Century* (Port Washington, N.Y.: Kennikat Press, 1971). pp. 173, 183–85, 198.

53. *Calendar of Plea and Memoranda Rolls of the City of London, 1458–1482*, ed. Philip E. Jones (Cambridge: Cambridge University Press, 1961), pp. 129–30.

11

"The Childe of Bristowe" and the Making of Middle-Class Adolescence

The behavior of middle-class youth became a prominent theme in the literature, laws, court cases, guild regulations, and thinking of fifteenth-century English society in an obsessive way uncharacteristic of preceding centuries.[1] Books of advice for youth aspiring to make their way up the social ladder proliferated in manuscript form and spread even more with the invention of printing. Among the dominant metaphors were the relationship of the young to the old, the apprentice to the master, the uncultivated to the cultivated. The process of forming a concept of a societal ideal of middle-class adolescent behavior was, as Norbert Elias described, one in which meaning and form were picked up and polished in speech and writing and "tossed back and forth until they became efficient instruments for expressing what people had jointly experienced and wanted to communicate about."[2] In this chapter I will look at this process of polishing descriptions of adolescent behavior as they were circulated between literary and legal creations, on the one hand, and the actual experience of adolescence, on the other. The game of exchange between the literary and the historical leads to a fifteenth-century construction of adolescence. Although the ideal type may be seen in a number of written examples, the portrait appears most fully in a popular poem, "The Childe of Bristowe" and in its variant, "The Merchant and His Son."[3] These didactic narratives are a fifteenth-century version of Horatio Alger stories, adventure tales in which an aspiring lad overcomes the obstacles set in his way to achieve good fame and fortune.

Seth Lerer was very helpful in reading a draft of this paper and sharing with me his own work on didactic literature of the fifteenth century. David Wallace, Ralph Hanna, and James Landman also offered considerable help in the final version. This version was first published in *Bodies and Discipline: Intersections of Literature and History in Fifteenth-Century England*, ed. Barbara A. Hanawalt and David Wallace (Minneapolis: University of Minnesota Press, 1996), pp. 155–78.

Historical conditions in the fifteenth century proved especially unsettling. In that century of disruption and transition, youth became a focus for anxieties about a better future. Disease and wars kept population low. The rise of new economic opportunities and the gradual demise of serfdom changed the social hierarchy. Political realignments in Europe and England and a heightened lay piety accompanied by criticism of the Church led to instability in the secular and ecclesiastical realms. It was a period of recognizable flux—one that inspired considerable comment from poets and moralists of the time. Among the concerns that occupied the middle ranks of English society, a rapidly expanding sector, were the values, virtues, and behavior that their class should maintain. Their anxieties centered on such questions as the most prestigious way of earning their wealth (law, trade, or landed estates), the appropriate education for their sons and marriages for their daughters, the type of clothing they should wear, the manners they should display, and their personal salvation. Fundamental to their unease was the shift in the old hierarchical order.

The predominant response of the middle class to the new social order of the fifteenth century was conservatism. In literature David Lawton has pointed to the general attribute of "dullness," not only as part of our modern reading of it, but as a desirable avocation on the part of its practitioners. Literature generally adopted a public rather than an individualistic voice. The message was an insistent one emphasizing morality, piety, and respect for hierarchy. In the writings of Lydgate, Hoccleve, and the other fifteenth-century poets, the moral lessons of books of advice were elevated to an elite version of public poetry for the monarch, among other powerful patrons. Literature for the education of princes was a grander version of the literature for the education of middle-class youth. The "dullness" of those poets was a virtue to them. While distorting their acknowledged master's, Chaucer's, writing to fit their own lessons in morality, they perceived themselves to be his dutiful apprentices, much as they saw master/apprentice relationships in general as the basis for a sound society.[4]

By looking at the various venues in which Chaucer's works appeared and were read, Seth Lerer has shown how Chaucerian tales were modified to fit with other "improving literature" and bound into books that were designed for the education of young readers of a household. Chaucer's texts became, in these versions, a vehicle for those compilers and authors who wrote "father Chaucer" as an instructor of youth. Although designed for children, the views expressed were not radically different from those found in the fifteenth-century poets such as Hoccleve and Lydgate. As Lerer points out, the thrust of so much of the fifteenth-century literary messages indicates a new importance for childhood training.[5]

I would go beyond that generalization to suggest that fifteenth-century literature, while it taught reading and conservative values to children, emphasized lessons needed in adolescence. The literature, along with and as part of historical experiences, produced the *Kulture* of which Elias speaks. The construction of middle-class behavior began to coalesce specifically around the adolescent years, and literature of all sorts, high and low, was directed toward an age group that was perceived to be most in need of instruction.

If authors aimed a major thrust of their moral messages at youth, so too did the regulations governing social life. Not knowing what the new social hierarchy would be, adults focused their attention on dictates of behavior that emphasized a public image, one that, as Elias points out, was self-conscious about the body and its uses. Guild regulations, even those of parish guilds, dictated the sober and pious behavior expected of their membership.[6] Sumptuary legislation attempted to enforce the social hierarchy of dress, the foods the population ate, and the places they sat at table.[7] Training for ritualized public behavior began with children and extended into adolescence in the form of manner books and moral tales for the literate and catchy rhymes for the illiterate.

THE PARAGON OF MIDDLE-CLASS ADOLESCENCE

To understand the process that produced a consensus on the making of middle class adolescents, we can follow the "tossing to and fro" of the ideal attributes from the popular literature, particularly the two variants of "The Childe of Bristowe," to the regulatory measures for apprentices and youth. Since the plot of the poem is not well known, this first section includes a narrative along with a comparison of it to the prescriptive literature and regulations. The poems begin with the Childe-William's background (the name is a shorthand that includes both poems, since he is baptized "William" in "The Merchant and His Son"). His birth and upbringing fit the ideal candidate for apprenticeship. His father, aside from his moral lapses into usury and neglect of charity and tithes, was "a squyer mykel of myght" with castles, towns, towers, forests, and fields. William's father in "The Merchant and His Son" was "a ryche franklyn of Ynglond" with many jewels, great treasure, horses, sheep, and land.[8] A fifteenth-century poem written for the mason's guild warns masters not to recruit from among serfs because the lord has the power to come and claim them. The demise of serfdom rendered the complaint out-of-date, but the lament rings true: "By olde tyme, wryten Y fynde/That prentes shchulde be of gentyl kynde." Part of the reason for preferring gentry was that they increased the prestige of the master and the guild.[9] Gentlemen's and yeomen's sons, like Childe-William, were more likely to enter prestigious guild, such as that of long-distance merchants than were those of husbandmen.[10]

Not only was the Childe-William well-born, he also met the physical requirements of the merchant class, being "semely and feyre" with "lymes large and long."[11] By 1510 the Mercers' Guild in London had spelled out similar specifications for their apprentices. They had to be at least sixteen years old, free of birth, tall, lith of limb, and not disfigured in body or members. But the Wardens despaired of honest recruitment because "daily there be presented and also admitted divers apprentices which be very little in growing or stature." When reality fell short of the ideal, the wardens considered compelling the apprentices' friends to swear to their fitness, but decided against it.[12]

Childe-William met the educational and courtesy specifications as well. During the fifteenth century the guilds had begun to require higher standards of literacy from their apprentices. The Goldsmiths, for instance, required apprentices to prove their skill by writing in "a book to be dormant in the treasury of the Hall." The book came to be known as the *Dormant*. The Ironmongers had an *Apprentices' Book of Oaths*, which served a similar purpose. One goldsmith claimed that an apprentice he had taken from Banbury was so skilled in engraving letters that he naturally assumed that the young man could read and write when he could not.[13] No such mistake could be made about Childe-William.

> When the child was xij yere and more,
> His fader put hym unto lore
> to learne to be a clerke;
> so long he lernyd in clergie,
> til he was wise and wittye,
> and drad al dedis derke.

The alternative version, the more lively of the two, says that William "cowde hys gramer wonder wele: hys felows cowde hym not amende."[14]

The literacy requirement coincided with the great popularity of advice and courtesy books that, like the household reading books described by Lerer, were designed to instill moral virtues along with instruction on polite behavior and proper public presentation for aspiring youth.[15] While the more famous of these books, such as John Russell's *Boke of Nurture*, were written for youth who planned to enter into noble households,[16] others, such as *The Young Children's Book*, were specifically adapted to middle-class ideals. These stressed such injunctions as "you must eat what you get with your hands" since "a man's arms are for working as a bird's wings for flying."[17] The poems assure us that Childe-William had learned all of the needful lessons recommended: "He wax so curteise and bolde, / all marchauntz loved hym, yong and olde."[18]

The merchants' superior moral values, in contrast to the usurious, impious, and uncharitable behavior of Childe-William's gentry father,[19] also find their place in the advice books: "Use no swearing of falsehood in buying or selling, else shall you be shamed at the last. Get your money honestly, and keep out of debt and sin. Be eager to please and so live in peace and quiet."[20] Law, the other alternative for obtaining middle-class wealth, which his father advocates, meets with Childe-William's disapproval because the youth is afraid he would endanger his immortal soul.[21]

The youth aspires to become a merchant, even though his father shrewdly points out that he has "Seyn men bothe ryse and falle; / hyt ys but caswelte" to be in "merchandyse."[22] "The Childe of Bristowe," however, claims an abiding desire to lead his life by "marchandise." As it turns out, Childe-William had made his own inquiries about a suitable master and tells his father that close by, at Bristol, there is a merchant who is a "just trew man" and that he wants to be apprenticed to him for seven years.[23]

The apprenticeship contracts presumed that the candidate was as well prepared and dedicated to middle-class values as was Childe-William.[24] While apprenticeship contracts contained economic elements involving fees, wages, and other payments, the emphasis was on the behavior expected from both parties. The apprentice swore not to marry and not to fornicate, including the wise precaution that he not have sexual relations with anyone of his master's household. He was not to engage in the temptations of the city such as drinking, gaming, and going to theater. He was not to gossip about his master's affairs, but remain loyal to his interest and not waste his money. He was expected to accept discipline without complaint and undertake not to leave the apprenticeship to serve another master or to run away. If he did run away, his sponsors could be fined and he could be barred from the craft.[25]

The master, likewise, accepted a series of obligations that regulated his behavior in this quasi-familial pact. He had to provide room, board, and clothing. He could not ask his apprentices to perform degrading tasks, such as carrying water, that were for menial servants.[26] He had to treat the youth as a younger member of his own status group. He had a duty, as did a father, to chastise his apprentice for wrongdoing, but he could not be abusive. Above all, he was to instruct the apprentice in his trade or craft without concealing trade secrets that would hinder the apprentice from becoming a master. Childe-William's father entered his son into such a contract: having traveled to Bristol he "with the Marchaund cownant made." It was for seven years, and the youth was to live with his master. The merchant thereby agreed that if he were paid "gold gret plente, / the child hys prentys should be, / his science for to conne."[27]

By the late fourteenth and fifteenth centuries entry into an apprenticeship was very expensive. The sponsor or the candidate himself would have to pay a varying amount to the master by way of an inducement to take the youth and to cover part of the expenses of lodging.[28] By the late fourteenth century the charge by the master was £2 5s. to £3 6s. 8d.[29] In their charter of 1393 the Goldsmiths tried to protect apprentices and their sponsors from unscrupulous demands by establishing a schedule of premiums to be paid to the master. If a ten-year contract was signed, then the minimum payment to the master was £5. If a shorter term was agreed to, then the premium was £6 12s. 4d. Fines of £5 could be levied on the masters for not abiding by those arrangements.[30] Premiums ranged from £2 to £6 in other guilds.[31] In addition, candidates or their sponsors had to pay the Goldsmith's guild 20s. to 40s. for entrance into the guild.[32] The Mercers' had similar entry fines for apprentices.[33]

The close, surrogate-familial relationship that developed between Childe-William and his master was not an unusual occurrence or simply a literary device, and it was certainly one that the middle class regarded as the most desirable outcome. The apprenticeship arrangement was a complex one. For the young person it meant leaving the natal home or school and moving into the house of a stranger. The master and his family would have a young, nonkinsperson in their household who would become a part of the family. For both the apprentice and the master the living arrangement was a potentially uncomfortable mix of familial and professional roles. The seven to ten years of working and living together could result in deep emotional conflict as well as attachment. The expenses of arranging the apprenticeship in a sense acted as a bond for the good behavior of the apprentice.[34] In Bristol, which was a much smaller commercial center than London, most masters would have one apprentice at a time. Masters with only one apprentice in their lifetime could form strong attachments to this surrogate son. Mortality of children in the cities of medieval Europe was very high, and therefore their inhabitants might not have surviving sons of their own, as was true of Childe-William's master. Thus their emotional investment in their protégés became intensified.

As the narrative technique of medieval popular poetry dictates, however, it is time to "return to the story of the boy's father." Childe-William is happily placed with his master, loved by the community of merchants, learning his trade, and well on his way to becoming an honest merchant, but his father lies on his deathbed with considerable anxiety about his own salvation. None of his fair-weather friends will act as executor. This leaves his only son, who "drad al dedis derke." What is our hero to do? What do the insistent voices of advice manuals and poetry tell him to do?

One of the main goals of the guides was to inculcate in the young an understanding of and reverence for hierarchy and authority. With this injunction, we must again pick up the narrative of the poems as a guide to readers unfamiliar with this piece of popular poetry. Injunctions to filial piety, such as that exhibited by Childe-William, were typical of advice manuals.

> And child, worship thy father and thy mother;
> Look that thou grieve neither one nor other,
> But ever, among them thou shalt kneel down,
> And ask their blessing and benison.[35]

This same obedience was to extend to a master who must also be treated with respect: "An thy master speak to thee, take thy cap in hand."[36] It behooved a youth aspiring to either maintain his parents' social position or achieve a better one to learn the rules and take advantage of the opportunity a master could offer toward this goal.[37]

Childe-William, of course, embodied these virtues. In spite of his father's sinful means of acquiring wealth, he agrees to act as his father's executor and save his soul at the cost of the inheritance he might expect. At the same time, he is completely loyal to his master and to his apprentice contract. Childe-William's master in return is continually described as loving his apprentice, even when he suspects him of gambling away his fortune.[38]

The two loyalties, to father and to master, dominate the poem, but the filial piety is expressed largely through the sacrifices that the young man must go through to save his father's soul. In this conventionally drawn center section of the poem, the Childe-William tells his father that he must meet him in the death chamber in a fortnight after he dies so that he can see if his soul has been saved.[39] When he is dead, the young man sets about an elaborate expenditure on a conventional funeral: masses for his father's soul, alms to poor women and children to say prayers for his father, repair of roads and bridges in his father's name, and so on until all his father's ready money has been spent. But when his father's burning soul appears in the chamber at the prescribed time, led by a devil with a chain and accompanied by a blast of lightning, the son promises to do more and asks him to return in another fortnight.[40]

Returning to his master, he explains that his father has died and that he must sell the whole of the inheritance he has gained, "croppe, rote and rynde." The merchant's response is anguished. Not only will his beloved apprentice be poorer, the young man will appear a fool to the merchant community.

> Thou schalt not selle they gode, Wyllyam, be the counsel of me;
> Men wyll sey that here therof, that thou art nevyr lyke to the.
> ["never like to thrive"]
> All thys cuntre wyll speke therof, bothe woman, chylde, and man,
> For to sele so sone awey all that thy fadur wan.[41]

The general anxiety about what others would think was also common to the advice literature.[42]

When arguments evoking public censure fail, the master suggests a loan to cover any short-term problems the apprentice may be having in trade. Loyal to his father's memory, the young man has not revealed what he is doing with the money, and the merchant assumes he has suffered a business setback. Apprentices at his stage of career did go to trade on their own if they had the capital, which Childe-William would have as executor of a wealthy father. The apprentice refuses the loan, arguing that if he must sell the land cheap, he would rather that the master own it than anyone else. The master pays him more than the asking price.[43] In the surrogate-filial relationship of apprentice and master, such an arrangement would be the most honorable.

Taking the money back into the countryside, Childe-William has it proclaimed in churches and markets that he would repay any man or woman whom his father had ruined, providing that they would say prayers for his soul. Penniless once again following this distribution, he awaits the second visit of his father's ghost. This time it arrives all black but without flames. His father is not yet saved, but the ghost realizes that his son's approach to fair dealing in life has been better than his own.[44]

A suspicion of a business setback was one thing, but when the apprentice returns the second time and wants to borrow money, the master becomes suspicious that he is behaving contrary to his contract, as a bad apprentice might do.

> [B]y my feith, y hold the mad;
> for thu has played atte dice,
> or at some other games nyce,
> and lost up, sone that thu had,

In the alternate version, the master suggests that he will end up on the gallows for whatever he is doing with so much money. Filial piety prevents the apprentice from confessing his drain of money, and the master says that he has heard that his "governaunce" was bad. When the apprentice suggests that he become his bondsman and servant in exchange for the loan, the master is forthcoming. Only in the alternative version does the author permit the master to make a sly comment to his wife that he is now assured of a reliable servant in his former apprentice.[45] That comment, in itself, is a hint about the problem of finding skilled labor in the fifteenth century that ultimately leads to strains between masters and apprentices.

Returning once again to the country he pays all of the tithes that his father owed to various churches and continues to give alms in his father's name until he is again penniless. Returning to meet his father's ghost for the final time, he comes across a beggar who claims that his father owed him for a measure of grain. With nothing left to give, he takes his fine clothing off his back and gives it to the beggar. Reduced to his underwear, he enters the death chamber and is, at last, rewarded with a vision of his father's salvation.[46]

If the merchant was bothered about lending money to his apprentice, his appearance before him in his undergarments leads to a lecture about keeping up appearances. In a society in which clothes make the man, Childe-William was not making a good impression.

> Wyllyam, he seyde, how ys hyt with the? thow arte a rewful grome;
> Hyt were almes, seyde the marchand, in preson the to caste:
> For moche gode haste thou loste, and broght unto waste.
> Y had thoght to have made the a man, y pray Got to gyf the care,
> Y wyll no more tryste to the, to go wyth my chaffare.[47]

His reaction was no different than that of the London Mercers, who required their apprentices and servants, when going to the Mart, to wear capes, partellettes of silk, furred gowns, and double-turned cappies shoes and slippers.[48]

The conclusion of the poem is, likewise, expressive of a middle-class ideal about how the master-apprentice relationship should resolve itself. The merchant has had his suspicions about the apprentice, but he has not been the financial loser in his arrangements with him. He also has never given up his quasi-paternal love. When the youth returns for the third time and explains his successful efforts to save his father's soul, all is forgiven. In "The Childe of Bristowe" he becomes the heir to his master, and in "The Merchant and His Son" he becomes the merchant's executor and marries his only daughter. In both conclusions he inherits all of his father's lands again in addition to the wealth of his father-in-law. In the merchant's appointment of William as executor, the alternative version once again permits a sly laugh; the merchant realizes to what lengths the apprentice's filial piety has taken him on behalf of his father and he presumes that he will do the same for a surrogate father. Both the merchant's present fortune and his afterlife are assured in the hands of this paragon of merchant virtues.[49]

Although the portrait may seem an overdrawn fiction, the master-apprentice relationship could result in such a comfortable conclusion in real life. Wills tell much about the familial bonds between the parties. Three percent of the 3,330 men registering wills in the Husting Court left their apprentices bequests. Money (28 percent) and goods (33 percent) were the typical bequests. John Claydish, a pewterer in London, left one apprentice 13s. 4d. and a more junior apprentice 10s. A goldbeater, William Wylewan, left his best mold and all other molds to his apprentice. His son would have the shop and other instruments. In other cases the apprentices received the shop (7 percent) and tenements (8 percent). Some men remembered all of their apprentices, thus indicating a generally good relationship within the shop and household structure.[50] The relationship could become so close that the apprentice was made chief heir to the master.[51]

With the intimate familial environment, one might also expect that marriages could result from the relationship built upon trust and acquaintance. Thus Thomas Wood, who had two daughters, married one to a former apprentice who went on to have a distinguished career in the Goldsmiths Guild. Harry ap Richard claimed that he had been apprentice to William Griffith, late tailor of London, who had released him from his indenture of apprenticeship. He had agreed with William's widow to marry her and take over the business, but, he complained, she broke the contract and married someone else.[52]

The filial relationship might also be carried to the grave. Thomas Gauder, a pouchmaker, died young with a wife but no children. He left his brother and nephew his inheritance and also made a number of civic bequests. At the end of his life his chief desire was to be buried in the same tomb as William Gauder, his late master. Richard Wycombe also valued the closeness of his relationship with his former master and his current apprentices and provided for prayers for his master's soul and gave each of his current apprentices 10s. each.[53]

NEGATIVE EXEMPLA: UNGOVERNED YOUTH

Although the poems about Childe-William as a paragon of mercantile virtue ring true with advice literature and historical prescriptions such as apprentice contracts and wills, one remains suspicious about the real and fictive fears railed against by all this assortment of evidence. Elias observed that books of advice used the ploy of holding up examples of the "uncultured peasant" or the obverse of the cultured to show how improved were the manners of the civilized. The rustic and rube were the negative examples that showed the positive virtues of culture to the consumers of manuals devoted to social-climbing. Negative examples were effective instructional tools. Likewise, guilds and cities made public examples of those youths who broke contracts or otherwise offended so that their punishment would be a lesson to others who might be inclined to offend.

John Russell's *Boke of Nurture* provides one of the most interesting contrasts between "governed" and "ungoverned" youth. A manual for the duties of a butler and carver to the nobility, its introduction creates appositions that give an insight into the sort of benign, adolescent savage who can be turned into a paragon of virtue. The introduction juxtaposes wilderness with noble household, poacher with servitor, unruly with well governed, and naive youth with civilized man.

Russell meets his candidate for conversion in a fittingly wild environment, a forest in the "merry season of May." The young poacher, armed with bow and arrow, has the right physical appearance—he is slender and lean. But he is in despair because he cannot find service: "I serve myself and no other man." Russell immediately asks the obvious question for any aspiring, medieval youth: "Is thy governance good?" This child of nature confesses that he has tried to get a master "but because I knew nothing good, and showed this wherever I went, every man denied me; day by day wanton [ill-bred] and not over-nice, reckless, lewd and chattering like a jay, every man refused me." Fortunately, he is educable and can come in from the wilderness.[54]

The contrast of wilderness to household provides an insight into the expectations that adults had when they viewed adolescents. The wilderness and the young savage's poaching stand for his disabilities in finding a position in civilized society. If he follows the advice of his adult mentor, he will no longer be an outcast, but can become a respected member of society.

The author of the fifteenth-century courtesy book, *Lytyl John*, uses a negative example whom he calls Ruskyn. Ruskyn is not an untutored child of nature waiting to be rescued, but rather he has only partially learned his manners and turns out to be foppish. Lessons must be learned thoroughly, not by halves. The author compares him to Absolon in the *Miller's Tale*.[55]

One large body of literature, that of the "ages of man," defined adolescence as a life stage both in terms of medical theory and of the type of behavior characteristic of each life period. Adolescence fell between the childish period of "wanton and wild" and the goal of adulthood to be "sad and wise." In the ancient physician's and philosopher's division of life stages into four (based on Pythagoras), adolescence was hot and dry as summer and fire and its humor was red choler. In the division of the life cycle into seven according to the planets (the Ptolemaic and Hippocratic periodization), youth's planet was Venus, which "implants an impulse toward the embrace of love."[56]

The morality play *Mundus and Infans,* captures the difference between the pranks of the child and the "love-longing" of youth. Smart little Wanton, a child of seven to fourteen, is an engaging figure. Wanton tells of all his secret games with relish. He can spin a top, but he also uses his "scrougstick" (whip for the top) to beat his playmates on the head. He manipulates his family by biting and kicking his brother or sister if they thwart him, but by pouting and crying if his father or mother should interfere. He can "dance and also skip, . . . play at the cherry-pit, . . . and whistle you a fit." On the way to school he has learned to do all those things that moralists told him not to do. He steals fruit from gardens, goes after birds' eggs, and ends up feeling the whip of his master.[57] Wanton is drawn along lines that can be seen in the behavior of real urban children of the time from the ages of seven to fourteen.[58] At fourteen Wanton changes his name to Lust and Liking. Mundus tells him that the next seven years are to be all games and glee, all "love-longing in lewdness." He sets out in pursuit of women, revel, and riot.[59] But the playwright does not dwell on his carousing and conquests.

Other late medieval popular poetry, however, takes up the theme of male adolescent behavior. "The Mirror of the Periods of Man's Life," a lively moral lesson in verse, divides life into stages by years and qualities. In the fourteenth year "knowliche of manhode he wynnes" (puberty) and through the early twenties the youth is a battle ground for the struggle between the seven virtues and the seven sins. Reason dictates an education at Oxford or the law, but lust has another institution in mind:

> Quod lust, "harp and giterne there may ye leere,
> And pickid staff and blucklere, there-with to plawe,
> At tauerne to make women myrie cheere,
> And wilde felaws to-gider draw.

Music, drink, mock fights, and wild companions vie with obedience, reason, and those other attributes that are to make one "sad and wise."[60]

Childe-William's master, curiously, was not worried about the sexual escapades of his apprentice, but suggested, instead, that he was unthrifty and had gambled away his money. Gambling, drinking in taverns, and wasting money on clothing was tempting. Three apprentices—Henry Pykard, Walter Waldeshef, and Roger Fynch—were charged in 1339 with being "addicted to playing knuckle-bones" at night and leading other apprentices into gambling. People in one ward found that Richard de Pelham was "a good man and true," but his son, Richard, was a "rorer."[61]

Apprentice contracts precluded gambling and unthrifty living, but the situation was hard to control when the older ones were abroad on their masters' business. The Mercers, in order "to avoid evil among the youth of the fellowship" when they were in Flanders, established six English houses there run by men of good reputation. The apprentices could eat only at those houses or face fines. They were to have only four groats worth of English beer (not the strong, continental beers) and no wine. They were not to play cards or other games for money and not to dance, revel, or sit up past nine o'clock in the evening.[62]

The problems caused by apprentices went beyond their wild living; they could defraud their masters and even beat them. Again, a few examples suffice to show the type of problem that could arise. While masters were much more likely to abuse the relationship because they had the greater power, apprentices could also cause problems. Edward Bowden violently and suddenly beat his mistress, reviled her, and tried to strangle her. The Goldsmiths were outraged and called together "worshipful men" to decide what to do about Bowden. They concluded that he would only get worse if they sent him to prison. Instead, they had him stripped and beaten in the Goldsmith's Hall kitchen until his blood flowed so that his own body's pain and bleeding would instruct him about the damage he had done to his mistress. Twenty years earlier the Goldsmiths had dealt with an attempted murder of a master by an apprentice.[63]

The story of Walter Prata indicates the sorts of ungovernable qualities in apprentices that scared masters. Stories like Walter's were reason enough to create literature and ordinances that emphasized honesty and obedience in apprentices. Walter was apprenticed in 1400 to John Lincoln, a liveried goldsmith. The two others, Henry Goldsmith and William Fannt, completed their apprenticeships a year after he joined the household but continued to work in Lincoln's shop as bachelors. Lincoln took in another apprentice as well, John Lannden, and so the business consisted of himself, two experienced workers, and two apprentices in training. The two apprentices lived with the master, as did Fannt, who occupied a separate chamber. They all took their meals together.

Prata was a precocious cheat. If a customer brought in silver to be weighed on the balances and turned into a new object, he knew how to steal a three- or four-penny weight at the scales. His master sent him off to get change for a gold noble, and he shortchanged his master by 7d. silver. When he went to a goldbeater on an errand to deliver silver-gilt, he returned short of silver. While the others were at dinner, he would excuse himself and go to the melting hearth to find grains of gold and silver that had fallen into the ash. These thefts were all performed in the course of his work as an apprentice, but he soon branched out beyond petty larceny. He went to a jeweler on London Bridge and claimed that he was borrowing a silver cup for his master. He sold the cup and kept the profits. As his skill developed, he made duplicate keys of his master's display chest and also of Fannt's chamber and chest. On one occasion he stole three ounces of gold from Fannt's chest and did not confess to it for three days, while they turned the shop upside down looking for the gold. He stole chemicals (sal ammoniac and saltpeter) and offered a man 10s. to show him how to use them for alchemy. His ultimate goal, he finally confessed to the Wardens of the Goldsmiths Guild, was to steal his master's gold and silver and go to Flanders with John Sasse, a Fleming. The account concludes that "in this wise he made much dis-ease among the men." The guild expelled him, with no possibility of gaining readmission.[64]

The "sad and wise" were continually bothered by the misbehavior of adolescents, particularly that of apprentices. Thus, the wardens of the Mercer's Company lamented to the membership that "they have lately known and herd that divers mennys apprentices have greatly mysordered theymself as well in spendyng grete Summes of mony of theyre Maisters goods in Riott as wel uppon harlotes as at dyce, cardes and other unthrygty games as in their apparell" to the great hurt of all. They needed some ordinances to deal with the problem.[65] A few years later on May Day 1517, a general riot among apprentices occurred, and the Mercers and others heard from the king that they must do something about the "wild, undiscrete Parsones named to be menes apprentices and menes servauntes of this Citie."[66] The concern over riot did not imply a decided culture of misrule among urban apprentices and, indeed, the literature speaks of individual rather than group violations of propriety. London's fifteenth-century riots lacked the carnivalesque features that early modernists like to refer to as typical of a "youth culture." The most serious riots were attacks on foreigners and involved guildsmen as well as apprentices and servants.[67]

Moralists could not accept that the planets alone made youth "ungovernable" and strove to educate them. Some writers argued that they turned out so badly because they were not adequately beaten. Others opined that their rebelliousness was the result of too much beating and that they became callous because of it. Still others felt that the home environment was so poisonous that young people lacked role models of how honorable people ought to behave.[68] How could they be expected to behave better than their elders? Medieval moralists, city fathers, and masters were perplexed about what to do with adolescents.

FIFTEENTH-CENTURY ANXIETY OVER ADOLESCENCE

Literary and historical examples of a new preoccupation with middle class adolescence abound, and it is quite clear that the adults were honing an image of the ideal behavior expected of this group of youth. The literary examples reinforced the regulatory ones, with each contributing to a unified image. But the investigation of this particular intersection of history and literature leaves two major questions unanswered: a historical one about the cause of sudden value placed on middle-class youth, and a literary one about the reason for the large audience for such poems as "The Childe of Bristowe."

A demographic explanation for the increased awareness of adolescence is initially attractive. If there were more adolescents in the population, then an older and smaller generation might feel threatened by their presence and feel that adult society could not properly assimilate or train them to be useful additions to the "sad and wise." Recalling the conflicts between youth and adults that our post-World-War-II "baby boom" occasioned in the 1970s, this is an attractive hypothesis. But the fifteenth century was a period of low population growth. The concern about adolescence arose, not because of an overabundance of them, but because they were a scarce commodity. Scarcity produced a sense of concern for their proper nurturing and training.

The plague of 1349 and the subsequent visitations reduced the population of England by about a third and in London by about a half. The plague did not visit once, but kept returning. There is even some evidence that the young were particularly vulnerable to mortality from the plague. In addition, a number of other diseases made their first entry into Europe and England during the fifteenth century.[69] With a scarcity of children who surviving into adulthood, parents in the country tried to keep their sons at home to compensate for the greatly reduced labor force.[70] The low rural population meant that opportunities to work for high wages or even to purchase or rent land made it easy for youth to marry and establish a family in the countryside.

From the point of view of the urban middle class, the scarcity of adolescents and the new opportunities in the countryside made it difficult to recruit apprentices. A husbandman's son would hesitate to accept a long-delayed adulthood required by an apprenticeship. The steep costs of entry were also a hindrance. If a youth persisted in the goal, he might have to work longer as an agricultural servant to earn the money and meet the new requirements of literacy. The chief suppliers of apprentices, the husbandman ranks, therefore felt a pull to remain at home. Some crafts, such as the Fursters (saddle makers), showed a reluctance to take apprentices at all. The city accused them of taking no apprentices in order to restrict the number of people practicing the trade and thereby raise prices. In their defense, they claimed that the pestilence had made it difficult to attract apprentices and that "they were feeble from a life of labor" and could not train them in any case.[71]

Other guilds responded by lengthening the term of the apprenticeship contract to ten years. By making the apprentices serve longer, they were able to rely upon skilled labor at a very low cost to themselves in the last years of the apprenticeship. The Goldsmiths by 1393 had already mandated that the term be ten years, but they agreed to reduce it for an extra fee or for sons of Goldsmiths. By their own records, however, the average term was 10.6 years.[72] The trend toward longer terms was established by the first half of the fifteenth century, when only 41 percent were for eight years and 59 percent were for a longer period.[73] Scattered references to contract violations and guild ordinances indicate that the average length of a term, in the fifteenth and sixteenth centuries, was ten years.[74]

Because the young people were staying in the country longer before seeking apprenticeships, the age of entry into apprenticeship rose. In the early fourteenth century fourteen was the usual age of entry into apprenticeship, and a city ordinance specified that thirteen be the minimum age. But the age of entry crept up to fifteen or sixteen by the end of the fourteenth century.[75] During the course of the fifteenth century the age of entry into apprenticeship increased to at least sixteen, but eighteen was more common. Many of the elite London guilds such as the Mercers, Goldsmiths, and Ironmongers began to require that their apprentices have an education before entering into their apprenticeships.[76] Thus, they spent longer in grammar schools than did apprentices of the previous century.

As the fifteenth century wore on, change in the composition of the apprentices can also be noted. More of the apprentices came from a husbandman background as opposed to that of gentry or a merchant. By the middle of the sixteenth century 47 percent of the apprentices were sons of husbandmen, 23 percent were of yeoman origin, and another 23 percent were native Londoners, with only 7 percent being drawn from the gentry. By the sixteenth century, then, husbandmen formed the predominant group, whereas townsmen and yeomen were dominant in the fifteenth century. Only the prestigious guilds, such as long-distance traders, could expect to recruit from the gentry and merchant class.[77]

We have, then, three factors that begin to explain this new-found concern with adolescence. The supply of adolescents appropriate for recruitment for apprenticeships was low until the end of the fifteenth century. Those who were recruited increasingly came from the husbandman class and, therefore, needed all the polish that the advice books could give to bring them up to the guild standards. Guild standards were actually rising as the supply of qualified candidates was shrinking. Finally, the guilds and masters were trying to dominate and assimilate an older population of adolescents. A young man who entered apprenticeship at age fourteen was easier to train and control than was a youth who entered apprenticeship at eighteen.

The lengthened terms of apprenticeship also created difficulties. In the fifteenth century apprentices did not finish their terms until they were twenty-eight, as opposed to twenty-one in the fourteenth century. Imposing the terms of apprenticeship contracts that delayed sexual activity, marriage, dress, and independent living arrangements was much more difficult for older apprentices. Guilds and masters were extending adolescent status to men who were essentially adult except for their dependent position. A combination of fear of and anxiety to do the best for these overgrown youths led to literature and public policies reflective of generational and social status clashes. Teaching a subordinate position and respect for social hierarchy was essential for middle-class adolescents.

Reinforcing the efforts to construct an ethos for middle-class adolescents were the conservative values and "dullness" among fifteenth-century writers. As Lerer has pointed out, Lydgate in his *Testament* used the technique of juxtaposing the unruly qualities of youthful behavior, including pranks and thefts, to the desirable "commercial, social, and religious spheres of action" that the youths should adopt. Lydgate casts his piece as "autobiographical," as does Hoccleve in *La Male Regle*.[78] The use of this personal approach, in contrast to *Ratis Raving* or Russell's *Book of Nurture*, adds a weight of first-hand experience to traditional themes.

Hoccleve describes in his "autobiography" the attributes of a prolonged period of youthful indiscretions:

> But twenti wyntir past, continuelly,
> Excesse at borde hath leyd his knyf with me.

Following the "ages of man" literature he speaks of the pursuit "of Venus femel lusty children deere," particularly at "Poules Heed" tavern, where he went "to talke of mirthe and to disport and pleye." He drank sweet wine, ate choice foods, and stumbled to bed to sleep it off.[79] It was Hoccleve's view that "for the more paart, youthe is rebel."

> O yowthe, allas, why wilt thow nat enclyne
> And unto reuled resoun bowe thee?
> Syn resoun is the verray, streighte lyne
> That ledith folk unto felicitee.

Even though friends and wise men tell youth that they will regret their excesses, they will not listen.[80]

The writings of both Lydgate and Hoccleve have elements that appear in books of advice, in popular poetry, and in urban regulations and court cases. Lerer even finds that popular literature and high culture intersected– the popular "Poem to Apprentices" borrows directly from the organization of Lydgate's *Testament*.[81]

The vast expansion of literature for instruction of youth in the fifteenth century suggests an audience of increasingly literate children for whom parents bought books, and authors and scribes found a profit in writing them. While some of the pieces were adaptations and infantilizations of Chaucer, as Lerer has shown, the scribblers were also busy with experimentation to make moral lessons palatable and memorable to their audiences. Even Russell's *Book of Nurture* engages a young reader with a positive image before plunging into technical descriptions of carving and serving.

Much of the popular literature was designed to be memorized and even recited orally, rather than simply read. For instance, "Symon's Lesson of Wisdom for all Manner of Children" did not presume a literate audience:

> All manner of children, ye lisen and hear
> A lesson of wisdom that is written clear.
> My child, I advise thee to be wise, take heed of this rhyme.

Other books organized the lessons in order such as "The ABC of Aristotle."[82]

"The Childe of Bristowe" and "The Merchant and His Son" are written in a way that would instill moral training and tell a good story.[83] The young hero is the ideal physical and social type—straight of limb, well educated, and gentle by birth—just the sort of youth with whom an aspiring apprentice might identify if given the poem early enough. His respect for father and master are tied into an adventure story, with the requisite three episodes devoted to saving his father's soul. The story carries the reader along with its adventure and rewards. The second version adds a touch of humor. Finally, Childe-William's patience and willingness to sacrifice any claim to his father's ill-gotten fortune is rewarded with the return of the property, a marriage, and full establishment as a merchant. In fifteenth-century fashion, the patience of the hero is likened to that of Job.

First was riche and sitthen bare,
And sitthen richer than ever he was.[84]

We cannot conclude that all of the fine lessons were picked up and put
into practice, or even that their chief consumers were children and adolescents. While undoubtedly the ideal presented in these poems was what the
"sad and wise" of the fifteenth century wished their sons and apprentices
to imbibe, the fact that the two surviving examples appear in devotional
rather than household books makes the reader wonder who was going to
learn the lesson. Certainly, the historical sources speak of numerous apprentices who showed no signs of moving along the continuum of behavior from "wild and wanton" to "sad and wise," but the story of Childe-
William does illustrate an agreement on an ideal type that can be found in
both literature and history.

NOTES

1. I would agree with Mary Martin McLaughlin that the eleventh and twelfth centuries can be characterized by a new preoccupation with the experiences of childhood. Mary Martin McLaughlin, "Survivors and Surrogates: Children and Parents from the Ninth to the Thirteenth Centuries," in *The History of Childhood*, ed.
   Lloyd deMause (New York: The Psychohistory Press, 1974), pp. 100–181.
2. Norbert Elias, *The Civilizing Process: The History of Manners*, trans. Edmund Jephcott (Oxford: Basil Blackwell, 1979), p. 7. His own study relies heavily on six-
   teenth- to eighteenth-century books of advice. His chapter on medieval manners
   (pp. 60–70) puts the advice literature, including John Russell's *Book of Nurture*,
   in the category of courtly behavior. He does not see the shift of audience of advice literature to the middle class happening until the sixteenth century (p. 70).
   Jonathan Nicholls, in *The Matter of Courtesy: Medieval Courtesy Books and the
   Gawain-Poet* (Woodbridge, Suffolk: D. S. Brewer, 1985), has pointed out that ci-
   vility is an urban term and that courtesy came to include not only courtly ideals,
   but skills needed for a new age (pp. 13–14).
3. "The Child of Bristowe" is preserved in the British Library Harleian MS. 2382 f.
   118. Those poems included within this manuscript are largely devotional literature such as Lydgate's "Life of Our Lady," "The Testament of Dan John" in
   various parts, poems to the Virgin Mary, Chaucer's the *Prioress's Tale*, and his
   life of St. Cecilia. In other words, the poems are associated with devotional tracts
   and with Lydgate. No doubt the selections from Lydgate in this manuscript led
   Joseph Ritson, in *Bibliographia Poetica* (London: Printed by C. Roworth for G. and
   W. Nicol, 1802) p. 71, to attribute the poem to Lydgate, as did Clarence Hop-
   per, who edited it in 1859 for the Camden Society (*The Camden Miscellany*, 4).
   "The Childe of Bristowe" is the ninth entry following "the Long Charter of
   Christ." "The Merchant and His Son" comes from Cambridge University Library
   ms. no. ff. 2, 38, f. 59. It too is bound with manuscripts of a moral and devotional nature, including part of William Lychfield's *Complaint of God*, proverbs
   of Solomon, meditations, mirrors of vices and virtues, several poems on the
   seven works of mercy, "The Charter of Christ," and several poems about the
   Virgin, St. Margaret, St. Thomas, Mary Magdelen, and St. Katherine. "The Mer-

chant and His Son" appears in the latter part of the manuscript, which includes "How the Wyse Man Taght Hys Son," "The Story of the Adulterous Falmouth Squire," and a variety of romances. The two manuscript sources are both of the mid-fifteenth century and contain similar collections. Both poems appear in W. Carew Hazlitt, *Remains of the Early Popular Poetry of England* (London: John Russell Smith, 1864), pp. 110–52. Walter F. Schirmer, in *John Lydgate: A Study in the Culture of the XVth Century*, trans. Anne E. Keep (Berkeley: University of California Press, 1961; originally published in German, 1952), lists the Ritson attribution in his appendix, pp. 275, 278, but does not consider the ascription as reliable. I am grateful to James Landman for looking up the two manuscripts in Cambridge and London.

4. David Lawton, "Dullness and the Fifteenth Century," *Journal of English Literary History*, 54 (1987): 761–71.

5. Seth Lerer, *Chaucer and His Readers: Imagining the Author in Late Medieval England* (Princeton: Princeton University Press, 1993). See Chapter 3 in particular. His study of the household type of manuscript collection could be of major importance in putting in context the preservation of such manuscripts as "The Childe of Bristowe" as well as the variant versions of Chaucer's works. As these are currently bound and catalogued, however the context seems to represent devotional literature rather than the sort of collections that Lerer has identified. It is possible that there were different levels of books for advice for the young and that adults would find some of the stories for adolescents instructive.

6. Barbara A. Hanawalt, in "Keepers of the Lights; Late Medieval English Parish Gilds," *The Journal of Medieval and Renaissance History*, 14 (1984): 137–48 speaks of the religious conservatism of the guilds. Barbara A. Hanawalt and Ben R. McRee, in "The Guilds of *Homo Prudens* in Late Medieval England," *Continuity and Change*, 7 (1992): 163–79 address the issues of social behavior in guild regulations. These are very close to the types of advice that appear in the general literature produced for the aspiring adolescent in that they address issues of behavior at table during guild feasts, moral relations with brother guildsmen, honor in business dealings, and so on. The guilds were, one may conclude, part of the general movement toward a definition of the middle-class, conservative morality that characterized the fifteenth century.

7. See Frances Elizabeth Baldwin, *Sumptuary Legislation and Personal Regulation in England* (Baltimore: The Johns Hopkins Press, 1926), pp. 73–119 for discussion of the Lancastrian and Yorkist periods.

8. Hazlitt, *Early Popular Poetry*: "The Childe of Bristowe," p. 111, l. 15; "The Merchant and His Son," p. 132, l. 2.

9. Henry S. Bennett, *England from Chaucer to Caxton* (London: Methuen and Co., 1928), pp. 149–50.

10. Steve Rappaport, *Worlds within Worlds: Structures of Life in Sixteenth-Century London* (Cambridge: Cambridge University Press, 1989), pp. 304–5. Among the skinners and tailors, 32 percent of the apprentices had fathers who were merchants or craftsmen, 30 percent had yeomen fathers, 19 percent were husbandmen, 16 percent were gentry, and the other 3 percent had fathers from miscellaneous backgrounds. See also Sylvia L. Thrupp, *Merchant Class of Medieval London* (Chicago: University of Chicago Press, 1948), pp. 211–19.

11. Hazlitt, *Early Popular Poetry*: "The Childe of Bristowe," p. 112, ll. 29–30.

12. *Acts of the Court of the Mercers' Company (London), 1453–1527*, ed. Laetitia Lydell and Frank D. Watney (Cambridge: Cambridge University Press, 1936), p. xi.

Charles Welch, in *History of the Cutlers' Company of London*, 1 (London: printed privately, 1916), p. 114, wrote that the apprentices were required to be "clean of limb and lith in their bodies without any deformity for the worship of the city."

13. Thomas Reddaway, *The Early History of the Goldsmiths' Company* (London: Edward Arnold, 1975), p. 147; Rappaport, *Worlds within Worlds*, p. 298; Walter Prideaux, ed. *Memorials of the Goldsmiths' Company Being Gleanings from Their Records* (London: Eyre, 1896), p. 28.

14. Hazlitt, *Early Popular Poetry*: "The Childe of Bristowe," pp. 112–13, ll. 37–42; "The Merchant and His Son," p. 134, ll. 29–30.

15. Alice Green, in *Town Life in the Fifteenth Century*, 2 (London: MacMillan and Co., 1894), pp. 1–12 first made this observation about the role of courtesy books in the fifteenth century and their importance in the formation of urban manners.

16. See for instance, Diane Bornstein, *Mirrors of Courtesy* (Camden, Conn.: Archon Press, 1975), ch. 4.

17. Edith Rickert, ed., *The Babee's Book: Medieval Manners for the Young, Done into Modern English from Dr. Furnivall's Texts* (New York: Cooper Square Publications, 1966), p. 22.

18. Hazlitt, *Early Popular Poetry*: "The Childe of Bristowe," p. 114, ll. 82–83.

19. Hazlitt, *Early Popular Poetry*: "The Childe of Bristowe," p. 112, ll. 10–16. The second version is more specific, explaining that when he lent 10s. he expected to get 11s. back, and he put the people under obligation and had them imprisoned when they did not make good on their debts. There is a whole catalogue of his deceits that are of great interest in themselves (see "The Merchant and His Son," pp. 133–34, ll. 11–24).

20. Rickert, *The Babees' Book*: "The Young Children's Book," p. 23.

21. From Rickett *The Babees' Book*: Hazlitt, Early Popular Poetry: "The Childe of Bristowe," p. 113, ll. 50–61: "they fare ful wel tha lerne no lawe." He goes on to say that he would never undertake a career that would "make God my foo." In "The Merchant and His Son" the boy makes less of a protest about the law but refuses to enter the profession (pp. 135–36, ll. 40–48.

22. Ibid., p. 135, ll. 45–46.

23. Ibid., "The Childe of Bristowe," p. 113, ll. 61–70.

24. A typical contract is that from the Merchant Tailors for 1451.

"John Harrietsham contracts with Robert Lucy to serve the said Robert as well in the craft and in all his other works and doings such as he does and shall do, from Christmas day next ensuing for the term of 7 years. He is to receive 9s. 4d. at the end of the term, and he shall work one year after the seven at wages of 20s. Robert is to find his apprentice all necessaries, food, clothing, shoes, and bed and to teach him his craft in all its particulars without concealment. During the term the apprentice is to keep his master's secrets, to do him no injury and commit no excessive waste of his goods. He is not to frequent taverns, not to commit fornication in or out of his master's house, nor make any contract of matrimony nor affiance himself without his master's permission. He is not to play at dice, tables, or checkers or any other unlawful games but is to conduct himself soberly, justly, piously, well, and honorably, and to be a faithful and good servant according to the use and custom of London. For all his obligations Robert binds himself, his heir and his executors, his goods and chattels, present and future, wherever found. (Charles M. Clode, *The Early History of the Guild of Merchant Tailors* [London: Harrison and Sons, 1888], p. 344).

The process of drawing up the contract is described in another case. William Morton and Robert de Eye, a cutler, came to a verbal agreement, and Robert had a scrivener draw up an indenture of apprenticeship that contained clauses William had not agreed to. The contract said that he would pay the usual £2 13s. 4d. for his first year, but Robert had added that he would have to pay a bond of £40 if he broke the contract. William refused and argued that his parents and friends would never have agreed to that. The Mayor overturned the bond. (*Calendar of Plea and Memoranda Rolls of the City of London*, 3, trans. Arthur H. Thomas [Cambridge: Cambridge University Press, 1929] p. 14 (1383).

25. George Clune, *The Medieval Gild System* (Dublin: Browne and Nolan, 1943), pp. 91–94.
26. Reddaway, *Early History of the Goldsmiths*, p. 147.
27. Hazlitt, *Early Popular Poems*: "The Childe of Bristowe," p. 114, ll. 71–78.
28. Sylvia Thrupp, "The Grocers of London, A Study in Distributive Trade," in *Studies in English Trade in the Fifteenth Century*, ed. Eileen Power and Michael M. Postan (London: G. Routledge and Sons, 1933), p. 255.
29. *Calendar of Plea and Memoranda Rolls*, 3, pp. 14–15. Public Record Office C1/67/144. *Calendar of Letter Books of the City of London*, Letter Book G, ed. Reginald R. Sharpe (London: John Edward Francis, 1905), p. 308 (1373) records an eight-year apprenticeship that went 46s. 8d. Hereafter these will be referred to as *Letter Book* and letter of the alphabet.
30. Reddaway, *Early History of the Goldsmiths*, p. 73.
31. Thrupp, "Grocers of London," p. 256.
32. *Memorials of the Goldsmiths' Company*, p. 15.
33. *Acts of Court of the Mercers' Company*, ed. Laetitia Lyell (Cambridge: Cambridge University Press, 1936), pp. 89, 193. Jean M. Imray, "'Les Bones Gentes de la Mercerye de Londres': A Study of the Membership of the Medieval Mercers' Company," in *Studies in London History Presented to Philip Edmund Jones*, ed. Albert E. J. Hollaender and William Kellaway (London: Hodder and Stoughton, 1969), pp. 157–58, records a 1347 entry of a 2s. fee from master and likewise from the apprentice; in 1348 it was raised to 20s.; in 1357 to £3 6s. 8d. About 12 percent were delinquent in paying fees, but most did eventually pay the fee along with a fine for delinquency. (Arthur H. Johnson, *The History of the Worshipful Company of Drapers of London* [Oxford: Clarendon Press, 1914], p. 272). Drapers set the fee at 13s. 4d. in the late fifteenth century but reduced it to 6s. 8d. in 1512.
34. One reason that the bonds could become close is that most business or craft establishments were small, and a master might have only one apprentice during his life time. In London between 1349 to 1410, 457 master goldsmiths took in approximately 1,120 apprentices. During the course of their active years as masters, half had only one apprentice, 19 percent had two, 10 percent had three, 7 percent took four, and 14 percent took five or more (see Reddaway, *Early History of the Goldsmiths*, p. 91). Reddaway warns that these figures must represent underreporting, since not all apprentices were registered regardless of the regulations.
35. Rickert, *The Babees' Book*: "Symon's Lesson of Wisdom," p. 123.
36. Ibid: "Rhodes's Book of Nurture," p. 132.
37. See Baldwin, *Sumptuary Legislation and Personal Regulation* for a discussion of the regulations on dress by age and status.
38. See Hazlitt, *Early Popular Poems*: "Childe of Bristowe," p. 122, l. 319, for an ex-

ample; or p. 126, l. 16 ("The burger lovyd the child so wele."). The youth always refers to his master as "dear master."

39. Ibid. The two poems deviate on the way the wealth is expended. In "The Childe of Bristowe" the youth expends all the cash on hand in the estate on prayers. He then sells his inheritance and finally his person, pp. 117–28. In "The Merchant and His Son" the action is compressed. He still meets the father's ghost three times, but the dispersal of cash on hand is omitted (see pp. 138–49).

40. Ibid: "The Childe of Bristowe," pp. 115–21; "The Merchant and His Son," pp. 137–39. In the latter, the son makes more of a protest that his father should amend his ways before he dies, but the old man will not and leaves the child with his estate and his benediction.

41. Ibid: "The Merchant and His Son," p. 140, ll. 110–14. In "The Childe of Bristowe," first version, the master simply says that he will be an unwise man if he sells his inheritance (see p. 122, ll. 298–300).

42. Rickert, *The Babees' Book*, p. 46.

43. Hazlitt, *Early Popular Poetry:* "The Childe of Bristowe," pp. 121–22, ll. 280–320; "The Merchant and his Son," pp. 140–41, ll. 106–27.

44. Ibid: "Childe of Bristowe," pp. 122–24, "The Merchant and His Son," pp. 145–47.

45. Ibid: "The Childe of Bristowe," pp. 125–26, ll. 388–427; "The Merchant and His Son," pp. 144–45, ll. 167–91.

46. Ibid: "The Childe of Bristowe," pp. 126–27; "The Merchant and His Son," pp. 146–49.

47. Ibid: "The Merchant and His Son," p. 150, ll. 54–58.

48. *Acts of the Mercers' Company*, p. 724.

49. Hazlitt, *Early Popular Poetry:* "The Childe of Bristowe," pp. 129–31, ll. 496–552; "The Merchant and His Son," pp. 150–52, ll. 250–90.

50. Guidhall, Commissary Court, 9051/1 18 (1393), 9171/5 225v. See Reddaway, *Early History of the Goldsmiths*, p. 285, on which Richard Bradcock left one existing and two former apprentices his best, second- and third-best anvils and his two last apprentices a clenching anvil each. See also, pp. 292, 294. In *Calendar of Wills Proved and Enrolled in the Court of Husting, London, A. D. 1258–1688*, 2, ed. Reginald R. Sharpe (London: John E. Francis, 1890), a goldsmith left tools to his apprentice, p. 144 (1371). Hereafter, this collection will be referred to as *Husting Wills*.

51. *Husting Wills*, I, p. 232 (1312); II, p. 233 (1383).

52. Public Record Office C1/64/313.

53. *Husting Wills*, I, pp. 19 (1361), 114 (1368), and 138 (1370) contains prayers for both master and mistress.

54. Rickert, *The Babees' Book*, pp. 48–49.

55. Diane Bornstein, *Mirrors of Courtesy* (New York: Archon Books, 1975), pp. 82–83.

56. John A. Burrow, *The Ages of Man: A Study in Medieval Writing and Thought* (Oxford: Oxford University Press, 1988), pp. 12–43.

57. *Three Morality Plays: Mankind, Everyman, and Mundus et Infans*, ed. Godfrey A. Lester (New York: W. W. Norton, 1981) pp. 115–16.

58. *Calendar of Plea and Memoranda Rolls of the City of London*, 2, ed. Arthur H. Thomas (Cambridge: The University Press, 1927), p. 36; *Memorials of London and London Life in the XIIIth, XIVth, and XVth Centuries*, ed. Thomas Riley (London: Longmans, Green, and Co., 1868), p. 268.

59. *Three Morality Plays*, pp. 117–18.

60. Frederick J. Furnivall, ed., *Hymns to the Virgin and Christ, the Parliament of Devils, and Other Religious Poems*, (London: Early English Text Society, o.s. 14, 1868), p. 61.
61. *Calendar of Plea and Memoranda Rolls of the City of London*, 1, ed. Arthur H. Thomas (Cambridge: Cambridge University Press, 1926), p. 113; *Memorials of London*, p. 88 (1311).
62. *Acts of Mercers' Company*, p. 724 (1526).
63. *Letter Book C*, p. 123 (1303). Warin Fatting, an apprentice of Matilda Fatting, maimed an index finger of her right hand. He was pardoned and paid 35s. in recompense. See Reddaway, *Early History of the Goldsmiths*, p. 147; *Memorials of the Goldsmiths' Company*, pp. 18, 22.
64. Reddaway, in *Early History of the Goldsmiths*, pp. 83–84, has reconstructed this young man's story from a lengthy record of his crimes that appeared in the court book.
65. *Acts of the Mercers' Company*, pp. 418–19 (1513).
66. Ibid., pp. 444–45. City fathers had good reason to fear riots among the apprentices as well as among other inhabitants of the city. The revolt in London in 1381 involved a number of servants. Trade fights led guild members to take to arms and attack one another. When adults began a fight, their servants and apprentices automatically joined in, and thus a crowd of 500 or more could assemble quickly, and deaths often resulted. If the riots became serious, the king could threaten to take away the city's charter, and sometimes he did. It was not, therefore, mere moralizing that led the guilds and the city fathers to take a keen interest in suppressing youth riots along with others. See Charles Pendrill, *London Life in the Fourteenth Century* (Port Washington, N.Y.: Kennikat Press, 1971), pp. 133–69, for a discussion of trade fights and their consequences for the city. The most unruly group of apprentices were those of the bench, that is, those young men who were studying common law at the inns of court. These youth were in their late teens or early twenties and lived just outside the city gates in the Holbourn and Fleet area. Unlike the apprentices associated with merchant and craft gilds, they did not live in the master's house and so were not directly supervised. Instead, they lived in rooms, often with their own servants, and learned case law with jurists and from attending court. Their living arrangements permitted them to congregate with each other easily at taverns or in the streets. Together with their servants, they contributed substantially to violent crime and riot in the city. (see *Calendar of Plea and Memoranda Rolls*, 1, pp. 156–60, 213). The apprentices of the Bench were as close as London came to having distinctive youth groups with a youth culture.
67. Apprentices as well as masters felt their wealth and grasp on London's markets and industries challenged by foreigners, particularly Lombards (Italians) and Germans (a lumping together of those from the low countries and German towns). In 1456 a major riot occurred between Mercers' apprentices and Lombards. A young man had taken the dagger of a Lombard and had broken it in two. He was immediately arraigned before the Mayor at Guildhall and was committed to the sheriff's custody. On his way home to dinner, the Mayor was held up in the Cheap by a crowd of Mercers' apprentices and other persons who demanded that the youth be released. The Mayor gave in, but this only encouraged the crowd, and later in the day they attacked the Lombards in their homes and took goods. Some rioters were arrested and put into Newgate, but when

the king's Justices proposed to try them, the crowd threatened to ring the Common Bell to signal that the city should arm. Although some of the offenders were eventually hanged, the situation was so unstable that the king and queen left London for a time. In 1493 the Mercers' apprentices rose against the German traders and collected a mob of servants, apprentices, and children. The merchants had prior warning and shut their gates in the Steelyard, which was the part of the city assigned to the Hanseatic merchants. The chronicler reporting the event was at pains to point out that no householders were involved in the attack, but only apprentices, servants, and journeymen. (see Pendrill, *London Life*, pp. 76–77). For an account of the alien merchants in late fourteenth-century London see Alice Beardwood, *Alien Merchants in England 1350–1377: Their Legal and Economic Position* (Cambridge, Mass.: Harvard University Press, 1931).

68. Gerald R. Owst, *Literature and Pulpit in Medieval England* (Cambridge: Cambridge University Press, 1933), pp. 460–68.
69. See John Hatcher, *Plague, Population, and the English Economy, 1348–1530* (London: MacMillan and Co., 1977) for a complete discussion of the effects of plague and the course it took in England.
70. Rappaport, *Worlds within Worlds*, p. 297.
71. *Calendar of Plea and Memoranda Rolls*, 1, pp. 235–39.
72. Reddaway, *Early History of the Goldsmiths*, pp. 73, 80.
73. *Calendar of Plea and Memoranda Rolls of the City of London*, 5, ed. Phillip E. Jones (Cambridge: Cambridge University Press, 1954), p. 184. See index under "apprenticeship, length of term."
74. In sixty-five scattered cases of broken apprenticeship contracts that appear in the Mayor's Court, Chancery Petitions, and surviving company records for the fifteenth century the average length of apprenticeship was for ten years. Sixteen years for a contract was not unknown (cf. Public Record Office C1/19/143). For writings on contracts in the sixteenth century see Rappaport, *Worlds within Worlds*, p. 109; George Unwin, *The Gilds and Companies of London* (London: Methuen and Co., 1908), pp. 91–92; and Welch, *Cutlers' Company of London*, 1, pp. 10–14. Cutlers required a seven-year term with extra service.
75. Rosamond J. Mitchell and Mary D.R. Leys, *A History of London Life* (London: Longmans, Green, 1958), pp. 46–47; Clune, *The Medieval Gild System*, p. 88; *Letter Book E*, p. 272; *Letter Book F*, p. 35; *Letter Book H*, pp. 165, 405.
76. Thrupp, *Merchant Class*, p. 193; Clune, *The Medieval Gild System*, pp. 87–88. By the sixteenth century the average age for entering an apprenticeship was 18 to 22, with some companies forbidding enrollment of apprentices under 16. The reason for late age of entry into apprenticeship was both the increased demand for literacy on the part of guilds and the need for adolescent labor at home. (Apprentices were mostly drawn from husbandmens' families.) (see Rappaport, *Worlds within Worlds*, pp. 295–98.
77. Rappaport, *Worlds within Worlds*, pp. 304–11. Thrupp, in *Merchant Class*, pp. 218–19, makes a similar observation about the lesser companies in the fifteenth century.
78. Seth Lerer, *Chaucer and His Readers*, pp. 108–10.
79. See Thomas Hoccleve, *Selected Poems*, Bernard O'Donoghue, ed. (Manchester: Fyfield Books, Carcanet New Press Ltd., 1982), pp. 50–53, ll. 111–209 for descriptions of his life.

80. Ibid., pp. 49–50, ll. 57–96. David Wallace notes that Hoccleve was only about 35 and still unmarried when he wrote this poem in 1405. He seemed to want to use this poem to distance himself from his own recent past and assert his adulthood.

81. Lerer, *Chaucer and His Readers*, pp. 109–10.

82. Rickert, *The Babees' Book*, pp. 22, 25, 122.

83. Lerer, in *Chaucer and His Readers*, pp. 95–96, shows how the *Tale of Sir Thopas* and *Melibee* become adventure stories as well known to children as were Robin Hood and other ballads.

84. Hazlitt, *Early Popular Poetry:* "Childe of Bristowe," p. 131. See also Lerer, *Chaucer and His Readers*, pp. 111–13.

Index